D0926824

RED PARTISAN

Related Titles from Potomac Books

Hitler's Bandit Hunters: The SS and the Nazi Occupation of Europe by Philip W. Blood

Images of Kursk: History's Greatest Tank Battle, July 1943 by Nikolas Cornish

The Eastern Front Day by Day, 1941-45: A Photographic Chronology by Steve Crawford

The Forgotten Soldier by Guy Sajer

Fighting for the Fatherland: The German Soldier from 1648 to the Present Day by David Stone

Blood and Iron: The German Conquest of Sevastapol by C. G. Sweeting

RED PARTISAN

The Memoir of a Soviet Resistance Fighter on the Eastern Front

NIKOLAI I. OBRYN'BA

Potomac Books, Inc.
Washington, D.C.

Translator
Vladimir Krupnik

Editors
Dina Chebanova
Sergei Anisimov
John Armstrong

Editor of the English Text
Christopher Summerville

Publication made possible by the I Remember website
(www.iremember.ru) and its director Artem Drabkin

Library of Congress Cataloging-in-Publication Data
Library of Congress CIP Data is available under LCCN: 2007060078

ISBN-13: 978-1-59797-125-6 (alk. paper)

Printed in the United States of America on acid-free paper that meets the
American National Standards Institute Z39-48 Standard.

Potomac Books, Inc.
22841 Quicksilver Drive
Dulles, Virginia 20166

First Edition

10 9 8 7 6 5 4 3 2 1

Contents

Preface by the Russian Editors

In 2001, I paid a visit to my uncle, a veteran of the Second World War, to interview him for my website. After a long and interesting conversation he mentioned: 'What a pity that my neighbour died some ten years ago! He could have told you some great stories ... But why don't we go to see his widow?' That was the day I first met Dina Chebanova, an amazing woman who recorded a lifetime's memories by Nikolai Obryn'ba and arranged them into a book after he passed away. The first Russian edition of this book was released in the early 1990s.

Although the book was printed in the form of a chalk-overlay album – the usual method for printing paintings – Soviet censorship had reduced the text to a banal collection of victory reports. Dissatisfied, I asked Dina to supply an uncensored version of the text and read it avidly in a few days. But by the end of the reading, I could not help asking myself: 'How could one man be so lucky? Was he really telling the truth?' These questions remained unanswered for a year, until, in August 2002, I drove all the way from Moscow to the Lepel district (part of a Belorussian province of Vitebsk), just to find out if the locals knew of Nikolai Obryn'ba.

In a local museum I found a photo and a few reprints of Obryn'ba's canvases. But most importantly, I was able to obtain the telephone numbers of some Partisan Movement veterans. Productive visits to these people resulted in numerous interviews, which are now available through my website (though in Russian only). From these, I was able to achieve my major goal: numerous details described in this book (e.g. the whereabouts of the Partisan artillery battalion and the existence of the telephone net) were fully endorsed. All these men remember the artists, Obryn'ba and Gutiev vividly: both from the war days and from their later visits to the area. I returned home satisfied and at the same time astonished ...

Artem Drabkin

The scale of warfare on the Eastern Front remains ill-conceived by Western society. Moreover, the brutality of the Second World War in Russia and fellow states (where the conflict is known as 'The Great Patriotic War') is often unjustifiably associated with the concept of 'Slavic barbarism': an idea established in previous centuries and still welcomed by many. *Red Partisan* by Nikolai Obryn'ba is therefore a highly unusual book for the eye of the Western reader – yet many Russians would recognize his story as being almost ordinary ...

The talented young artist Nikolai Obryn'ba had no doubt which path to choose when war broke out. Like many men of his generation, he volunteered for the front line. In those days, the path was clear for men who had already served mandatory duty within the Armed Forces or possessed skills considered useful for respective branches of the service. And at the same time, men of humanitarian professions (like the students of Moscow Art Academy) made the only choice that would grant them the possibility of combat: volunteer units. Standing little chance against the battle-hardened units of the German Wermacht, under equipped and poorly trained, Russian volunteers played their bitter role in the days when the Soviet State faced military defeat. Volunteer units became yet another last-stand effort by the Soviet Union: an attempt to throw the enemy off balance and to stop the German juggernaut. The volunteers were used as a military asset to buy time, enabling the Soviet Union to recover from the unprovoked German strike of 22 June 1941. Thus, tens of thousands paid with their lives, wearing down German divisions, destined to fall under the Red Army's blows in the years that followed.

But the days of victory seemed far away for Nikolai Obryn'ba, and hundreds of thousands of his fellow countrymen, who were unfortunate enough to become prisoners of war on the Eastern Front – the only major front in Europe for three consecutive years. The fate of Slavic people (including Russians, Ukrainians and Belorussians) was pre-determined by German war planning: they were to become obedient slaves or be annihilated. To survive, to remain human, to escape: these were three mottos Nikolai was able to keep as a promise to himself through his time in captivity. Being able to escape with a small group of comrades, he made contact with a Partisan unit deep in the forests of Belorussia, and here the second part of this breathtaking story begins.

Mostly autonomous and relying on the support of local peasants, Partisan detachments were a military asset behind enemy lines. Inspired by the example of the Patriotic War of 1812, when armed Partisans or 'guerrillas' helped evict the Grand Army of Napoleon, the Partisan Movement soon became a major force. Teasing extended German communications with great success, the Red Partisans perfected their tactics, forcing German commanders to divert considerable resources and manpower from the front line. Never in modern history had a Partisan Movement played a larger role than in Belorussia, the true 'Partisan Republic', situated as it was, well behind the official front line. By reading the pages of this remarkable book – sharing the pain of bitter defeats and the pride of bloody victories – the reader follows the odyssey of Nikolai Obryn'ba: from a young and inspired artist to a hardened and determined veteran of many battles.

Sergei V. Anisimov

The Partisan Zone or '*Island of Soviet Power*'

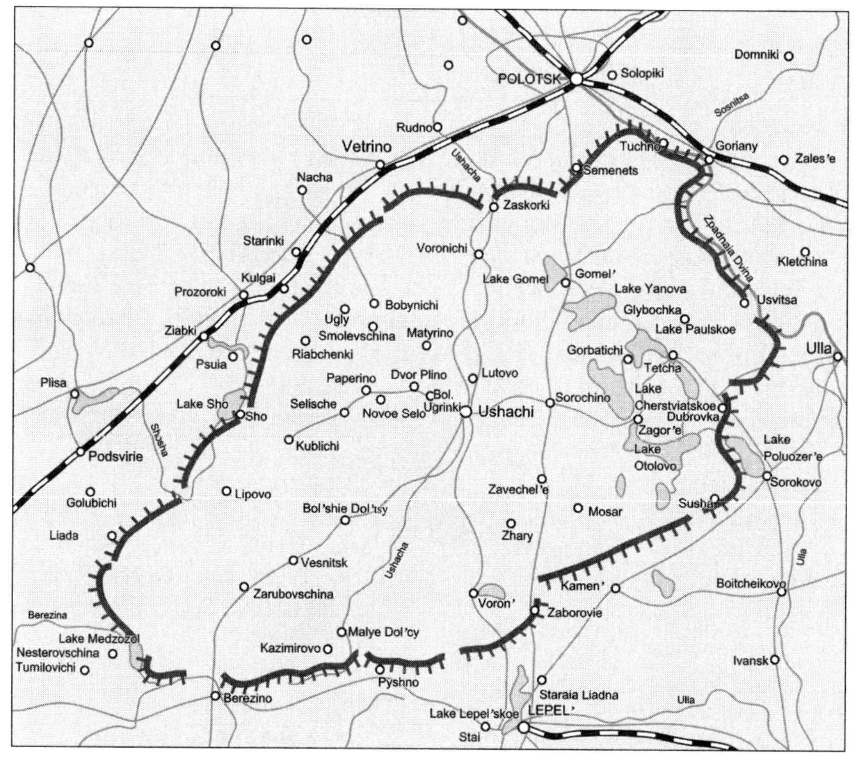

In early 1943 the Partisans of the Lepel region wiped out German and Polizei forces to create a 'Partisan Zone'. By the end of 1943 the 'Zone' consisted of 250,000 square kilometres. In April 1944 German forces consisting of the 15th, 56th, 82nd, 195th and 252nd Infantry Divisions, the 201st Security division, the 6th Luftwaffe Field division, the 2nd, 12th, and 24th Waffen SS Regiments and supporting Russian Polizei units, cracked the 'Zone'. The Partisans, though lacking heavy weapons, put up a stiff resistance, but by the end of the month were cornered in the Ugly–Selische–Kulgai area. On 3 May 1944, most Partisan units broke through in the direction of Novoe Selo, the rest were dispersed or killed. At the end of June 1944 the region was liberated by the Red Army.

Note on Russian Names

Russian names are made of three elements: an individual first name, a patronymic second name in honour of one's father, and a family surname. Referring to another person by use of their patronymic name implies a mark of respect. For example, author Nikolai I. Obryn'ba frequently refers to his Partisan Commander as Fedor Fomich, or Fedor Fomich Dubrovsky.

Meanwhile, Russian forenames have several diminutive forms, which are not always obvious to Western eyes. For example, the name Alexander has Sasha, Sashka and Shura as diminutive forms; while Nikolai has Kolya, Kol'ka and Kolen'ka. For the reader's convenience, the following list contains most of the diminutive forms used in Nikolai I. Obryn'ba's text, with the full form in parentheses.

Afonka (Afanasi)
Allochka (Alla)
Anya (Anna)
Dimka, Mitya (Dmitri)
Fedya (Fedor)
Galya, Galochka, Galka (Galina)
Grisha (Grigory)
Katya (Yekaterina)
Kolya, Kol'ka, Kolen'ka (Nikolai)
Lena (Yelena)
Lesha, Leshka (Alexei)
Leva (Lev)
Liza, Lizka (Elizaveta)
Lyuba (Lubov')
Masha (Maria)
Misha, Mishka (Mikhail)
Nad'ka, Nadechka, Naden'ka, Nadia (Nadezhda)
Nastya (Anastasia)
Olen'ka, Olya (Olga)
Pasha (Pavel)
Petya, Petro, Petr (Piotr)
Sasha, Sashka, Shura (Alexander)
Senya (Semen)
Serezha (Sergei)
Tanya (Tatiana)
Tolya (Anatoly)
Tonya, Nina (Antonia)
Valya (Valentina)
Vanya, Vanyushka, Vanechka (Ivan)
Vasya, Vas'ka (Vasili)
Vera (Veronika)
Volod'ka, Volodya (Vladimir)
Yura, Yurka (Yuri)
Zhenya (Evgenia)

Those are thrice cursed by me
Who make me slay,
Thrusting me into war . . .

N. I. Obryn'ba

Part One

Captivity

CHAPTER ONE

First Night of the War

For many Muscovites, 22 June 1941 will forever stand out as the most memorable day of their lives. Suddenly, one sunny morning, the announcement of war burst into our lives, wrecking fates and shattering dreams, hopes and expectations. The day was bright and sunny. My wife and I were going for a holiday to the Dniepr. I had been chopping wood in the yard since morning and discussing with the neighbours what kind of camera would be best for photographing landscapes. Suddenly a boy ran into the yard: 'Uncle Kolya, the wireless says the war's started!' Everyone rushed to the loudspeakers: 'Today without any declaration of war ...' From this moment our lives changed. From this moment we all faced the question of 'tomorrow' and our place in the war.

Galochka ran up, out of breath: 'I couldn't get through! There were vehicles with soldiers on the road. One threw me a letter and yelled, "get it to a post office!" Then another one, and another one! They started throwing down envelopes from all the vehicles. I didn't have time to catch them all – they were falling and everyone was picking them up.'

We had to get ready, to stock up on food. We rushed to the shops. People were running about, buying all that was available. None of it was left for us – only sets of mixed pastries. We bought five boxes and returned home.

I set about ringing the guys and we decided to go to the Revolution Museum. I was friends with some people from Kiev, with whom I had transferred to the Moscow Arts Institute. They were: Leva Naroditsky, Nikolai Peredny and Boris Kerstens. We had all finished Year Five and 'reached the diploma,' as the saying was then. I had studied in the battle painting class, run by Petr Dmitrievich Pokarzhevsky and worked with him on the panorama, 'The Defence of Tsaritsyn' [an episode from the Russian Civil War – Trans.]. All four of us had been working in the Revolution Museum, making copies of pictures and some pieces for the exposition, so we went to the museum to join in the work for the front.

Everything was in turmoil. Everyone was in a hurry. Yet complete strangers were stopping each other in the street, striking up conversations about the same thing: the war. In the museum we were told to make posters on the following themes: 'All for the front!' 'Have you volunteered?!' and 'Productive work will help the front!' I started drawing a picture for the museum exposition, entitled: 'The German Occupiers in the Ukraine in 1918'.

When I came home in the evening I told Galochka that we had already got jobs. My mother-in-law was at home with the kids. We began to make blackout sheets and stick up the windows with criss-crossing bands of paper. But we couldn't stay at home for long. We longed to see people, so we ran to Sretenka, to a movie-theatre. Having spent about fifteen minutes there, we suddenly realized our four-year-old son, Igor, was at home: what if there was a bombing raid? We rushed back. Our boy was asleep, the window curtained by a bedspread. But we couldn't sleep. Sirens wailed, announcing that everyone should go down to the bomb shelters.

We sent Mum and the kids to the bomb shelter while we stayed in the yard. We sat on a bench and ate the pastries bought that day. It was the first night of the war. A sort of fireworks festival broke out in the skies: searchlights were swinging about, intertwining and criss-crossing; flak guns were banging from the roofs of big buildings; shell bursts were flashing out like white flowers in the searchlights. We heard the sound of footsteps running down the street, but in the yard it was quiet. Around us the apartments were empty. It seemed like only we two were left on the surface – my wife and I. We began feverishly discussing the war: it would be fine to go to the front together, the only concern was to make arrangements for our son. That same night it was decided I would join the army and go to the front. I would refuse my draft exemption papers [awarded to men with certain skills and trades – Trans.], give up art, and become a soldier.

The sirens sounded the All-Clear and the crowds headed home. Everyone was excited and only the sleepy kids, nodding in weary arms, made people go back to their flats. We rushed to our kinfolk, bunked the kids down, and went out onto the street. No one could sleep ...

CHAPTER TWO

Movie With a Happy Ending

In the morning I ran to work and announced our decision. Leva said: 'Galka [a diminutive of Galochka – Trans.] is right, we have to join up.' The four of us – Leva, Nikolai, Boris and I – went to the *voenkomat*. The *voenkom* [i.e. military kommissar, a voenkomat being his office – Trans.] said everyone should go home and work, instead of holding up mobilization. We returned to the museum dissatisfied. An idea entered our minds. We could petition the Editor of *Pravda* [the main organ of the Central Communist Party Committee – Trans.] – perhaps he could get us to the front! We ran to the editorial office and insisted on being seen. The Editor listened to us and said he would do everything possible. Four days later we were called back and told we could work in the voenkomats, drawing slogans and posters. We wanted to join up for combat! But diploma students were exempt from the draft and would not be taken to the front. Instead, we produced placards – the first placards on the topic of the war in the exposition – and I returned to my picture about the German occupiers in the Ukraine ...

But one day, as the four of us were walking to the Institute, recruiting for the *Opolchenie* [i.e. Territorial Army or Home Guard – Trans.] began in a small office in Pushkin Square. When we arrived registration was under way. The place was noisy and crowded. People mobbed around a desk and we joined the queue, rapidly making our way to the front. All the time, men were arriving, taking their places in line. Soon the room could not hold them all, and those who had already enlisted were glad to get out of the crush and into a crowded corridor. Enough people had gathered for a whole platoon, or even a company, and it seemed to us that this would be a mighty force; that it would play an important part in the war; that all we had to do was turn up at the front and the war would be over (that was what we told our wives). Before we left, we were told to show up at the Hotel Sovietskaya next day: that was where the Leningradsky district Opolchenie Headquarters was located.

I came home and proudly told Galochka that we had enlisted in the Opolchenie. She immediately began to sew a backpack with straps: the kind a soldier would need for storing all necessities. Galya also wanted to enlist as a nurse. But what to do with Igor? Mum didn't want to look after two children – her own ten-year-old Dimka and our four-year-old – because on top of everything, she had a job to go to. Then, in the morning, it was announced that all women with kids were to be evacuated from Moscow. Galya would go to Penza with Igor.

As for me, at last I was signed up and shorn. The first night as an Opolchenie soldier I should have spent in the school, but I ran away and came back at dawn. I jumped out of a window and returned the same way. I was not yet used to the fact I was now a soldier. Also, it seemed pointless to sleep on the floor in the school when I could go home and see my wife off to the evacuation, and carry her trunk to the assembly point. When I came home, Galya's mother took the children out, leaving the room free for us to say goodbye. It was our final farewell and we both understood it might be for good. At that moment I felt the war more keenly than when I was issued with a rifle. We couldn't fall asleep on this last, so short-lived night. Tomorrow I would not be able to come home again ...

We were in the Opolchenie now. Our formation was dressed in a variety of suits: pants, jackets, shirts all different shades – white, black, grey, dark-blue. The only uniform thing about us was our close-cropped heads. They marched us through the beloved streets of Moscow: 'Left foot! Left foot! One, two, three ...' And led us into the hall of what had been a first-class restaurant, full of joy and music just yesterday, but now there were no white tablecloths, and the tables were lined up in a row. And it wasn't a ceremonial dinner: motley-dressed men with shaved heads sat at the table, jammed up against each other, while our section leader ladled pearl-barley soup from an aluminium saucepan. We courageously held out our aluminium bowls and chewed our black bread. Well, if this was what it took to achieve victory, we would eat this 'shrapnel' with great appetite; we would scrub the bowls clean and ask for a second helping, tapping with our aluminium spoons. Where had they dug up this amount of aluminium crockery? It was amazing!

Before leaving for the front we were lined up in the school yard. The street beyond the fence was packed with women and kids, who were standing devouring us with their eyes. We were trying to stand still, while displaying a good deal of bravado, to let them see what good warriors we were, despite being dressed so diversely. I was wearing white pants and a brown jacket. My head was shaved smooth as a watermelon, and a straw hat was perched upon it (those without hats had peaked caps or skull caps, for it was no good having a shiny new-shaven head).

We had been marching in the streets, singing songs, keeping in step, which did not come at all easily for me. I tried to tap with my left foot as firmly as possible, but it was painful. And I was frequently mixing up my feet, which seemed unfair! Now, standing on one spot, I was trying to keep in step on the turns, so as not to bring shame upon myself in front of the women who had come to see us off. We were facing the fence and I saw hundreds of eyes staring at us, some sparkling with tears. Women were nodding to us, waving their handkerchiefs, and trying to cheer us up with smiles. I noticed the radiant blue eyes of my wife in the crowd, she too was smiling, all the while gripping the iron rods of the fence with her thin hands. After the command, 'Count off!' the words 'At ease! Break up!' came like music.

And that was it. The string of shaven heads broke up, dispersing into small, individual beads, like drops of mercury, and we ran to the gate and into the street. The women were crying, standing with bowed heads in front of their men. One of them, as if apologizing, silently stroked his wife's shoulder. Another had a child in his arms. Yet another was consoling his wife, trying to impart cheer and unconcern to his voice. But a heavy weight lay on everyone's soul. Everyone understood that something serious was happening, yet couldn't believe it. And somewhere, in a corner of one's mind, there was still the idea that all would pass and not turn out for the worse; that it would all finish like a movie with a happy ending.

We were consoling our wives that soon we'd come back with victory. I told mine: 'Don't take any winter clothes for the evacuation – everything will be over by autumn.' We had got used to believing our government knew some secret way to win, and even if a retreat was under way, why that was no more than a strategic move, and before we had time to reach the front the war would be over and the enemy on the run. Everything would be fine, like in a good film. And our wives were going to the rear in an orderly fashion and would be waiting for us to come home, battle-seasoned and grown stronger with victory on our steel sabres. Well, if need be, we could go into combat for victory and endure the pearl-barley porridge and the separation.

But in the eyes of the older guys – amongst us there were many who had been through the Revolution and the Civil War – there was disquiet. It seemed to me that their wives had packed their bags more thoroughly, not forgetting even a trifle. They were bringing their handkerchiefs up to their eyes more frequently, and looking at their husbands with longing. Some of them couldn't restrain themselves and began to cry, throwing their arms around the necks of their shaven husbands.

I pushed through to my wife and embraced her. We kissed, there in the crowd, the same way as the rest, feeling shy before no one. I was hugging her and we were trying to retain, to absorb, the memory of every touch. We came out of the crowd and stood under a tree. It was growing dark and the command to return was imminent. I was kissing my wife and we were both feeling a keen lust for each other. Standing in the shade of the trees she was prepared for anything, but then a thought rushed through my mind: what if someone saw? And so I didn't take what a person can give as the best feeling in the world, if born of love. I always regretted that. I regretted giving in to embarrassment and the fear of violating the rules of behaviour. Whether I was lying under falling bombs, knocked about by typhus, or blinded and ready to take my own life, I always regretted not making love to my wife back then . . .

CHAPTER THREE

Here, There, and Somewhere Else

On the night of 5 July 1941 we were marching along the blacked-out high road. Fedya Glebov was singing, jauntily starting one new song after another, including our favourite, 'Along the Valleys, Across the Uplands' [a popular soldiers' song of the Russian Civil War of 1918–22 – Trans.]. Our company, which included students from the Surikov Institute of Arts, was part of the 11th Rifle Division of the Opolchenie [renamed 18th Rifle Division on 26 September 1941 and later reorganized into the 11th Guards Rifle Division – Ed.]. We marched smartly, our light-coloured pants visible in the darkness, moving away from Moscow ...

By the time daylight dawned we weren't singing anymore. There was no more familiar bitumen beneath our feet, and we were falling out of step. The rear of the column was lost in a grey mist, and we – sick of tramping – began to wonder: why are they driving us so hard? It's time to have a rest! Well, if this was what it took to win the war, we could march till morning. But we had been on the move both night and day, and we were sleepy.

During the march we had been overtaken by the first trucks carrying weapons and uniforms. Since we were Opolchenie, and a newly formed division, we were being armed and fitted out on the road. Trucks would drive up, the column would stop, and packs would be thrown down from the vehicles so we could be issued with their contents straightaway. Initially, we had been a motley and colourful crew, armed with Polish rifles, then with old German models – though there was no ammo for them. But day by day we were getting everything we needed for the war. We got ten-round SVT rifles [a Soviet semi-automatic weapon of the early war period – Trans.] and uniforms. At first there wasn't enough for us all, but gradually we received blouses, pants, foot-wrappings and puttees. All of this changed our appearance and we looked at each other as comparative strangers. There were many funny moments with the foot wrappings and puttees, the handling of which required practice, so as not to get mixed up, and not to rub one's feet sore.

Our life, difficult even without this, was complicated by the fact so many different things had been accumulating in our backpacks: clothes, hand grenades, Molotov cocktails, and so on. On top of all this we were issued with ammo: a common individual allowance plus a reserve, which was supposed to be carried in the unit transport. But when we had no transport everything had to be carried on our backs. Then our leading singers would strike up songs and we would join in. If you didn't sing you'd be in a stupor. Songs helped us to march, to hold out.

The sun, the heat, of that July – who of my generation could forget?! The road was white with dust, which shrouded us. We were constantly thirsty, but even the most disciplined among us had an empty flask. Suddenly, a shriek! Someone would reel, stagger a few steps, and fall into the dust. Medical orderlies would run up, drag the invalid to the roadside and bring him to his senses – it was sunstroke. But we were not allowed to stop, to step out of formation. Even if your comrade fell, you couldn't help him. You had to march on. Just keep going, the orderlies will deal with it. 'Don't fall out of step!' And so the column flowed around the fallen and moved on. This was the rule of march. Back then it shook me. I even had a quarrel with a *starshina* [i.e. sergeant major – Trans.] when I tried to help a guy who'd fallen next to me.

On the fourth day of the march they gave us a treat. They took some heavy English 'Hotchkiss' machineguns and boxes of ammo from the vehicles. To carry all this would be unbearable. The machinegun shield – the heaviest thing – was carried by one man, the tripod by another, the ammo by two others. Machineguns would be disassembled and the parts distributed between the soldiers. Heavy machineguns, company mortars, ammunition, all were loaded on the soldiers' backs. The amount carried by each of us, when put on a blanket and tied in a bundle, was difficult to lift off the ground. On top of all, we were laden with hand grenades and Molotov cocktails for anti-tank combat. And marches were long, 50–70 kilometres each. It was beyond one's power to hold out a whole day on the white-hot road. Yet we kept marching, filling the air with our songs.

Time and again our unit was shifted from one sector of the front to another. From near Vyazma we were sent on trucks to Orel, then to the Bryansky Front, then to Elnya, and then back to Vyazma again. We dug defence lines and anti-tank ditches. As soon as we were ready to face the enemy, an order would come and we moved on. We understood that this fever gripped not only us but those above. No one knew how to stop the enemy. It seemed to me that we were rushing around like hares in a circle: we'd been here, there, and somewhere else, and kept coming back to Vyazma.

They were always hammering into us: 'Hard at drill – easy in combat' [an aphorism of Field Marshal Alexander Suvorov, *b.* 1729, *d.* 1800 – Trans.]. But we were incapable of distinguishing the two. We were on the march twenty hours a day. We would have only one stop: an hour for lunch. But it was not easy to provide soldiers with food on a forced march. We were fed with millet gruel. Yet these marches trained us well and we learnt a lot: how to wrap our legs with puttees, how to handle a shovel, how to construct dugouts.

Our nurse, Tonya, a young, thin woman (though tall and well-proportioned), reminded me of Galochka in height and appearance. It drew us together straightaway, and when we were stationed in the forests near Elnya, she talked me into becoming a medical orderly. She had been given the task of selecting volunteers and training them to drag the wounded from the battlefield and provide first aid. I learned to apply bandages and splints quickly and correctly. Using a sharp shovel, which I always kept well honed (I could even sharpen a pencil with it), I could make wooden splints from any tree branch, in order to immobilize a broken leg or arm.

The main thing during training, apart from transport, was dragging a wounded man over broken ground. If the man was conscious, he would try to help you with a hand or a foot. But if he stopped helping you out, it was hard to drag him. If the man had a trench coat or a groundsheet, you could use it to lug him over bumpy ground. But if he only had a blouse, there was no choice but to grab his belt or collar. And you had to take into account what kind of wound he had. Certainly it was proper to select and train soldiers for this kind of work. I can't believe our girls used to do that sort of thing.

Initially I worked because I liked Tonya and wanted to help her somehow. But when, in training, the commanders mentioned me as the best orderly – issuing me with a medical bag – I felt proud. I felt pleased with my mission as the saviour of wounded men. And my comrades began treating me like one who could be of a great use. I received gifts from everyone: bandages, iodine, pills, and we took turns carrying my stretcher on our shoulders.

One cloudy morning Tonya told me the commanders had ordered that a hospital operating theatre be built in the village we were stationed in. The locals advised: 'Our *kolkhoz* [collective farm – Trans.] has a storehouse for potatoes. It has log walls, timbered partitions and a lot of earth strewed on top. And you could put in a two-layer ceiling, although not too thick!' The commanders approved, the location suiting the battalion well.

Work went ahead. We sawed and hewed with axes. We made an operating table, cleaned up the compartments, covered everything with fresh thatch. The brass hats – a young Georgian *kombat* [battalion commander – Trans.] and a colonel along with him – came over. They spoke about something and examined everything meticulously. Then Tonya said our operating post had been judged the best in the battalion. We rejoiced, for such praise was like a decoration for us. And next day Tonya brought me her blanket as a gift: 'Go on, take it, I can see you have no warm things at all, but it's already cold.'

Oh God, how important for life even a small kind deed is, and how little we know its consequences! This small blanket of Tonya's would save my life. And not only mine.

At dawn, as usual, it began to rain. We were lined up and directed somewhere. On the march again ...

CHAPTER FOUR

Remains of a Soldier

We were on the move again. We'd been told the Germans had broken through near Vyazma and we had to eliminate the breach. We were not far from the town of Kholm-Zhirkovsky. Approaching a forest we saw blackened buildings – or to be more precise, kitchen stoves surrounded by piles of charred logs: all that remained of the peasant dwellings. At the forest edge the earth was torn up by bomb craters. In the burnt-out houses, and lying around, were the corpses of Red Army soldiers: blistered, dark-blue bodies. Their helmets, rifles – even their shovels – were scorched. In the houses coals were still smouldering. Everything had obviously happened recently. The place stank. We stood in a stupor. In our minds, scenes unfolded: scenes of soldiers, just like us, resting or hiding from a raid, caught by death. It was here we sensed the fear of death for the first time. Many threw up. I simply wanted to sit down and go nowhere. But the column marched off and in a few minutes we began talking again, swapping jokes.

The sun was low and people were moving wearily. I watched the swaying heads and shoulders, trying not to think about my first close view of death – a helmet, a shovel, several charred pieces of iron: the remains of a soldier. Passing a forest we came upon an open space. In front of us, a field with bushes and the yellow grass of a dried-out swamp. On the horizon a village stretched out on a hill, silhouetted against the glowering sky. There the enemy lay. We were regrouped into battle order and tasked as follows: we must cross the field and consolidate near a thicket of alder trees, our start line, then the attack would begin. But we were hungry and more than anything in the world we simply wanted to eat.

We had to run to the right. Jumping a fence, I saw two women burying a trunk – probably containing their only belongings – in a hole in a vegetable garden. Here cabbages were growing. I pulled out my dagger and without asking the owners, cut off a cabbage. Slicing it into four pieces, I threw my mates a piece each, and we chewed the crunchy leaves while dashing towards the ditch near the alder trees, where we were supposed to lie down.

I was lying near Tonya with my medical bag. She began to cry softly. I pulled out an album and began writing a letter to my wife. This was a stereotype fostered by movies and literature: it was the way to behave before an attack. Should I die in action, they'll find the letter when burying me and send it to my wife: everything will be according to the rules and I'll be up to the mark. But in my soul I didn't believe in death or in the reality of the attack. I dug in my pocket, pulled out my NZ [i.e. *neprikosnovenny zapas* or reserve stock – Trans.] of sugar, covered with tobacco crumbs, and handed it to Tonya. She looked at me with bewilderment but took it. As she nibbled, she gradually calmed down, wiping her blue eyes with a small fist.

We stood up and rushed across the dried out swamp, overgrown with bushes. Suddenly, I saw a soldier carrying two loaves of bread. He said that on the forest edge there was a destroyed vehicle full of the stuff. I quickly returned with Lesha Avgustovich. We picked up a whole stretcher-full of bread and caught up with our line. I handed my end of the stretcher to a soldier and threw the loaves around to our comrades: the whole section was soon chewing, without letting go of their rifles. I saw two soldiers holding up our arts critic. The poor man suffered from angina and was having an attack of crippling chest pain. I quickly pulled the valerian drops out of my medical bag, poured some into a flask, dripped in some water and gave it to him. The guy was embarrassed: 'Well, you know, that wasn't the right time for that to happen ...' I took his rifle, gave him my arm, and we moved off together.

Moments later we lay down to wait for the rest of our group to catch up. Many soldiers used this stop to adjust their puttees (these puttees annoyed us greatly, unravelling at the most critical moments). Someone found a leaflet dropped by German aircraft: 'Red Army soldier, hurry up and surrender! The German Army is advancing, you may not be on time to get your parcel of land, which the Germans will provide you with.' The little nurse Masha was outraged and tore the paper apart. But many other leaflets were lying around, and some soldiers took them, as if for cigarette rolls. The unease with which this was done betrayed a suppressed thought, an echo of something I'd heard from a peasant near Orel: 'Oh well, it can't get any worse ...'

The Starshina – we nicknamed him 'Samovar' for his low height, red face, and golden hair combed straight back – ordered: 'Get ready!' We moved into the attack at a quick walk, which broke into a sprint: 'For Stalin! For the Motherland!' My hands gripped the rifle ever tighter. I felt myself overwhelmed by some wave. I wasn't the same person as a moment ago. Something had taken me over and I was aware of only one desire: to run straight at the enemy. It was a similar feeling to that experienced in my first bayonet drill, when I found myself rushing at a dummy with a screaming impulse to run it through. Behind me, Leshka was dragging the stretcher as he ran. We kept swapping over and carrying it in turn.

At last we made the brow of the hill, met only by a row of derelict sheds. All was quiet – no one was shooting from the village beyond. That meant it had all been a false alarm! I noticed it was raining; that I felt chilled inside; that I was exhausted. We set ourselves up in a barn, crawling into the hay so as to warm up a bit and snooze. Samovar sat on the doorstep and ordered a reconnaissance of the village. Two soldiers went: Misha Volodin, the tallest in our platoon, and another, much shorter man. We envied them. It was always worthwhile going scouting: one might find something to eat. We were always hungry.

It was getting dark, rain continued to drizzle, and the grey silhouettes of village shacks could be seen in the distance. Our scouts returned, leading a soldier from our company: an ageing, stooping, *Opolchenets* [a soldier of the Opolchenie – Trans.] with a broken rifle. We clustered around and asked what had happened. It turned out that two German motorcyclists, riding through the village, had seen the old soldier. Snatching the rifle from him, they broke the gunstock apart on a rock and said: 'Go to bed, Rus.' We asked him: 'Why didn't you shoot?' 'I don't know. They were laughing and shouting, "Rus, Rus, come here," so I went. Then they . . .' He held up the rifle and looked like a frustrated kid who had broken his favourite toy.

The village was named Staroye Selo. Suddenly, machineguns opened fire from the place, tracer bullets falling almost next to us. Samovar's first reaction was to yell: 'What the f*** are you doing? There are soldiers here!' And he added a few more strong curses. But then, green and pink flares flashed in the darkness, followed by the roaring of tanks and more machinegun fire. Everybody rushed from the barn down the hill. I caught sight of a deserted machinegun and a wave of exhibitionism (as Galochka would have called it) came over me: though it's not easy to say where exhibitionism ends and duty begins! It was as if I could see myself in action: my comrades would say, 'Well done – the medical orderly kept his head, grabbed a machinegun and was ready to beat off a tank attack!' Taking cover behind a rock, I tried to familiarize myself with the weapon and open fire. What a shame I knew so little about machineguns! To my dismay, I found I couldn't work it. I couldn't even attach the ammo drum, which for some reason had been pulled out of place. Someone began pulling my leg from behind: 'Kol'ka, give me the machinegun before Samovar sees it.' But I held back, annoyed that I had found the gun but would have to let someone else fire it. And yet, I felt shame at the thought of letting my comrades down, and the machinegun was taken from me.

Meanwhile, lines of our soldiers were advancing, as the Germans shot at them from tanks and armoured vehicles. We had no artillery: the boys were driving off the tanks with Molotov cocktails. All around, fires flared up, lit by the fuel mixture.

It turned out that many were killed and wounded on our right flank, but joy and excitement broke over us: the German attack had been successfully beaten off. Everyone exchanged stories, and laughing, said what a fine fellow Mishka Udaltsov was, who had outflanked a tank with his section and made the Fritzes retreat with the fuel mix. Each man told of all he'd been through, making up heroic details on the spot.

And so the battle we had just been through was something of a dress rehearsal. Before it, we hadn't seen the enemy, and even when he was shooting at us, we couldn't believe that he might be killed. Putting on a trench coat doesn't make a soldier. To kill – even to save your life – means turning upside-down all the thoughts and feelings in your mind and heart. Deep inside we had not been ready: just like the old soldier who, having been summoned, approached the German motorcyclists and gave away his weapon; and the Starshina, who, when the firing started, had yelled at the enemy. Indeed, there had been doubts inside each of us regarding the Germans: maybe they were not such beasts as the papers said, maybe it was just a misunderstanding? But after this battle something changed. Before the attack, each of us was silently asking if he would be able to kill. Now there was a reply: I can if I have to. At the start of the war, getting people ready to kill – hardening them to it – was a reconstruction of the whole human mentality. And it was a long, painful process. We had been unready for the war, not so much technically as morally, and it took time to re-educate people. It seems to me this was one of the factors that enabled the Germans to overwhelm our army during the first days of the war.

CHAPTER FIVE

Circle of Fires

Leshka and I were transferred to the 4th Platoon as medical orderlies. In combat conditions medical orderlies were placed in the rearmost platoon, making evacuation of the wounded more convenient. When we arrived, the command to dig trenches was given. The sticky yellow clay did not succumb easily to shovels, while the driving rain soaked our woollen jackets, making them heavy and cumbersome. The guys from the 3rd Platoon were around somewhere, chopping with their shovels, but now we were in the 4th and everyone was a stranger to us. Leshka and I dug a knee-deep sitting trench, but as we were in a hollow, water seeped up from below. Why we were digging defences at the bottom of a hill no one knew ...

The command 'Rest!' found us standing in water, soaked to the skin. We brought bundles of flax and spread them on the floor of the trench. Then we lay down inside, pulling our trusty stretcher across the top in an effort to keep off the rain. A heavy sleep descended upon us after an exhausting day: the march, the attack, the digging – as well as the rain and constant hunger (our field kitchen had been lost God knew where).

I was woken by water, dripping down on my face from the stretcher above. Alexei opened his eyes too. It was light but strangely quiet. No commands could be heard. Looking around, we were surprised to see lines of empty communication trenches, half filled with water. Soldiers had been sleeping here, but where were they now? Again and again we looked about us, unable to believe we were alone. The platoon had vanished and we'd been left behind! Covered by our stretcher, we must have slept unnoticed as our comrades slipped away. We had arrived at the 4th Platoon during the night, so we were probably not missed at reveille. I had reported our presence to the platoon commander, but perhaps he had forgotten about us. Maybe he had other things to worry about, but if so, what? Yesterday we had seen fires on the horizon: they were not burning for nothing! And so we stood in a daze, trying to work out why we had been left behind, and which way the platoon had gone. We could not have known this night had changed our lives, separating our fates from those of our comrades, who were now far away, on the march somewhere . . .

We grabbed our gear, threw the stretcher on our shoulders, and rushed into the forest. Having gone a short distance, we came upon an officer, lying beneath a groundsheet in the bushes. He saw us and called out. We ran up to him joyfully. He was the commander of a neighbouring battalion. His first questions were: which battalion were we from? And which company? But when we replied that we didn't know where our battalion was; that we had fallen asleep and been left behind, he looked bewildered. He didn't scold us, as we'd expected, but said: 'What? There is no one on site?' Then he explained: 'I sent messengers out to nearby units, but they only found the catering platoon. The other battalions must have left without informing us . . .' The fact he was talking to us plainly, without regard to rank, made the situation tenser, and more serious. Just then a messenger ran up, and reported that our right flank was deserted: the neighbouring battalions had left.

The Kombat told us to fall in, then ordered a march. The battalion pulled out of a hollow in front of Staroye Selo. Stretching along the edge of the forest, our column included many carts carrying wounded men: we had not imagined so many casualties after yesterday's battle. Marching with our new-found comrades, we wondered: how could it happen that when our unit received the order to withdraw, they didn't warn the neighbouring battalion? But already, the fact we had been forgotten no longer seemed so horrible and unjust.

Daylight grew and a *rama* [literally 'frame' – a nickname for the twin-fuselage German FW-189 reconnaissance plane – Trans.] appeared in the sky. Minutes later a Messers [nickname for the German Me-109 fighter plane – Trans.] arrived and machinegunned our column, making one pass after another, adding more wounded to our numbers. German bombers – 'Junkerses' – were moving eastwards, high in the sky, heading for Moscow. The Fritzes likely had an airfield nearby, as the rama had directed the Messers at us so quickly. This level of efficiency was depressing. Now we couldn't march on the roads for fear of being spotted, so we had to make our way through the woods. Yesterday we had been hunting the enemy, searching for his sabotage groups, and being led into the attack. Suddenly we were retreating east, hoping to squeeze by unnoticed, avoiding combat, and losing casualties to enemy fighters.

We were moving in groups to a river crossing. Reconnaissance patrols returned with distressing news: the Germans were already there, a tank column supported by a unit in grey vehicles. No point heading in that direction – so we continued through the forest, skirting round blast craters made by 500 kg bombs. We came across a glade. As soon as our leading troops tried to cross it, a machinegun opened up from the opposite side.

We immediately fell back, turning sideward again. Then we bumped into a group of Muscovites from the Opolchenie, coming from the Dniepr. The Fritzes were there too! Where could we make a crossing? The situation was becoming increasingly confused. Near Kholm-Zhirkovsky our column was surrounded. No one knew what was happening. Lesha and I lost contact with our new comrades and were washed away into other units.

Alexei and I were walking, dragging our stretcher, still hoping to find our battalion. It was clear to us we were wasting time searching for a crossing: the situation was changing hourly as the Germans tightened their grip, closing the circle. Meanwhile, each man became a strategist, sharing his ideas on how to act and what to do. Some said we should fight our way through, others that we should stand firm. But we were in the realm of uncertainty: what lay ahead of us? How far had the Fritzes advanced? Where were our troops? We decided to push on as fast as possible. Perhaps we would get lucky and break free? But every misfortune, every encounter with the enemy, every time we came under fire, our faith was eroded, making us prey to panic, fatigue and hunger. Panic leads to alienation, loss of faith, the single-minded drive for self-preservation: a return to the animal condition for people bound by fear and having no future.

During the night we were joined by a group of Opolchenie men from our battalion who, as it turned out, had left the night before. Some of them had managed to get as far as the river, but light tanks had struck, blocking access to the bridge. Now an enormous quantity of enemy armour had built up there.

In the hours of darkness everything began to move – soldiers, guns, hospitals – all crawling along in one particular direction. But when the columns were met by men and vehicles coming the other way, the whisper would go round: 'The gap is not there, it's in another direction . . .' And an hour or two later, the main flow would have turned to the right about. Thus we would rush round the whole night. And in the morning we would be bombed. Lesha and I were no longer trying to find our battalion: it seemed to us that a small group would have more chance of filtering through the encirclement.

Why did we want to break out rather than stand and fight? We hadn't yet learned to resist regardless of the odds, as we later did with the Partisans. And the very word 'encirclement' was paralyzing. The old habit of thinking and fighting by the rules was still alive in us: we were in a unit and the top brass would tell us what to do. If they were not around, we would have to find them, in order to learn what to do. Yet we should have decided and acted that day, that moment. Meantime, the Messers kept screeching over, scattering the columns into separate little groups.

There were so many German aircraft that even if they found a small party – or even a single man – they would attack, machinegunning us in formation. The flyers hunted with impunity. They dropped not only bombs, but leaflets: 'Fighters, surrender and you will be freed!' 'We're not fighting the Russians but the Communists!' For the peasants, they would drop children's shoes and white bread buns in bags. And special leaflets: 'If you don't want to get bombed don't let soldiers in!' Our soldiers abandoned heavy guns and tanks without fuel, blowing up our first *Katyushas* ['Little Kate' – nickname for the BM-13 rocket launcher – Trans.]. Hundreds and thousands of men were rushing about inside a circle of fires, frightened by the shooting, and the tanks of the enemy.

A group of Moscow Opolchenie men formed up. They wanted to head directly east through the forests, bypassing any settlements. Alexei and I joined them. As we walked, we anxiously peered at the sky, so as to determine east and west. But the heavens were grey with slow, soggy clouds. We looked at the trees, trying to remember if moss grew on the northern side . . .

It was difficult to navigate the forest without a compass in summer. Suddenly, the forest ended and a field opened up. German vehicles were rolling across it. We dashed back among the trees and turned leftward, where the woodland stretched to the horizon.

We had been walking a long time when we came across a forester's shack. We knocked at the door but no one answered. We sat on the doorstep. The guys emptied their pockets, shaking out flakes of *Makhorka* [type of cheap tobacco – Trans.], then set to work making roll-ups for everyone. Suddenly, I noticed a fleeting shadow at the window. We began knocking again, threatening to smash down the door. An old man in a white shirt and a waistcoat appeared at the threshold. He glared at us with angry eyes. 'What!' we exclaimed, 'an old man scared of his countrymen?!' 'You are loafing about,' the old man replied, 'and you want food too! I'm sorry we haven't had time to ask – there have been a lot of you today . . .' We felt ashamed. We were retreating, looking for a way back to our lines, leaving these folks behind. We tried to explain, to break down this hostile barrier: but the harder we tried, the brighter his animosity burned. Of the Germans, he made the following observation: 'What's there to be afraid of? They're people too. It can't get any worse.'

He was actually looking forward to the Fritzes! But we needed to find a way out – though we hadn't lost hope of lodgings for the night, and maybe some potatoes. The old man said there was a village nearby, free of Germans. Alexei and I decided to go over. We would find out what was going on, ask for food and shelter, and return in the morning to pick up the others. The old man had a daughter in the village: 'There is a shack next to the well. Pop in, maybe she'll take you in. There are plenty of your lot in the village, both wounded and stragglers, not knowing where to go. Scarpering towards Moscow . . .' We left with heavy hearts.

We approached the village in a state of exhaustion. It stood on a hillock and looked very familiar. We couldn't believe our eyes: it was almost identical with the one where we had beaten off the tank attack. Was it possible we had come full circle?

We trudged along an empty street, still clutching our stretcher. It was growing dark. Only the puddles shone on the road, while the dead windows reflected the dull glow of sunset. Not a single fire burned in the windows. Local men stood in the middle of the street, chatting quietly among themselves. They replied to our greetings with bitter words: 'You're wandering around still armed – we're gonna have lots of trouble because of you. There are enough of your sort in the village already, without you . . .'

We didn't stop to talk. We moved further into the village. The doorstep of one shack faced the street – the old man's daughter lived there. I went up a couple of steps and knocked on the window. A grey face flashed behind the pane, then the hostess opened the door:

'What are you mooning around here for? This place is full of your lot!' I was flustered by her words and only said: 'Can we stay overnight at your place?' 'No, sweetheart, you can't. What if the Germans turn up? I've got kids! No way! You'd better sleep in the bomb shelter, in the vegetable garden. Lots of you guys have been staying overnight in the bomb shelters. What are you carrying a stretcher for? You could give it to a poor old woman – I'll make a skirt out of it if nothing else.' Only then the thought entered my head: what do we carry the stretcher for? The hope that we might find our unit somewhere was still alive – how could we abandon our equipment? But the woman's words made me see the absurdity of our situation. I told her: 'Take it, maybe you really can find a use for it.' She became more talkative and suggested sending her son to show us the bomb shelter. She said there'd been fighting three days ago, many wounded men remaining on the battlefield. Some of them had been picked up by women, some had crawled into holes: 'Many of them hide in vegetable gardens and in the woods. They all want to get out of the encirclement.'

After her story, we were convinced that having wandered so long, we had returned to Staroye Selo, the village where our first combat had taken place. The woman called her son: 'Andrei!' A lad of about fifteen came out, putting on his jacket, readily agreeing to accompany us. We walked down the street, announcing we were hungry enough to chew out a boot heel. Andrei suggested going to the abandoned kolkhoz beehives. We went in, pulled out several honeycomb lumps, shook off the bees with our field caps, and squeezed sweet, fragrant, autumn honey from the combs. Having eaten my fill, I stuffed some combs into a medicine jar that served as a glass.

We talked with the lad: 'So, are you afraid of the Germans?' 'Of course I am! Look how many soldiers are hiding, and they all want to get away, but the Germans are holding them tight.' We crossed a potato field, the leaves entangling our feet. At last, Andrei said: 'Here . . .' It was a small hump with a hole underneath, covered by logs and strewn with earth, with a chute masked by an oven door. Andrei went down with us, asking where we were going and what would happen if the Fritzes found us. We learned from him where the roads from this village led to. But we couldn't talk too long, for our legs were aching and our eyes were closing. Andrei shut the door and all was silent and dark. We couldn't imagine that tomorrow, the Germans would be around here, in this village ...

CHAPTER SIX

Souvenir, Souvenir ...

We were woken in the morning by the roar of engines. Our first thought was of Messers – but the ground was shaking. Sticking our heads out of the door we saw silhouettes of tanks and vehicles. We were not sure what kind of units were moving down the road – ours or German? An hour or so passed before we could plainly see black-and-white crosses on the tanks. It was obvious the Fritzes had already settled in the village, but new columns kept moving down the road. Screening ourselves off with potato leaves, we watched the Germans running about the village, catching hens and laughing. Two of them were washing themselves near the outermost shack. If only we could last till night and clear out: we'd be more careful in future, we would not make such a foolish mistake again – walking so long, just to return to the spot we started from!

We took turns to creep out and watch, sharing our impressions. We considered shooting, but banished the thought immediately: we'd be pinned down straightaway – it would be a senseless end. Perhaps we could become Partisans? But the forest we had come through was not big enough to hide in. No, we had to escape across the front line as soon as possible. But for now we were sitting in a mousetrap. How could we have chosen a place so exposed on all sides to stay overnight?! And next to the road! We'd been trained to fight, but our experience was limited. In the dark it had seemed like a safe place ...

A woman was walking towards us across the field. Leaning over the door she asked: 'Is there a pot down there?' This woman has nothing to boil potatoes in?! We tried to drive her away: 'Get out of here, do you want to lead the Germans onto us?!' She left, quietly mumbling, 'I thought it was here ...'

Ten minutes later, to my horror, I saw the Germans. In their square helmets, sleeves rolled up and submachineguns in their hands, they were moving in file, firing bursts. Our soldiers were creeping out of their hideouts here and there. Leshka, scrambling backwards, fell on top of me: 'They are right next to us!' I quickly hid my rifle under some straw, but above us a voice barked: 'Rus! Out, out!'

I crawled out first. Leshka passed me his backpack and bags, I gave him my hand and helped him out. The Fritzes laughed. They sent us to join a group of our soldiers, standing some distance away, watched by two guards. This group grew steadily, as the German line advanced across the field, catching our men, who were hiding in bomb shelters and under bushes. There were many wounded. Some were supported by their comrades, others were carried on trench coats. I noticed that a number of these casualties had dressings made from their puttees: I understood then just how important these annoying items were, how useful they could be to a soldier wounded in combat.

We were led along the street we had traversed the day before. The roads were lined with vehicles, motorbikes and tanks. Field-kitchens were smoking, filling the air with the savoury smell of roasted meat. Red cigarette packets with silvery foil were scattered all around. The Fritzes, happy to be at rest, were washing, cleaning up, and smartly saluting their top brass. My God, it was just like the newsreels we'd seen in the cinema! I was watching it all with detached curiosity, as if I were someone else: consequently there was no fear, just a kind of frozen incredulity. Did I really have to suffer so many ordeals to join the Opolchenie with such faith? Did I really have to go through all that drilling, all that marching – tramping hundreds of kilometres, twenty hours a day, with no transport – to take part in just one action? Just one action! And then suddenly to stop, like a broken watch, and with no future?

We gathered in a yard enclosed by a fence. The wounded were carried into a house. A German stepped out onto the doorstep and said in pure Russian: 'We're gonna search you. You are not allowed to have knives, razors or weapons.' Suddenly a woman shrieked near a shack across the road: a boy all covered in blood was with her. It turned out he'd blown something up and two of his fingers had been torn off. I immediately imagined that he'd picked up my hand grenade primers, which I'd thrown away in the vegetable garden when we were caught. Pity, guilt, and the thought I might be able to give him aid, propelled me across the street. I rushed into the shack, took out a bandage and iodine, and began treating the wound. Everyone in the room was yelling. Suddenly a cry came from behind my back: 'Quiet!' And a shot rang out. A German interpreter – it was he who fired – grabbed me by the sleeve and pushed me towards the door: 'Let's go!'

Out on the street, he began to interrogate me, poking his pistol into my chest: 'A kommissar? An officer? Where are you from?' I didn't dare say I was from Moscow, so I answered, 'From Kharkov. And I'm not a commander at all, I'm a private, I used to be a student in an Institute of

Arts.' 'Where was the Institute?' 'Kaplunovskaya Street, number eight. And I lived in the "Giant" building, at number ten.' I was speaking of the time, six years before, when I studied at the Kharkov Institute of Arts and lived in the 'Giant' communal hall – a massive place, built for all the students of Kharkov's institutes of higher education. The interpreter replied: 'And I studied in the Polytechnic and also lived in the "Giant". I know that a student is promoted to a commander's rank after graduation from an institute. And another thing: you've got a moustache and long hair – it means you are a commander, because all soldiers have shaved heads.' As bad luck would have it, we had grown 'Chapaev' moustaches [after the legendary hero of the Russian Civil War, renowned for his enormous moustache – Trans.] and it had been three months since our first and only haircut. I explained: 'My friend and I are both artists and volunteers: that's why we've got moustaches – because we were allowed. As for our hair, it's simply grown out.' 'If you hadn't come across me, your fellow-countryman, they would have shot you straightaway. Tell no one you're volunteers – we shoot volunteers immediately. Call yourself a commander and have a haircut as soon as you can: or you'll be in trouble.' But then the interpreter warmed up: 'We used to go to your institute to dance with your girls. You used to have dancing nights and the masquerades were magnificent. I studied in Kharkov for eight years and was a spy.' 'Pity I didn't know back in Kharkov what you were!' I broke out. He looked at me narrowly: 'And what would have happened?' My mouth went dry. I realized my words were out of place and simply said: 'I've just never seen a spy ...' 'Watch out then! And when you're searched tell them you're a painter, a Kunstmaler.'

He left me near the shack with the other POWs and disappeared: but the chill of the near fatal experience that had just touched me did not leave with him. What had stopped him, a spy and a Fascist, from putting a bullet through me on the spot? Could it be that, after hiding so long, he wanted to say openly: 'I'm a spy'? Was he just showing off his power? And these guys were on their way to Moscow! I felt sick and disgusted, as if a viper were crawling on me.

Rejoining my comrades, I saw that Alexei was talking to Sashka Lapshin (I have changed the original name) from our platoon. Great was our joy on being reunited. It turned out he'd been captured at the river crossing. The guys asked me what the interpreter had said. I told them, and we decided to call ourselves 'Kunstmaler Academy Moscau' – 'artists from a Moscow Academy,' which was about as much German as we could manage. This, however, would explain our presence at the front as artists. We had just talked this through when Sasha was counted off and shoved into the shack. Alexei and I were to be in the next group.

We stood before the shack, into which people were being called in groups of three or four. As soon as one group was released, another would be marched in. They were searching for documents. Suddenly, Sashka strode out, hoisting his backpack onto his shoulder without stopping, while holding his gas mask container and an album for drawing. Sashka said that when he told the Germans he was an artist from Moscow, they became very interested in his album. But a German was already counting us off: 'Ein, zwei, drei ...'

I entered the shack. There was fresh yellow straw on the floor and one window was curtained with a blanket. There were about five German soldiers inside, accompanied by a young junior lieutenant. We were ordered to place our backpacks and gas mask bags on a table, where they were disembowelled energetically. One German found a small piece of lard in my kit, all covered with crumbs, and took it away – as well as a piece of sugar left from my reserve stock. Then they rifled through my medical bag. Finding my jar of honey with the medicine label on it, they turned it over, sniffing at it for some time: but having decided it must be some kind of medication, they tossed it back into the bag. One German took the belt from my pants. This belt had Caucasian brass panels and was a gift from my brother-in-law. The German tried it on, repeating: 'Souvenir, souvenir, gut ...' I realized they were taking anything that seemed to be of use. I was astounded by their pettiness: how could one soldier take from another a piece of dirty sugar? Or a piece of lard? Or a handkerchief folded into four?

But then a red-haired sergeant major with freckles took an album containing front-line drawings from my gas mask bag. He began looking through it, repeating, 'Kunstmaler, Kunstmaler ...' His comrades forgot about the other bags and gathered round, pointing at my pictures and laughing cheerfully. Then the Lieutenant took the album, and consulting his phrase book, asked me: 'Where from?' I answered. Then an idea struck him. Opening the album at a blank page, he pointed at it, then at himself, repeating: 'Draw me! Draw a portrait!' I took out a pencil and began sketching. The Germans and our POWs stood stock-still, staring at me intensely. Five minutes later, everyone recognized the Lieutenant's likeness and began clamouring: 'Gut! Prima!' I tore out the sketch and gave it to the Lieutenant. He looked at it thoughtfully and stuck it in his pocket. But immediately recalling something, he produced some photographs and leafing through them, selected one of a beautiful woman. Handing it to me, I understood he wanted me to draw her too: so I did. Again, everyone approved, and it seemed to me that a good contact had been set up: they sympathized with me and were already returning our backpacks and gas mask bags, having thrown the gas masks into a corner of the room.

But then the red-haired sergeant major remembered that all documents had to be checked, and reached for the pocket on my blouse where I kept a packet containing photos of my wife and family. It flashed through my mind that now these bandits would see a precious picture of my wife, taken on a riverbank, where she stood naked, putting on her white dress, while the wind tousled her hair and bent the reeds down to the water. I loved this photo more than any other, Galya was so pure. It was a memory of the best time of my life, the days of my first love and joy. And now they would be looking at it, snatching it away as they had my belt, saying 'Souvenir, souvenir ...' Instinctively, I covered the pocket and turned his hand aside – the hand of this red-haired one with the freckles. I saw the smile disappear from his lips in a second, and he jabbed his finger into my chest: 'Communist! Communist!' He assumed that my Party membership card was in there. Everything changed. The soldiers who had been laughing a moment before, pressed against me and I stepped back into a corner. I couldn't have explained it, but I knew something had snapped inside me: I wouldn't back down, even though I knew they could do anything to me. All this flashed through my mind like a filmstrip, reeling at a mad speed. Meanwhile, they had already seized my arms, and the red-haired one had pulled out his pistol. He was about to press it under my chin when the Lieutenant waved him aside, and studying his phrase book, found a question and showed it to me: 'What is that?' I answered, remembering only two words: 'Photo, frau ...' He burst out laughing and produced his pack of photos once more. He deliberately turned them over, backside up, and leafing through them, indicated I should do the same. As I did so, everyone stepped back, and though it was clear they remained uneasy, we were allowed to go out. It was my first encounter with the Germans.

CHAPTER SEVEN

A Harsh Lesson

In the morning we were herded down the road. The first transit camp was near the town of Belyi. We were kept there for ten days. We were not fed or given water, and we were exposed to the elements. The camp had been built on a potato field: we survived on the leftover spuds, scraped up from the cold earth. Snow fell early that October. Here for the first time, I saw young, healthy men dying of starvation.

After the first few days in camp, Lapshin, Lesha Avgustovich and I came to the conclusion – and it would have been unwise not to have come to it – that our lifespans were limited by the torments of hunger and slow dehydration. Our end was near. This meant we had to ask the Fritzes to give us work: in other words, to produce pictures for them. We approached a Polish interpreter and told him the truth about our feelings towards Stalin. Back in 1941, after we had been thrown into battle against German tanks armed with only Molotov cocktails, I understood what kind of man Stalin was; and that all his agitated claims about our country being ready to beat off the invasion was a bluff. In truth I had been astounded: for we had been led, not so much to battle, as to slaughter. The wireless and newspapers had clamoured before the war: 'Our borders are unassailable! We will destroy the enemy on his own territory!' And yet the Germans advanced, and we poor, hungry, untrained Opolchenie had been used as a shield against the enemy's armada. It was then I understood there had been no plans for the war, no leadership of the *Stavka* [i.e. the Central Soviet Military Command – Trans.], and that Stalin was a fictitious Supreme Commander.

And so we told the Polish interpreter we had no chance of surviving unless work could be found to earn us food. We told him we did not like Stalin, for he had ruined lots of people, and Lesha pointed at himself, saying that his father had been arrested by the State, and never seen again. The interpreter astonished me with his answer, which was a harsh lesson for me. He simply said: 'This is your opinion, your feelings. But the Germans don't need to know about them. I will try to find a job for you myself. Right now you have to survive and I'll be helping you out. And later on you'll find where you fit in ...' I was astounded. Suddenly I understood that even in this situation, without food or water, when life itself was at stake, one had to hold out to the end. If I wanted to survive this hopeless state of affairs, I had to clear my soul of all doubts. Whatever feelings I had towards Stalin at the moment, there were only two camps, two ideas, and two leaders in charge. And for this reason, I had to suppress my feelings and stick to only one idea, one camp, and one leader. It became a law for me and remained so forever: neither death nor torture would provide me with any kind of justification.

Fortunately, this Pole wasn't a scoundrel. Moreover, he understood our condition and decided to support us – as well as teaching us a lesson. He was a Polish officer who had betrayed his country. What had led him to this path? Maybe his own circumstances helped him understand that we were in a desperate situation, and knowing his new masters, he did not want us to get close to them? But where did this charity, this mercy come from? He had said nothing to shame us, but simply promised to help out. This encounter had a major effect on my life, especially during captivity.

The Pole brought us photographs, from which we would make drawings, and he himself passed them on to the Germans, paying us for the work. And then we said goodbye to this man. We were watching from behind the barbed wire as vehicles and tanks rolled past. The Germans were heading for Moscow. The Polish interpreter was leaving with them and said this to us at parting: 'In two weeks we'll be in Moscow!' He was smiling and waving: but strange to say, I saw him as a dead man, a corpse with no eyes.

After ten days behind the wire, where some of the 350,000 POWs who'd been encircled by the Germans near Vyazma were gathered, we were sent west. I understand now why the Fritzes moved us gradually, in stages: it was in order to 'process' us. It would have been impossible to shoot us all, but equally, it would have been impossible to advance with so many POWs in the rear. Having weakened us in that first camp, to prevent us from escaping in all directions, they drove us still farther. We were starving. On the way, people would throw themselves on the corpses of horses, tearing off chunks of frozen meat: the guards would shoot them.

A street scattered with shreds of bodies; water-filled grave ditches; burnt-out shacks; charred and scorched animals; and suddenly, lying in the slush, I saw books. We were trudging past a village library that had been torched. A book by Stendhal, with a gilded cover, and *War and Peace*, were in the mud. I picked them up and stuffed them into my backpack. It was my dream, before the war, to buy *War and Peace* and suddenly I saw it, in a leather binding, lying in the road. I couldn't step over it. I snatched both these books without hesitation, although every gram in my backpack felt like a kilogram and we had been ditching all we could. But these two books would save the lives of all three of us.

We had been marching towards Smolensk for four days, stopping in specially erected enclosures fenced with barbed wire. Watchtowers with machinegunners would illuminate us with flares at night. A column of wounded, on foot and in carts, had been dragging along beside us. The tail-end of this column, stretching from one hillock to another, was hidden beyond the horizon. Thousands of people, dying of cold and hunger, were left at the stopover sites all along our route. The Fritzes finished off those who were still alive: a guard would kick a fallen man and machinegun him on the ground. Before each new march, guards with sticks lined up on both sides of the column and the command 'All run!' would be given. The mob ran and blows rained hard upon us. This kind of beating would last for one or two kilometres before the word 'Stop!' was announced. Gasping for breath, hot and sweating all over, we would halt – and be kept standing in this condition, in the biting-cold wind, rain and snow, for an hour. The exercise was repeated several times, so only the fittest would survive and march on. But many remained behind and solitary shots would ring out, as the Germans finished them off. Sometimes, we would be herded onto the roadside and marched through minefields: but although our feet could detonate anti-personnel mines, our weight was insufficient to trigger anti-tank mines: consequently, German vehicles were still blown up in this way.

The column stopped. I took my notepad and began to draw. Suddenly, a cavalryman rode up and threatened me with his whip. Fortunately, he was called aside by a colonel, riding in a convertible. The Colonel asked me what I was doing: I answered that I was an artist drawing pictures. He looked at my sketches and said: 'It's not allowed. You shouldn't draw dead German soldiers.' I threw myself into the crowd of POWs walking on the mined roadside – no one would search for me there. The road was crammed with German vehicles: their convoys moving in both directions. It seemed they were everywhere. As we hiked over a hill, we noticed the Germans were laying signal cables. We tramped over a cable that was caught on a stump. I saw some Fritzes at the foot of the hill, tugging at this wire, which did not want to yield to them. But I bent over automatically and released the cable. When our column descended the slope, walking past the signallers, a soldier caught my eye, shouting, 'Come, come!' I went across and he shoved a box of matches in my pocket.

In the evening we were herded down to the River Dniepr. And again, having not reached a camp, they drove us into enclosures fenced with barbed wire and began lining us up. They formed up a long column of fours. Then they made us turn to face the river, our front rank within a metre of the water. A guard yelled: 'Down on your knees!' Perplexed, we knelt on the riverbank. I was fourth from the water but I immediately felt my knees were soaked. A German yelled: 'Schlafen!' – 'Sleep!' – and the command passed along the column. Sleep? But how?! The sand was wet and subsiding under the weight of so many people, icy water oozing out. And yet, standing on our knees in an icy mixture of snow, sand and water, we spent the bitter night. If anyone stood up or lay down, he was shot. By morning, many had frozen to death. Any who could not get up and unbend their knees when commanded, were finished off with submachineguns. My life – and those of my two friends – were saved by the matchbox presented by the signaller and the two books I found on the road. Having covered ourselves with Tonya's blanket, we burned Stendahl's *The Red and the Black* and Tolstoy's *War and Peace*, page by page. These two books, picked up from the mud, breathed out warm air and we did not freeze to death. At dawn we were allowed to cross the river, where we found a village and some shacks.

Our shack was crammed with people, but we rolled under the steps leading up to the door and beneath the floorboards. Suddenly, lying on the cold earth under the shack, I had to answer the call of nature. I felt it so strongly that I had to get out as soon as possible. But the other two didn't want to quit, as our place might be taken by others. Nevertheless, we all crawled out, so as not to lose sight of each other. We had only walked a short distance, when suddenly something happened. We looked back, and to our amazement, saw that our shack had collapsed! Immediately the air was filled with the angry shouts and commands of the Germans and the *Polizei* [a German-organized force of collaborationists – Trans.]. The wounded were moaning, while the uninjured were dragging the wreckage apart, carrying out the casualties. One man, white as chalk, had a broken arm. I began making a splint for him but he said: 'No problem! It'll make me fiercer!' His words astounded me, sounding like a pledge of revenge in a situation where death was constantly at our backs: the most any of us could hope was that death would spare us for at least another moment.

A column was forming up. The shouts of the Germans and the blows and curses of the Polizei were in the air. Near the river-crossing I heard, for the first time, the sound of someone being systematically beaten. A sergeant major was yelling that the Russians were swine and they – the Germans – were the master race. A motionless body was spread on the ground. Two Polizei brutes sat on the legs and head, while a third battered the quivering body. The Sergeant Major counted the blows. When I heard these sounds for the first time, I thought someone was beating dust out of a mattress. Seeing with my own eyes where the sounds were coming from, I felt sick to the stomach. So disgusting was the sight of a beating, death was a better choice ...

Our column stretched out, people walked clasping each other, supporting the exhausted. Grey vehicles flashed by, full of Fritzes roaring with laughter, pointing their cameras at us. Yes, the war was on, and we were threatened not only with physical annihilation but moral annihilation, as the Fascists tried to destroy our dignity and our faith in everything that was good. It would not be easy to survive in this hell, but it would be a hundred times harder to remain a human being.

CHAPTER EIGHT

Dante's Description of Hell

A pale sunset, a high embankment peopled by silhouettes. A bridge was being built, its ribs emerging like the skeleton of a gigantic, stranded fish. We had arrived at Yartsevo. The column of POWs shuffled into a barbed wire enclosure. Built on the site of a former brickworks, it was divided into sections overlooked by watchtowers on stilts, resembling huge spiders, a machinegunner in each one.

During the whole march I had been carrying my medical bag, containing dressings, cotton wool and manganese powder. The wives of my comrades used to send parcels, including dressings and medications, with a note for me: 'If my husband gets a wound, please dress it.' I had been storing it all in my bag, which was now heavy, weighing down my shoulder. I had not dared to get rid of it before, but now I no longer had the strength to carry it. Then an idea occurred to us: we could ask to be sent to a hospital for wounded POWs. We approached a guard with this request: he called up a Polizei and sent him for a doctor. We waited, crowds of emaciated scarecrows lurching past, trying to stop their legs giving way. At last a doctor, who was also a POW, came up. He told us there were more than enough surgeons among the prisoners, let alone medical orderlies. But suddenly recalling something, he offered us a barrack for the seriously wounded. We joyfully agreed.

A Polizei led us through several barbed wire fences to the barrack. It was already dark. An enormous guy opened the door – he was the orderly here. He let us in and immediately shut the door. We couldn't see a thing in the dark, but the stink of rotting bodies struck our senses. We pressed against the wall of the shack, which, being made of wooden planks, let through a little air. For some unknown reason, the orderly looked at us with undisguised animosity. At last he said: 'There's no place to sleep in here. The doctors don't come. And these guys are all goners.' He didn't even bother to lower his voice. We were dumbstruck by his brutal frankness: 'They're all doomed,' he continued, 'what are you going to do in here?' I spoke up: 'We will be doing everything possible to alleviate people's suffering, and, generally, everything in our power. We'll sleep in here and tomorrow we'll start work.'

The plank beds were arranged in three tiers with a gangway, seventy-eighty centimetres wide, stretching along the whole shack. People lay pressed against each other in the dark, trying to keep warm. Someone touched my sleeve: 'Doctor, doctor, save me. I want to live, I've got a house with a garden and kids, three of them, cut my arm off, it's burning! Only let me live ...' A lump came to my throat, but I answered as firmly as I could: 'I'll be examining everyone tomorrow and will help you. But now it's dark.' I couldn't find the guts to admit I wasn't a doctor. My two comrades were rooted to the spot, silent, torn apart by pity and helplessness in the face of this suffering. The orderly climbed onto his bunk in another part of the shack, and we crawled under some plank beds, squeezing into a tiny space, and settling in somehow. It was stuffy, but the pungent smells seemed to be diminishing: fatigue was having its effect. I shut my eyes and immediately the wet, slippery road began to flash through my mind – and corpses, corpses ...

We were lying motionless in our hole, beneath the suffering, raving, dying people. But despite the horror it seemed almost cosy. We warmed up, and gradually, drowsiness began to win out. Suddenly, some warm fluid began dripping onto my leg from above. At first I couldn't understand what it was, but then Sashka said: 'I'm wet all over – the wounded are pissing on us!'

The morning came, grey and dank. When we crawled out of our shelter everyone had already heard that some 'doctors' had come. I discovered that the Germans had not been giving them water. Instead, every morning, they would each get a mug of tea or coffee – or so they called these brown slops. But I needed boiled water for my work. I had to make my way to the camp kitchen to get it. The kitchen was located in a big shack. Everything here was covered in smoke and soot. The corpses of horses, picked off the road, were brought here and butchered: huge pieces of horseflesh were thrown into cauldrons full of water, then the meat was taken out and cut into small pieces. I was astonished that horses were brought in two-wheeled carts harnessed to people! Meanwhile, firewood was piled under some twenty dangling cauldrons. There was no chimney here, so dense grey smoke, tinged with pink and pierced by sparks, swirled over these cauldrons, while tongues of fire licked them from underneath. Dark, sallow figures, with field caps folded down over their ears, were rushing about flaying suspended carcasses. Giant shadows, swaying fantastically in the smoke and vapour, rose to the roof of the huge shack. All this recalled Dante's description of hell. But the most horrifying thing was that everything seemed to be done in silence, as if everyone was mute.

With great difficulty I obtained a bottle of boiled water and set to work. Most of the wounded were still in their original dressings, applied on the battlefield. When such a dressing was removed, one felt sick from the smell. Sasha and Alexei dropped out straightaway, and I had to lay them in the corridor by the wall. Meanwhile, my dressings were turning out well. I would clean a wound with manganese solution and dress it up properly. The sight of a fresh dressing would awaken hope in the hearts of the wounded. But when I found my fellow-countryman with the 'garden and kids' he was already dead from gangrene.

There were seriously wounded men here, and I even had to carry out an operation, amputating the remnants of a smashed arm. My patient lost consciousness. I gave him liquid ammonia to smell and went on with my work. When he saw his crippled arm wrapped in a snow-white dressing, the gleam of a smile flashed on his grey lips – or it might have just been my fancy, for suddenly everything began to swim before my eyes and I felt nauseous. When I came to, someone had shoved a roll-your-own of Makhorka between my teeth. Tobacco was precious, so this was an expression of the highest appreciation from my patients. And then it was back to dressings. Either head or stomach or scrotum – oh, what an inconvenient place for a dressing that was! Alexei and Sasha were giving the wounded food, having discharged the orderly, who had been rapaciously ripping off the dying.

It was sleeting outside. More and more columns kept arriving. A group of new POWs rushed up to our shack, knocking and demanding to be let in. I knew that if just one of them began tearing off planks to get in, the whole lot would be pulled apart for firewood. Picturing this, I put on my bag with its red cross and came out, blocking the door. The crowd of desperadoes began pushing forward, raising a horrible din. Suddenly, one of them threw himself at me: 'Let us in!' I kicked him in the stomach and he fell to the ground, bursting into tears. I felt ashamed. Looking at the hostile faces, blue from cold, staring at me from hollow eyes, I said: 'There are seriously wounded soldiers in here, and there's no room even for us, the medical orderlies. We have dressed them, and if we don't take care of them, they'll all die.' The mob wavered. But then somebody piped up: 'Why are you listening to them bastards?! Smack these scumbags down!' It flashed through my mind that calling for an attack using the plural was horrible and unjust, given I was alone against them. It was as if they were trying to justify themselves with this plural, for to kill me would be to kill some dark force, which they perceived was killing them. I could not show my weakness and began yelling at them, accusing them of cruelty to the wounded. It had the desired effect, and the crowd took a step back, then dispersed. Afterwards, I began to shake uncontrollably from all I'd been through. We kept watch all night: but no one came back to threaten us.

On the third day, my stock of medications was exhausted. I was suffering from physical and moral fatigue. It seemed to me that I myself had begun to decay, like my wounded.

The pallid light of a sickly dawn was seeping through the chinks of the shack. Sasha was shoving me, whispering that it was time to leave; that we could do no more for the wounded; that we were in danger of perishing ourselves. Suddenly, an imperious knock at the door. I clambered out over Leshka, who tried to push me away with all his might, being half asleep and confused. At last I reached the door and opened it. The doctor who had sent us here stood before me. He was surprised to see me, but we both rejoiced to meet again. The doctor had managed to obtain permission from a German brass hat, to add a group of walking wounded to a column of POWs bound for Smolensk. He wanted to take us along as medical orderlies.

It is painful to remember selecting patients for the journey. Everyone knew that to remain meant certain death. People were stretching out their hands to us, assuring us they felt well, faking cheerful and courageous looks. But I had not forgotten the dressings I had made for their stomachs and shattered limbs. I knew what superhuman efforts these smiles cost them. And yet, even if selected for the march, any one of them might be finished off with a bullet at the first fall. But no matter how hard I tried to convince myself that all these guys were doomed anyway, it didn't make the job of selection any easier.

It was cold. A light sleet was falling, turning the road to yellow slush. The column set off for Smolensk. Scenes of all I'd been through, here at Yartsevo, cycled through my memory: I saw myself cleaning wounds, making dressings, repositioning bones; I saw faces twisted with pain, the infernal camp kitchen; and scenes of degradation, punishment, and brutal beatings. A passing truck splashed us with cold mud, spattering the white dressings of the wounded. We heard the laughter of the Germans, the sound of a mouth organ ...

CHAPTER NINE

A Handful of Cottage Cheese

We were loaded onto a train in Smolensk. They drove us like cattle to the carriages, shoving rifle butts in our backs. The crowd pressed forward. One had to remain upright on two sloping planks, but people were stumbling and falling off under the Germans' shouts of 'Schnell! Schnell!' and the curses of the Polizei. Alexei, Sasha and I were among the first few dozen to clamber in, managing to occupy a place in a corner. We were able to sit with our legs crossed beneath us, but they kept stuffing POWs into the carriage and most of them had to stand. The medical orderly girls were the last to be wedged in – about twenty of them. At last the door screeched and the lock clanked. But the train remained still.

Everyone was exhausted, field caps folded down over ears. The Fritzes had removed most of our possessions, even the belts from jackets and trench coats, leaving a mess-tin dangling in front of each of us: our only utensil and reason to live. An ageing, emaciated man dropped down on his knees beside me. He wore spectacles but one glass was shattered, and he was tilting his head, trying to take a good look with one short-sighted eye. He couldn't speak because his lips were swollen, but with great difficulty he managed to articulate – in a kind of hissing rattle – the word 'W-a-a-a-ter . . .' But no one had water, or if they did, they were keeping it hidden: saving it for the moment when they too were on their knees.

The buffers clanked, there was a push, then another, the carriage shuddered, and the train grudgingly spluttered into motion: 'Where are they taking us?' my neighbour on the right whispered. 'What do you care?' said a stooping, grey-stubbled Opolchenie man, 'there's no difference once we're in a cage. Where to? Probably to Germany.' The wheels kept grinding on the rails . . .

My neighbour on the left had stopped wheezing, but I felt his weight pressing heavily against me. I tried to release myself but there was no room to turn. Suddenly, a spurt of fluid flowed from his bloated lips and his head fell. He was dead for sure: 'This man just died!' I yelled, but no one reacted. Leshka winced from pain, whispering: 'Nikolai, what should I do? My guts are bad, I need to get out.' I pulled a towel out of my gas mask bag and said: 'Use this – put it underneath you.' Leshka managed to make use of my towel, but it wasn't enough, for he had diarrhoea. A young soldier, almost a boy, had already lain down on my dead neighbour. He was looking around with wild eyes. He too was thirsty.

An hour went by, then another, and another. I noticed no one was standing any more, everyone having squirmed around to take up less space. Only the group of nurses remained on their feet by the door, hiding behind each other as they tried to tidy themselves up. Sasha was sitting with closed eyes. I, too, was drowsy and ready to sleep – or maybe I was just stupefied by the heavy smell in the carriage. Eventually the train slowed down and we stopped – shouts in German, tramping on the platform – what's happening out there? Where were we? No one had a watch (all had been taken away). Someone shrieked then abruptly fell silent. I was no longer surprised that my neighbour was sitting on a dead body – he was behaving oddly in other ways, frequently choking and gasping for air. His blue eyes glittered, even in the semi-darkness. Suddenly, he tore off his field cap and began fumbling about with his hands, unbuttoning his blouse. Then he grabbed hold of my head: 'Drink, dri-i-i-nk ...' I tried to break loose but he seized my hair. I strained every nerve to unclench his grip but failed. Leshka came to my rescue and at first we didn't notice the boy was already dead. We disentangled my hair from his fingers and his hand fell down. His head dropped too, a gleam of light from the window burning in his sightless, staring eyes. At that moment one of the girls in the group of nurses fell into hysterics ...

The train halted. They started hammering at the door with rifle-butts, knocking out the bar and yelling: 'Los, los! Schnell!' The door screeched along the iron grooves and fresh air rushed into the carriage. Sasha began tugging Leshka, who was completely exhausted. Neither he nor I could get up: our legs were asleep and we were trying to get on our knees first. The girls had already left, the rest were moving towards the door, stepping over dead bodies.

A tumbledown station. It turned out we had been dispatched to Vitebsk. We were glad not to be in Germany. Polizei were helping the German guards, yelling and beating with sticks any who fell behind. We were marched to a POW camp through the bombed-out streets. Blackened buildings were all around, but here and there some houses had been miraculously spared by the flames. The bright arrows of German road signs could be seen on telegraph posts, emphasizing the city's destruction. The earth beneath our feet, covered by ashes and pounded by rains, had become hard and smooth: I was astounded by it back then. Gazing round, my impressions were vivid and intense, like a memory from childhood. There were no fences: only yards overgrown with tall weeds, marking out the streets.

Our column pulled into the gates of the camp. Its huge expanse was fenced with several lines of barbed wire. Watchtowers with machine-gunners, and guards with dogs, were here as well. I walked as if in a dream. But Leshka felt better, and was even joking: 'We won't be washing ourselves because we no longer have a towel . . .!' We were escorted to the parade ground and lined up. An interpreter shouted: 'POWs! The German command cannot tolerate officers and political kommissars being held with soldiers! We want to create proper conditions for them! Better ones! As it should be for officers! Political kommissars and officers – one step forward!' But nobody made this fatal step. The command was repeated. Suddenly, several men stepped forward, looking suspiciously fit and well-fed. The interpreter said: 'Are you kommissars?' They replied: 'Yes!' An officer barked: 'Fill their mess-tins up with broth!' I was all for saying I was a kommissar too, for the smell of the soup had turned my wits, but Sashka knew better: 'Don't you see they are provocateurs? And over there is fresh earth – that's a grave for real kommissars.'

Having achieved nothing, they led our column away to issue bread and gruel. I nearly lost consciousness. Leshka and Sashka supported me, to prevent me from falling, but someone had already stolen my mess-tin and I was left with no container, and hence with no prospect of food. But Sasha joined the queue, dragging me with him. Leaving me behind, he forced his way forward, got his ration, and returned. Then he gulped it down and handed his mess-tin to me . . .

I felt better after the gruel, but the good life at Vitebsk didn't last long. Early in the morning we were herded back through the ruined streets to the station. We already knew we would be sent to Germany. This time we got an open carriage with high walls. Loading took a long while, German and Russian curses filling the air. Meanwhile, the Polizei's whips were cracking and POWs were moaning, falling from the planked footway, unable to sustain the pressure from behind. The Germans shot the weaker ones without mercy. Consequently, when we finally settled ourselves in a corner, we almost felt comfortable, for violence no longer threatened.

The sky was overcast. It was cold, and the drizzling rain began soaking Tonya's shabby red blanket, our only protection from the elements. The heavy iron door closed, whistles sounded, and posts began flashing by faster and faster. Soon we could see nothing, shrouded by the thick smoke that covered the long iron body of the train. As usual, a bustling movement started up, as everyone tried to settle more comfortably. Suddenly, Sashka had an idea: 'Guys, let's do some trading!' 'Trading?' I asked through a kind of fog, 'trading with what? And with who?' 'With the locals!' Sashka replied. 'What locals?' I had no idea what he was up to. Neither did Leshka, who piped up: 'They won't let us out, will they?!' Sashka pulled a piece of laundry soap from his backpack. Leshka and I stared at it stupidly while Sashka developed his idea: 'The carriage is uncovered – right? We'll put the soap into a mess-tin, hang it over the side during a halt and shout: "Swap, swap!"' Immediately our imaginations were fired, as we pictured local peasants putting bread into the mess-tin. It was decided that Sasha would stand on my back, so as to reach the top of the carriage wall, and lower the mess-tin down on a line made from the straps of our backpacks.

We came to a station. The train stopped and we heard the sound of soldiers and women yelling nearby. Sashka clambered on top of me, let the mess-tin down and began swinging it, so as to attract attention: 'Swap! Swap! Give us some bread!' No response. Lesha took my place but still we had no luck. Everyone in the carriage stared at us: then, understanding what we were about, and realizing the business required two or three people, they began organizing themselves. But the train jerked forward, Sasha pulled the mess-tin back, and we were rolling along once more.

Suddenly, shooting broke out. I asked Sasha to go down on all fours, climbing on his back to peer out of the carriage. The train was traversing a high embankment, which formed a bend. Several men, having tumbled over the top of their open carriage, had bailed out. One of them landed badly, clearly hurting himself, but two others sprang up and started running towards the woods, falling then scrambling up again. My heart was pounding so hard, it was ready to jump out of my chest: here we were, right now, we had to do something! More men jumped out of the same carriage, scooting like hares over the snow-covered grass. Shooting opened up from a tower fixed to a carriage in the middle of the train – our carriage was near the end, so I could see everything. First, two submachineguns started slamming away, then a machinegun went to work. Two men dropped, but three others kept running. More gun bursts. Two more fell wounded: they tried to get up but were finished off by rifle shots. Now the hunt for the last one began. He reached a ravine – one more step and he'd be safe! But he was killed before he made it. I dropped down to the floor in despair. My neighbour, sitting above me, his jackboot almost touching my lips, droned instructively: 'Don't fuss, sit quiet or they'll shoot you like a rabbit.'

Some time went by, the rain stopped, and the day slid towards evening. Again, rumbling and clanging shook us up, the train shuddering to a halt at some station. Sasha and Lesha opened the 'trading post' again. This time, Lesha stood on Sasha's back, dangling the mess-tin over the side and calling out: 'Swap! Swap! Soap . . .!' Suddenly, Leshka felt someone tugging on the tin. Frantically pulling it up, he leaped back down: inside was a handful of cottage cheese! Leshka and I hadn't noticed a gang of onlookers pushing towards us, but Sasha did: and as one of the interlopers shoved me aside, Sasha poked his hand into the mess-tin and grabbed the curd. Several hands seized him but Alexei tried to beat them off. Soon everyone was rolling on the carriage floor, a big lad screaming: 'Give it u-u-up!' But no one knew who had the curd. The useless fight lasted several minutes before petering out, everyone crawling away exhausted. Hiding in a corner of the carriage, Sasha sat with his back against the wall. We screened him from suspicious eyes as he spat out white curds and clots of crimson blood: 'I hid it in my mouth.' We shared Sasha's bounty – a pinch each – holding it in our mouths as long as possible. We had nothing else to barter. The train kept going ...

It was dark. And drizzling again. We lay on the ill-fitting planks of the carriage floor in our jackets and summer pants, pressing against each other under the blanket, trying to keep warm. A tall skinny guy moved next to us, and by way of introduction, began to recite Tolstoy's poetry. We liked him and accepted him straightaway. His name was Volodya Shipulya (I have changed the original name). He was from Moscow and a biologist by trade. The chill did not permit us to lie quiet, and those who were nearby kept trying to creep under our blanket, which I was afraid would be torn to pieces. We were exhausted, but everyone was trying to huddle closer for warmth, constantly crawling somewhere, while I badly wanted to sleep.

The train stopped again, remaining stationary for a long time. It was night. The rain grew stronger, and we were sitting by the wall, hunched up, holding our backpacks above us. Our knees were numb, we were half asleep. Dead bodies lay around. Earlier they had been fully clothed, but now they lay naked: pale ghosts in the gloom, stripped by shivering shadows, hungry for warmth. The train moved on, stopped again, and we, stricken by slumber, slept in a heap, rolling over the carriage floor.

Dawn broke. Our train was again still. The wind, which had risen in the morning, was driving dark clouds through a cold sky. We were starving. We began tossing the mess-tin over the side in desperation, without hope: though on one occasion, someone put five potatoes in it. The potatoes were raw and hard to eat – no one tried to rob us this time – and we swallowed with difficulty. The train took off again. Large snowflakes began to swirl. First they fell lazily, and then they flew in our faces, stinging as the train sped along. Now there were four of us. We chatted quietly, hungry and sleepy. The number of corpses kept growing: they were dragged to the back of the carriage to be unceremoniously stripped. But I noticed that boots were not removed: people probably thought their own would not have time to wear out.

The train stopped in an open field covered by wet, thawing snow. From the shouts outside we understood we were not allowed to move further, as our track had been damaged and a flood of 'specials' from Germany was using the other. Trains were rumbling past. Pressing one's eyes against a chink, one could see platforms with tanks, troop and freight carriages – everything bound east. Would it ever be possible to stop them? In the corner of my mind was a hope that something – I didn't know what – would eventually stop this avalanche; that one day the enemy would be smashed. But for now we were unable to resist, to rise above cold and hunger, unable to unite. We had been enslaved by the instinct for survival, incapable of self-sacrifice. In that jumble of bodies, everyone was dying alone.

The carriage doors clanged open and they began letting us out – as it seemed to us – into a field. It was hard to stay steady on your feet, even harder to climb down, to slide out of the wagon into the wet slush of mud and snow. They began lining us up next to the carriages, giving each of us a hunk of warm bread – real, fragrant bread, the like of which we had long forgotten. Wrapping the bread in our rags, we consumed it crumb by crumb, afraid it would disappear too soon. But some guys with vacant eyes stuffed chunks into their mouths: they were already in agony and doomed. The Polizei yelled but did not swear. One of them shouted: 'Russians, you have to pull yourselves together and get to the camp! Help the exhausted men out or they'll be shot dead!' Which of the Polizei dared say this? He was a brave man. I would remember these words, and this voice, till the end of my days.

We were walking with difficulty, dragging ourselves along a road trampled into slush. Someone fell – the guard shot him. And that voice again: 'Russians, help your comrades out!' Yet I was unable to help anyone, for my legs were giving way from weakness. But Sasha helped me, and Volodya supported a guy next to him. By the roadside I saw the protruding stump of a cut-off cabbage. I bent over and tore it out. Sashka hid it, for I was exhausted by the effort. We approached a barbed wire fence, amidst high pine trees, and the head of the column disappeared through a turnpike gate.

CHAPTER TEN

Soul of a Jackal

The Borovukha-2 POW camp was situated in the Polotsky district. It was a former frontier-guard station, now fenced with five rows of barbed wire. There were up to 20,000 POWs in the camp. We were marched to the parade ground, formed into squares, then divided into companies and battalions. We were supposed to remember their numbers. Battalion commanders were assigned and they began moving us into the former barracks. A *Polizeitruppe* had been formed beforehand. We were led to a house and billeted. I found myself on the second floor [i.e. the first floor in British English – Trans.], Sasha, Volodya and Lesha were with me. The room was about 40 square metres, not counting a small space near the door. The whole room was taken up by a plank bed crammed with people. We were warned not to lean out of the windows, and were permitted to use the toilet only once a day. No water was provided, but there was snow outside, and those brave enough to try, would tie some belts together and toss mess-tins out of the window. If they scooped up some snow their luck was in: but they could also catch a bullet, for the guards would shoot.

Nothing in the world is so excruciatingly unbearable as the lack of water. Oh God, how badly it burned! And people here were dying of thirst more than anything else. Dead bodies were brought out time and again. We all huddled on the plank bed: sitting, lying, hardly speaking at all. I took my album and sketched the skeletal, emaciated faces of the dying.

Meanwhile, some kind of trade was taking place nearby. Someone was selling a cigarette and wanted twenty-five roubles for it. Another, having tied up some belts, threw a mess-tin out of the window. He bucketed up some snow and lay down behind the window-sill: a submachinegun burst smashed through the casement, and plaster rained from the ceiling. But the mess-tin in this man's hands contained a couple of spoonfuls of snow. He immediately swapped one spoonful for the cigarette. Everyone watched enviously, unable to take their eyes off him. Suddenly, the guy came to me, and lifting a spoonful of snow to my mouth, said: 'Here, eat.' I shrank from him: 'I have no money, I have nothing.' 'It's free, eat it up, you need it. You are an artist, and although we will all die here, your pictures will remain – they will know we were not traitors.' His words shook me: I felt ashamed, but knew I must respond quickly. My parched lips touched the spoon and the icy moisture melted in my mouth, while tears fell from my eyes. And so, that which all the horrors had failed to achieve, was accomplished by this simple swallow of water: a swallow for my comrades, for their torments and shame. I felt sorry for them all – and for myself. I felt desperate to do something, to change something. Maybe at that moment I became truly aware of what was happening to me; aware of my responsibility for everything, and for always. This moment would remain with me my whole life, and this man's words became my commission, my command, to draw. There are moments in life when suddenly all becomes clear; when one comprehends the truth of one's situation and one's destiny is revealed. This guy's words returned my human dignity; returned to me the confidence that I would escape as soon as I gained enough strength. As if one could get away ...

Everyone spoke freely in the camp – but only about the past. All feared speaking of the present, though we lived in isolation, like lepers. I had come to know a Muscovite, Tolya Vedeneev, skinny and tall with a boyish face. Tolya was from the Polytechnic Institute and knew German well. He lived on the ground floor. One day, I went down to see him in the huge hall, crowded with prisoners. There were four tables in the middle of the room: two for billiards and two plain wooden ones. Prisoners lay sleeping on all of them. Dim bulbs hung down from the ceiling, casting sharp shadows and amplifying ugliness, gouging out hollow cheekbones and sunken eyes.

Tolya and I talked about the defeat of our army. Those around us pitched in, examining the reasons from every angle. One old-timer, a frontier guard, told us they used to catch saboteurs who had been sent across the border: apparently, Hitler had ordered the invasion for 14 June but the date was changed. 'But the strange thing is,' whispered a lieutenant (now in a private's uniform and unwilling to admit he was an officer), 'time and again we sent information to Moscow, stating that the Germans were preparing to cross the border: but we only heard that our troops were being sent for training, and more importantly, were not given ammo – only enough for target practice. Here was Stalin's ingenious plan to reconcile Hitler.' A stocky officer of about fifty, who was also hiding his rank (though it was clear from his speech his rank could not have been lower than a captain), broke into the conversation: 'Stalin had nothing to do with it. Pavlov betrayed us!' [General Dmitri Pavlov, the defender of Minsk, was recalled to Moscow in 1941, when Stalin falsely accused him of treason and had him shot – Trans.] But before he could continue, others attacked Stalin and Molotov for the pact with Hitler, and for strengthening the

German economy with our supplies. Then yet another voice chipped in: 'Take the Finns – they held us on their fortified border for such a long time [a reference to the events of the Russo-Finnish War of 1939–40 – Trans.] – had we looked after our frontier sensibly, we wouldn't have let the Germans across . . .'

This kind of talk went on all the time, everyone trying to understand how it was that we were in prison, while the enemy was almost at Moscow: what was the secret of the Germans' rapid advance? Two names – Stalin and Hitler – personified the opposing camps, and were on every prisoner's lips. Some violently cursed Stalin and our unreadiness for war: they were trying to find their bearings – for a soul torn to shreds needs to pull itself together. They were patriots of their Motherland and they would rise to defend it again. But the curses of others were a means of self-justification. They had made their choice and were now concerned for their own skins, their own bellies.

It grew late – time passed quickly in these exhausting arguments. But over and again the same question rose before each of us: what did you do yourself, and why are you here? One might refer to the stupidity of our top brass, or the superior tactics of the enemy: but in one's soul there was no excuse – though all were trying to conceal it, saying, 'I was wounded' or 'I was knocked unconscious' or something else. Humankind had fallen apart here: there was no uniform mass, only alienated individuals, and each of them had to be responsible for himself.

Suddenly, a commotion was heard, followed by loud curses: the Polizei Colonel's nightly progress through his realm. It was better not to catch the eye of this flaxen-haired fellow with the bellowing voice and lascivious lips. The guys hid me under some rags as soon as they heard the louse coming, and from my hiding place I watched him enter the room. He strode in wearing a leather jacket, blue riding breeches and boxcalf jackboots, a map-case on his hip. The Fritzes had assigned him Colonel of Police, but he was just a bookkeeper from Central Asia with the soul of a jackal. There was gold in his map-case: teeth, watches, crucifixes – all plundered from the POWs. A Polizei gave a frenzied shriek: 'Stand up!' The men rose to their feet and froze in the cold light. 'Attention!' The lousy Napoleon inspected their ranks, a riding-crop in his hands. Suddenly, an idea entered his skull, animating his whole frame: 'Why do you look bored?! Why are you not cheerful?! You're with the Germans! Show your joy! Up on the tables, f**k you! Drive these swine up on the tables!' The Polizei were whip-happy and immediately began lashing about. People threw themselves onto the tables, pushing each other aside so as to climb up faster, but it was impossible for everyone to do it at once. Presently, however, the floor cleared and the prisoners packed themselves onto the four tables, clinging to each other for dear life, waiting for whatever would come next. 'Dance, you f**k-wits!' shrieked the Colonel. No one understood – not even the Polizei – yet they rushed to the tables, cracking their whips, the Colonel all the time yelling: 'Dance! Cheer up, you scumbags!' He proceeded to pile one curse upon another, reviling all the saints, God himself, and the Holy Mother – a towering Babel of blasphemies that filled the room. The creatures in his thrall slowly started to stamp their feet: the Colonel burst into hysterics. Slapping the riding crop across his hand, he burst into 'The Kamarinsky Mouzhik', a bawdy old Russian folk song. When he'd done, he screamed: 'Enough fun! Off the tables! You bastards are getting too excited!'

I was lying quietly, for if I had been found hidden away from the rest, I would have been killed. From under the rags I saw people falling, trying to get off the tables. One man wanted to jump off but fell flat on his face, sprawled out on the floor. Others fell on top of him, unable to resist the pressure from those behind. Men were tumbling, struggling to find their feet, while the Polizei dashed about, thrashing them with their whips: either for being too slow to get off the tables or for being too slow to get off the floor. I felt a chill down my spine: it seemed to me that I would be discovered and dragged into the light. Meanwhile, the exhausted prisoners crawled away, avoiding each others' eyes; the Colonel swaggered about; and a Polizei announced: 'If a watch is found in anyone's possession he'll get fifty lashes, so hand it over to Mister Colonel! And it is forbidden to have gold in your mouth or elsewhere. Hand it in now, because if we find it, it'll be so much the worse ...'

Some guy – toothless and hollow-eyed – shuffled up to the Colonel: he was informing on those who had gold teeth. The day before, his teeth had been pulled out, but he'd been left alive. Now he was doing his best to repay. The Polizei grabbed an old man with a beard, dragging him to the door with a whip handle jammed in his spine. At the end of the corridor was a room where a dentist pulled teeth: it was handy for the cellar where corpses were dumped, and where his unfortunate patients were thrown after their operations.

One after another, several people were taken away. At last, the Colonel abruptly turned on his heel and strutted to the door, followed by the remaining Polizei. Everyone sighed with relief and the guys uncovered me carefully, so as not to let anyone notice. Now we knew there were some among us who counted gold teeth, we had to be more wary: doubtless there were other rats willing to whisper in the Colonel's ear. Meanwhile, our friend, the stocky Captain, remained frozen on the floor, face down in shame that he had been obliged to suffer such humiliation.

The time came to queue for the toilet. We were allowed to go once a day and had to queue for two or three hours. Having parted with my comrades, I walked into a dingy, stinking corridor, joined the queue, and stood half-asleep. The toilet was at the end of the corridor and I could hear the shouts and curses of the Polizei: 'Come on, come on, don't stay too long, others need it too!' It seemed to me I was delirious. How long had this nightmare lasted? We'd been here for three days: but one day here was like a year, when death could come at any moment. And I badly needed the toilet, but my turn was still far away. Suddenly, somebody smacked me on the cheek. I lashed out instinctively, my hand striking someone in the dark. Caught in a strong grip, my hand was twisted sharply and a voice bellowed: 'Polizei, come here!' And before I came to my senses I was dragged away and thrown into a square room.

A neat Polizei in a trench coat and peak cap stood before me, wiping his cheek with a white handkerchief. I looked pathetic in front of him, in my unbuttoned jacket, and vest made from a single piece of grey broadcloth, a hole cut out for the head. I stared at him as if hypnotized by my own humility. Behind me there was a plank bed with a Polizei lying on it. Those who had escorted me down were grinning, and I guessed that in front of me stood the Chief of the battalion Polizei: 'Didn't you see who was coming through?' I wasn't looking for trouble but it burst out of me: 'You've got a star shining on your forehead, haven't you?' Laughing, he addressed his colleagues: 'Boys, it's not long since this scumbag lost the star from his forehead [a reference to the red star insignia on the Soviet uniform – Trans.] but he's looking for it on mine.' A blow immediately shook my head, but I stayed on my feet. My mouth filled with warm bitterness: I spat out a tooth, blood flowing down on my chin. But I kept looking into his eyes. Again a blow, this time from the other side. And I began to choke, losing my breath. I opened my mouth and spat out two more teeth. I summoned my last strength and stood firm, knowing that I must not fall or I would be kicked to death. The Polizei were guffawing: 'You're a dentist, sir!' And 'sir' gave them a gracious order: 'Boys, give it to him in turns.' They lined up, each of them eager to give me a blow: but I was losing consciousness and fell.

They probably dragged me to the end of the corridor and threw me into the pit for corpses, wherein the 'daily rate' was dumped. I came to my senses in the morning, though the cellar was pitch-black. I sensed someone's legs on me and began shoving them away: but a searing pain in my side brought my movements to an abrupt halt. Fearing they would begin dumping bodies on top of me, trapping me for good, I somehow forced my way out, finding myself in the corridor again, which was surprisingly quiet. Without strength to get up, I crawled back to my barrack-room, resting against the wall of the deserted corridor. I heard footsteps from a side door. Too exhausted to lift my head, I sensed a man standing next to me: 'What are you doing here?! Why aren't you at roll-call?!' Wearily raising my eyes, I saw the Chief of the battalion Polizei. The urge to crack a joke came over me again, though it always led to trouble: 'I'm taking a walk.' Recognizing me, he calmly replied: 'Keep walking. Which room are you from?' I told him and he left. I crawled towards my room.

I tried to climb up on the plank bed but it was too difficult. After several attempts I got up on the first level and collapsed. I was in such pain that I could only lie on my right side. Apparently, when I had fallen, the Polizei had kicked me and broken my ribs. I calmed down a bit and wiped the clotted blood off my chin. My mouth was burning – I felt there was a bloody mush in it, but I had no water to rinse it or to quench the fire inside me. Suddenly the door opened and my tormentor came in. He came up to me, sat on the plank bed, and began scrutinizing me. Gathering all my strength, I tried to look at him quietly too, as if I hadn't recognized him. He asked me: 'Where are you from?' 'From Moscow, from the Institute of Arts.' 'I'm from Sverdlovsk. I used to be a second year student in the Medical Institute. For two years I was a spy for the Germans. They should have sent me to the army as a lieutenant, but the documents I used for spying have been lost. They sent me here, to be the Chief of the battalion Polizei, until my papers are found.' I could not understand why, after beating me within an inch of my life, he had come to talk to me, to admit his treachery. Then he started chatting about literature: he didn't like Gorky, who he thought too biased; while Chekhov was too 'slobbery'. I strained to maintain a decent accent, feeling good that I had not succumbed before this betrayer, either yesterday or today. Suddenly he stood up: 'You know, you can drop in, I like you.' 'As soon as I have a chance,' I replied politely.

He left me alone with my bitterness and joy: bitterness because of my suffering, and joy because I had not demeaned myself. But the pain was so strong, I soon lost consciousness . . .

CHAPTER ELEVEN

Tolya's Plan

They herded us out to the parade ground. It was drizzling, the morning grey and overcast. All stood sleepy, with field caps unfolded over ears, collars turned up. My wool-lined jacket was disintegrating, and my only salvation was a piece of grey fabric – my father's old army blanket. I had sewn pants for myself from half of it and made a kind of vest from the rest, cutting out a hole for the head. They kept us standing a long time in the autumn rain. At last, the Chief of the battalion Polizei appeared and gave the following speech: 'The great German Army keeps advancing towards Moscow so quickly, it has become necessary to form brigades of POWs – former signallers who will follow the German troops to lay communication lines. The signallers have to be selected, and forms for them have to be filled out. Those who can use the Roman alphabet may become clerks and get gruel twice a day. Those who can do that, step forward!' A number of prisoners stepped forward, including me and Tolya. We were lined up in a column of fours and led to a former mess hall of the military station. There we would be tested, just in case we were trying to cheat an extra helping of gruel. But Tolya, who knew German, had conceived a crafty plan to outwit our captors ...

The hall was as huge as a riding school. At the far end were tables where candidates would be seated, and next to the windows were stools for those who failed: they would be tormented later. I had already seen this procedure. One Polizei would sit on the victim's neck, another on the legs, while a third would give blows with a stick, counting up to twenty-five. I immediately lost any desire to become a clerk. Besides, I had never learnt German, and one mistake would be enough to trap me under a Polizei's arse, counting up the blows – if one lasted till twenty-five, that is.

Karamzin, a colonel of our army – an ageing man who was obviously a cadre officer – was the examiner. He was walking along the long tables where the candidates were sitting. We already knew that each of us would have to provide personal details written in Latin script [as opposed to Russian Cyrillic – Trans.] such as: name, rank, home address, nationality and pre-war occupation. A German was present at the exam but did not interfere, merely exchanging a few words with Tolya Vedeneev, commenting that he spoke German very well. I told Tolya my details: he wrote everything down and handed the crib sheet to me, which I hid under the cuff of my blouse. The German said that those who succeeded would start work tomorrow, filling in questionnaires for the would-be signallers.

Karamzin handed over our completed forms to the German. A minute later, the Polizei snatched someone from a table and dragged him over to the window. The Colonel, pretending not to notice, strolled along the tables, cursing us with choice Russian oaths: 'For twenty-five years you've been doing nothing under Soviet rule! Now the Germans will teach you how to work! You'll learn what clubs are for! For twenty-five years no one has had a right to touch you! From now on you'll be beaten at every step! You'll be taught to work for the Great Germany!'

A guard counted off another group and I remained sitting at the table. I did my best to calm down and concentrate, but kept staring at the miserable body twitching on the stool by the window: I couldn't take my eyes off it. The Colonel paused behind my back. Then he took the questionnaire from me and looking through it said: 'Look, you can tell right away the man knows!' I couldn't believe he had spoken to me without jeering, but he simply praised me and told me I could quit the table. I returned to the line, wondering what would happen tomorrow if they found I had made some mistakes. I whispered my fears to Tolya, but he replied: 'I have worked out what to do tomorrow, just rely on me.' At that moment, a German sergeant major came up to Tolya and talked about something. Tolya translated: 'The Sergeant Major's name is Willi, he's an Austrian from Vienna and will be our escort.' It gave me hope, for everyone was saying the Austrians were kinder than others. After the exam we marched back to the barrack escorted by Willi. Tolya kept reassuring me: 'Don't worry, I've worked everything out. In the morning, when everyone sits down to fill in questionnaires, you'll start drawing Dimka the violin player . . .' Dimka was from Moscow too, a second year conservatory student.

In the morning, Willi escorted us to the hall again. We returned to our tables and prepared to write down the details of the signallers. But there was no queue of POWs eager to lay communications for the Fritzes. Dimka and I had found a place by a window, and in accordance with Tolya's plan, I began sketching his portrait. Willi came in and shouted a greeting to Tolya. 'Mister Sergeant Major,' said Tolya, 'there is an artist from the Academy of Arts among us, he wants to make a drawing of you very much.' Willi came up to me with a satisfied look: 'Sit down and draw my portrait.' I said

I had no time to draw, for I was supposed to fill in questionnaires for the signallers. Willi waved his hand: 'Draw! No point writing!' So far, so good. I seated him in Dimka's place and began drawing. The other guys bunched around, watching as I drew, and I was relieved that the portrait developed into a good likeness, and that I hadn't let my 'team' down.

When I finished, Willi looked at the portrait and praised it highly. Now he wanted me to draw his wife's portrait from a photograph, making it the same size as his own. He wanted to send both portraits to his Frau in Vienna. The woman in the photo was beautiful, and it was hard to imagine that Willi – a jackbooted guard in a POW camp – could have such a nice wife. What could he write to her about? What could he tell her? Nothing poetic or heroic, just mundane service for someone else's Führer: a humiliating job, for he had to humiliate other people. The portrait of his wife left Willi delighted. He immediately gave me two packs of thin cigarettes, containing fifty-one smokes in all. This was not quite enough for two cigarettes each, for there were twenty-seven clerks and I had to share everything equally. But drawing lots for the booty would help, though some would have to wait for the next pay from portraits.

In the evening we, the crew of clerks, were issued with a 'nourishing dinner'. Each of us got a mess tin of rich fish soup, a piece of jam the size of a matchbox and dense as jelly, and quarter of a loaf of bread. Generally speaking, it was a royal treat, and we couldn't have dreamed of such a feast. We ate slowly, being afraid of overeating – after starvation it is dangerous to eat rich food. And so we kept putting our mess tins aside, but our hands always returned to them and we would start supping again. We decided to leave the jam till the following day. And yet we wanted to taste it so much! So we took a little onto our spoons, and holding them in our mouths, let the slivers of jam melt away.

There was a roll-call in the morning, as usual, and we clerks were again led to the hall of the former mess-room of the Borovukhinsky garrison. Tolya Vedeneev sat next to me, in case he had to interpret something, as our guard often brought soldiers' photos, requesting that I make drawings from them. But I felt sick that day. I had sore guts and my loins were in pain. I sat quietly, trying to control myself: I had likely eaten too much fat the night before, being out of the habit. Fortunately, we were not required to work and were sent back to the barrack. I felt bad and kept running to the toilet. Tolya brought a young, skinny doctor from the hospital. They'd been friends back in Moscow and had been reunited on the train ride here. His name was Petr: recently he'd been a student of medicine, but when the war broke out, joined the Opolchenie like the rest of us. Petr touched my belly: 'It's common dysentery. A serious problem in these conditions. I can't take you up to the hospital and there's no point being there. The only available method of treatment is to drink distilled water and eat charcoal from burnt bread – this will clean the infected gut.'

But where to get distilled water? And how to burn bread? Tolya suggested walking me to the boiler room, as he had a pass into the kitchen yard, where he worked as a woodcutter.

Tolya Vedeneev was tall and blond. His freckles made his complexion golden. He had big hands and feet, clever blue eyes, and a slightly pugged nose. He was a young and charming man. They'd taken him to the kitchen to chop wood, but he was no good at it, his skinny, enfeebled frame making him completely useless. The kitchen chef was Karl Kuntzel, an Austrian, who was an amazingly kind, cheerful, lively man. Once, he stood and watched as Anatoly chopped wood, then resolutely came up to him, took the axe, and chopped the whole lot himself. He did it with artistry and said to Tolya: 'Go and tell them in the kitchen that you've chopped it all, otherwise they'll kick you out and you won't get any tucker. I'm used to chopping wood from childhood – you are no good at it, but you're a good chap.' Thus, Tolya began to earn his gruel thanks to the kitchen chef: he would stand on watch so that no one could see, and Kuntzel would chop the wood. Tolya told me all that on our way to the kitchen.

We went down a steep stairway to the huge boiler room. Two men bustled about near the furnace. One of them was a broad-shouldered man with flaxen hair, soft features and a flattish nose. This blond fellow – who spoke with the distinctive Volga accent – was nicknamed 'Asmodey' [from 'Asmodeus', a Russian name for the Devil – Trans.] because he worked in the basement all the time. The other man – skinny and graceful – was our own Dimka, the violin player from the Moscow conservatory, whom I had sketched only days before. Having found what we needed, Dimka filled a mess-tin with hot distilled water and Asmodey shoved some bread on an iron stick into the furnace. The bread burned and blackened. It was a pity to waste this bread, but we had no choice.

Having cooled my supper down, I began to nibble the charcoal, washing it down with small gulps of water. Bits of coal crunched against my teeth. I felt gripes in my stomach. Asmodey was looking at me with pity: 'Certainly, if it helps, come again whenever you want.' Dimka turned his head away and winced: I guess I didn't look too good, with a black mouth and coal scrunching against my teeth!

Next day we came to the hall again, waiting for someone to volunteer as a signaller: but once again, there were no questionnaires for us to fill in. Willi came around and took me up to the administration block: *Hauptmann* Heinrich, the office manager, wanted to see 'the artist'. The Hauptmann [German equivalent to the British rank of captain – Trans.] took me to his room, where there were several other men, and suggested I drew a portrait from a photograph. I spent two hours on the portrait and it was already lunch time. All the officers ate in this room, their batmen bringing them food. The Hauptmann gave me half of his lunch and bread. I sat in a corner of the room near a bedside table and began to eat. The officers were lying on the beds, breaking wind from time to time. Heinrich was trying harder than the rest. I was bewildered and disgusted by this. I couldn't do anything about it, nor could I keep eating, despite being hungry. I put the bread in my pocket and decided I would burn it for charcoal ...

CHAPTER TWELVE

Victim of the Mad Lance Corporal

A few days later, Willi appeared with a message for me. In an excited manner, he asked Tolya to interpret: 'The order for today is to direct Nikolai to the camp Commandant, Major Menz. Nikolai is to draw Herr Major's portrait.' I asked if Tolya could come too – he would be needed as an interpreter – and Nikolai Goutiev, who was also an artist. Willi agreed, but then added: 'I will have to ask the Commandant's permission first ...'

... I had become acquainted with Nikolai Goutiev the previous week, when I was first taken up to the administration block to see Hauptmann Heinrich. A strange figure had been led into Heinrich's office: a POW with watchful, inquisitive eyes, black as olives. His field cap was folded down over his ears, a mess-tin was attached to his belt, and one leg was bandaged with a piece of a groundsheet. A Lithuanian pointed at him, telling the Hauptmann: 'This fellow calls himself an interpreter but understands nothing!' My fellow-POW looked at me enviously: 'I am an artist from Rostov and can draw portraits as well.' When the interpreter translated this Heinrich laughed, as if to say: 'If you're as good an artist as you are an interpreter, then you must be no good at all!' Nevertheless, he told Nikolai to sit down and draw. We sat together and sketched the Hauptmann's portrait. He liked both drawings. We were given three cigarettes each and told to call again the next day.

A guard walked us back to the camp – a talkative Austrian. But to my surprise and grief, Nikolai 'the interpreter' could not keep up a conversation. He knew only two phrases: 'Mein Mutter geboren Baden-Baden' ('My mother born Baden-Baden') and 'Strauss – gut, prima.' We kept repeating 'Strauss' over and again, along with 'gut' and 'gross Musik' – 'great music' – rolling up our eyes and raising our thumbs. The Austrian pulled out a mouth organ and tried to play 'Tales from the Vienna Woods'. He was playing the waltz and I kept saying: 'Strauss – gross, gut Musik!' Adding some Russian words in the hope their meaning might be apparent to our jolly guard. It must have been an amusing scene: the Austrian guard playing a mouth organ to two POWs! Suddenly, the Austrian stood stock-still, the mouth organ pressed to his lips. He became serious: 'Krieg nicht gut!' – 'War no good!' Then he lowered his voice to whisper: 'Hitler scheise; Hitler, schlecht.' ('Hitler shit; Hitler bad.') He looked around, saw two soldiers approaching from the camp, and pulled himself up. When they had passed, he pulled out some bread and cigarettes and gave us the lot.

At last we reached the gates, the turnpike was raised, a sentry let us in, and we entered the camp territory ...

... And now we were on our way to the office block again, this time to draw the camp Commandant. We walked through slushy snow and puddles. I felt bad. Although I'd managed to stave off the first bout of dysentery with distilled water and charcoal, gripes kept tormenting me, and I didn't know if I would ever recover fully. Tolya was worried I might not be able to work, as I kept squatting, but I hoped to hold out during the portrait session. If they found out I had dysentery I wouldn't see the Commandant or my pay for the portrait – and all the guys back in the barrack were waiting for us to bring something to eat.

I carried with me all the art materials I had: three pencils – a black one, which the Hauptmann had presented to me, plus a blue–red one and a green one (both from the office) – a piece of chalk found in one of the bedtables, and a piece of charcoal. But I hadn't yet decided what to draw on: the leaves from my album were too small, while writing paper was both too small and too thin. But as we entered the office block (the former Red Army Club of the Borovukhinsky garrison) the first thing my eyes caught was a piece of grey cardboard lying on the floor of the corridor: it was apparently used for scooping ashes from the fireplace. I was in luck! I grabbed the piece of cardboard, shook off the dust, and saw that it was a 'Diagram of Industrial Development in the First Five-Year Period'. But its back was pasted with excellent porous grey paper, and its size was just right for a portrait. I already had chalk and charcoal – what could be better?

The guard led us into Hauptmann Heinrich's office: 'You will draw a portrait of Major Menz,' he announced with authority, 'Major Menz is a very important person, the Commandant of the whole camp ...' Gripes struck me in the pit of my stomach and I strained every nerve to hold out and not give away my condition. Heinrich escorted us to Menz's office through a corridor. We had heard rumours about Menz to the effect that he was an aristocrat, a baron from a noble family. The first thing the Baron did when he took command at Borovukha was organize a kennel and stables, so he could start hunting hares and foxes. Indeed, everything was as it should be on a baron's estate: but the Red Army Club served as his castle, and instead of serfs he had POWs – walking corpses. When you saw the Baron on his horse, you couldn't help but admire his bearing. He behaved with such dignity that we grudgingly sympathized with him as a victim of the

Mad Lance Corporal – Hitler. Menz no doubt resented his assignment and simply wanted to make the best of it, napping in the afternoons or going hunting. It all helped create a kind of an aura around him: as if he were suffering at Hitler's hands as well!

Hauptmann Heinrich knocked on the Baron's door. We heard a 'Yes?' from within and Heinrich entered. The office was not large. At a desk sat a neat man of about fifty or fifty-five with greyish hair. Raising his hand to Heinrich in greeting, he asked: 'These are the artists, are they?' Then, addressing Tolya, who he immediately took to be the interpreter, Menz declared: 'The artist can spend twenty-seven minutes on the drawing.' When Tolya translated this command I was taken aback: why only twenty-seven minutes and not thirty? Then I realized the Major was erecting a barrier between him and us, suggesting that every minute of his time was precious and granted to us as a favour. The three of us were marking time in front of the Baron's desk. He was sitting quietly, sifting through his papers. He behaved with such simplicity and natural grace, he was immediately distinguished from all the other Germans we'd seen so far. Neither before nor after, neither in real life nor on stage, did I see such a classic type of aristocrat: natural, at ease, unselfconscious. Yes, our task would be hard – we had to hold out and not demean ourselves or humiliate the name of Russian artist. Yet my gripes were so strong, and as the seconds ticked by, my mind kept returning to one thing ...

I took a chair and sat down, placing the scrap of cardboard litter against the back of another, so as to capture the image of the demigod in German uniform. As I took up my piece of charcoal, the Baron again addressed Tolya once more: 'Herr Major has no time to pose, so he will continue his work.' These were completely draconian conditions! But the gripes in my stomach disappeared as I strained every nerve in order to concentrate. When Menz raised his head I drew his face; when he bent over his paperwork I drew his uniform – collar badges and the gleaming silver eagle with outspread wings.

Then I swung my eyes to the side: to my amazement, a chubby, red-haired German *Obergefreite* [German equivalent to the British rank of corporal – Trans.] with a pig face and a Swastika armband was sitting in the corner, watching us with his bloated eyes. I hadn't noticed him in the shadows. Why was he here? How could the Baron tolerate his presence? But I could not afford to lose seconds as Menz momentarily raised his head. Meanwhile, Nikolai was toiling hard, sketching on white paper with a pencil.

The clock struck eleven. Major Menz made a sign with his hand and said something to Tolya. We stood up. I understood two words: 'rauchen' and 'essen' – 'smoke' and 'eat'. Without waiting for Tolya's comment, I emphatically pronounced: 'rauchen' and 'essen'. The Major pressed a button. In a minute a batman entered and clicked his heels. Menz ordered him to walk us to the canteen and feed us. The batman reported that the canteen was closed and breakfast was over. The Major ordered cigarettes brought and something else. Our hopes were raised again! And the batman justified them, bringing a pack of cigarettes and a paper cone of candies for each of us. That was great! At that moment it seemed to me I wanted sweets even more than a smoke: maybe because it seemed such a fanciful dream. The Baron requested we show him the portraits. I saw that he liked our drawings. Tolya interpreted: 'Herr Major says that the artists may finish the portraits tomorrow, he gives you another twenty-five minutes.'

Hauptmann Heinrich and Willi were waiting for us in the corridor. Heinrich was delighted the Major had asked us to finish the portraits: he had done the Major a favour and obviously felt some self-satisfaction. Willi was also pleased, but for a different reason: for he knew in what kind of condition we had worked. But as soon as we left the office my pain intensified and I had to ask for permission to relieve myself among the pine trees ...

I caught up with Nikolai, Tolya and Willi strolling slowly along the slushy footpath. I heard Tolya ask: 'Who was that man with the Swastika armband in the Major's office?' 'A pig!' Willi answered crossly, 'a Fascist pig!' Willi told us that the Nazi Corporal had been planted in Menz's office to spy on him – Hitler hated and distrusted the nobility, appointing his own people to watch over them. This was a revelation for us. We even felt sorry for the Baron: this exemplary aristocrat, watched by a swineherd.

CHAPTER THIRTEEN

The Best Gift in Forty Years

I was still going to the boiler room each day, to see Asmodey for a drink of his curative water. One day, as I entered the kitchen yard on my way to the boiler room, I was stopped by a POW. He was a man of medium height, in a broadcloth blouse and dark-blue officer's breeches. A trench coat was draped over his shoulders and his field-cap sat at a jaunty angle – it looked like the star had been removed recently, leaving an unfaded patch. The man's neat appearance – so unlike everyone else – indicated he'd been a professional Red Army officer. Only the absence of collar badges showed that he was a POW too. His face was handsome, his expression calm. He looked straight into my eyes: 'Are you drawing the Major's portrait?' Expecting an ugly conversation, I replied, 'Yes, I am.' But the officer smiled faintly: 'I used to be an artist in a club when I was a serviceman. My name is Grigory Tretiak.' I stretched out my hand and said I was from Moscow, an Arts Institute student named Nikolai Obryn'ba. 'Come to my place,' said the man, 'I live in the second room down the corridor where the kitchen workers live. Tell them that you want to see Tretiak, let Asmodey walk you to me.' Thus I met Grisha [a diminutive of Grigory – Trans.] Tretiak. I didn't yet know that life would bring us together in the clandestine struggle.

Nikolai Goutiev invited me to see him in the working team – an area where the interpreters' quarters were situated. The camp had its own interpreters – internal ones who had nothing in common with the Commandant's office interpreters. The working team was separated from the rest of the camp with barbed wire, but a Polizei Nikolai knew let us in and we entered an area where there were several four-storey buildings – formerly the garrison officers' quarters. The interpreters – who more or less knew German – lived in one of the houses. Some knew only a few essential German phrases; others, like Tolya Vedeneev, knew the language better than the Germans themselves. Fate had brought them here by different roads, but all wanted to survive, and for this reason called themselves interpreters. It wasn't considered a sin among the POWs to be an interpreter, for we knew very well the difference between the Commandant's office interpreters, who'd come with the Germans into Russia as jackals to live off the Russian land, and the in-camp ones, who interpreted orders and tasks given by the Germans to the working team to chop firewood, shovel snow, mop the floor, and so on.

Kolya introduced me to some people. It was already late and as it was forbidden to walk through the gates without a pass, I decided to stay overnight at Nikolai's place. I lay on a table, my backpack under my head. I had just fallen asleep when a shout of command rang out and the Polizei Colonel appeared right in front of me: 'Get up you Jewish conk!' I managed to get my legs down from the table, knowing he could hand me over to the Polizei brutes, standing nearby like a solid wall. Instantly, a thought struck me. Filling my lungs, I bellowed out a barrage of filthy Russian curses. The Colonel smiled: 'Well, this one's no Jew! Let him sleep.' They left me alone, my body shaking and trembling from the evil that had just passed me by.

In the morning Willi picked me and Nikolai up and escorted us to Heinrich. We continued sketching in the Commandant's office and I asked the Hauptmann to assign me to a working team, so that Nikolai and I could report straightaway and guards wouldn't be searching for us in all the buildings. The Hauptmann ordered Willi to walk me to the workers' quarters and assign me to a working team.

The working team had its own quarters and its own leader – at that time a Muscovite named Vasili (I don't remember his surname). Before the war he'd been the chef at the 'Moscow' Hotel. By his looks, I judged him to be about twenty-six or twenty-seven years old. He had a handsome Russian face, light hair brushed backwards, white even teeth and a charming smile. His manner was friendly and he didn't try to play the big boss. When Willi brought me to Vasili, he accepted me as a mate and fellow-Muscovite, introducing me to his interpreter, Nikolai Orlov. I liked Nikolai immediately. He had black hair, dark-brown eyes and a husky voice. He had been an artilleryman with the rank of senior lieutenant. The names of Vasili's assistants were Alexander and Vanya. They were both from Donbass and had served in the same unit with Vasili. Alexander was a sprightly lad, but Vanya was quiet and gentle, older than the others, but shy and kind. I was lodged in a small room, 6 square metres in size, but I didn't need any more! There was a small room next to mine, with several men from the same unit as Sasha and Vanya, plus another guy with flaxen-white hair – Volodya from the Volga. An old Jew lived in the kitchen. He was a watchmaker, which was useful for Vasili and for the Germans. The Fritzes were wild about Russian watches and Vasili had been collecting them: and for this reason needed a watchmaker. He hoped to collect enough watches to buy himself out of prison and become a 'prima': in other words, to marry a local woman and live near the camp.

Meantime, I was invited to play cards and we sat to have a game of 'Preference'. But I didn't know how to play and soon pulled out of the game. Nikolai Orlov and I went to my room. He told me whereabouts he had fought; how he had tried to break out of the encirclement, but having run out of ammo, was forced to blow up his Katyusha rocket launcher. He told me about Vas'ka [a diminutive of Vasili – Trans.]; that he was a harmless guy, and that the other guys were not bad either: 'Don't worry that some are Polizei – they earn extra gruel but they are not scumbags.'

The working team was under the command of the red-haired *Gefreiter* [German equivalent to the British rank of lance corporal – Trans.] Bormann. He had blue–green eyes, slightly protruding from his eye sockets as if he had Graves' disease. His character was as colourful as his red hair. If someone was late for roll-call, Bormann would yell, goggle and make horrible faces at him, looking for all the world like a madman and sadist. But then he would suddenly come back to normal and give a crafty smile, as if to say: 'Scared you, didn't I?' Bormann was the supreme commander of our working corps and we all knew that in spite of his yelling and eye-rolling he wasn't that bad. We discovered this a few days after his appointment. Bormann had sent five workers from our team to wash floors and nail down some boards. One of our guys saw a white poodle, which belonged to one of the officers, running about and contrived to knock it dead with a log, hiding it in his backpack. When he returned to quarters we skinned it like a rabbit and set it cooking on the stove in our mess-tins. The poodle had disappeared! A hue and cry went up and the Polizei were looking for it everywhere. We hadn't finished cooking it when Bormann entered with some Polizei. They fell upon the woodcutters straightaway, grabbing them by the collars and dragging them off to the guardhouse for twenty-five lashes each. But Bormann stopped them, suddenly shouting out – the interpreter hurriedly translating – 'We can't beat them now! Make them eat the poodle first and then beat them! Otherwise it'll come out that Bormann bashes the POWs unjustly!' And then Bormann and the Polizei stood patiently and waited till the poodle finished cooking and was eaten up. Then sentence was pronounced: 'Ten days confinement with no food and twenty-five lashes each.'

Five or six days went by. Lance Corporal Bormannn appeared, smartly dressed with all his decorations, and lined up all the guys from the working team. He announced that he had turned forty years old that day, and wanted to see how much we all loved him. The working team leader gave us a sign and we cheered loudly. Bormann remained impassive, listening. The leader gave the order again and we cheered once more. This was repeated several times. At last, Bormann said he did not feel we were happy, and sadly nobody was enjoying himself much. Then he suddenly began goggling and rolling his eyes, as if some idea had dawned on him. He called up the Polizei Chief and ordered him to bring up all the prisoners from the guardhouse – there were about thirty men at the time. Everyone thought there would be a big beating now. The Polizei rushed to prepare stools and fetch whips. The prisoners were brought up to await their fate. Bormann addressed them via his Jewish interpreter, Boris Levin: 'Today is my birthday. I want to see people who will be sincerely happy to congratulate me, and I hope to find them. I want to be greeted by the prisoners first.' They bawled out at full strength: 'Good health! Long life!' Levin translated the message for Bormann. 'No one has ever congratulated me so sincerely before!' Bormann beamed, 'even the Polizei didn't wish me long life! For this reason sentence is to be suspended! All prisoners to be released from custody!' Now such a cheer went up that Bormann smiled: 'I have received the best gift in forty years!'

We understood that Bormann was pushing the limits of what he was permitted to do for us, and covering his kindness with this kind of crankiness. A German from the Commandant's office had already demanded that Bormann replace Boris, sending the Jewish interpreter to the ghetto. The demand was repeated at least three times in my presence. But Bormann kept stubbornly rejecting it, making the point that he couldn't get by without an interpreter and hadn't found a new one yet. Boris – an engineer from Leningrad – had been captured in the encirclement, like most of us.

The search for Jews was organized on a regular basis. Recently there'd been a check in the working team. Doctors selected by Bormann himself sat at a desk, and those suspected of being a Jew stood in a queue, passing one after another in front of the commission with their pants down. Bormann turned his head away as the Jews passed by, so as to let the doctors do the same. But it was also necessary to divert the attention of the 'Little Lance Corporal' in Berlin, whose intentions were entirely different. The doctors remained silent and all passed before the commission in safety.

I saw Boris Levin again after the war, when he came to Moscow from Leningrad to find me. He came to tell me how he escaped from captivity. When the final order came to send him to the ghetto, Bormann gave him a pass and left a pistol under his pillow. By such means Boris escaped to the Partisans. Bormann was a special man who risked his life for others.

CHAPTER FOURTEEN

A Sacred Mission

I moved into the living quarters of the working team. Kolya Orlov lay on my bed with a fever and couldn't get up. At first we thought he had a cold, but our doctor came up and said he had typhus. It meant we had to hide him, to avoid sending him to the hospital. While the word 'hospital' sounds like a word of hope, suggesting survival and care, here this horrifying word meant death. There were doctors and orderlies in the hospital – a big hall with no beds – but there was no food, and no possibility of protecting the sick and wounded from lice. The lice here were more dangerous than wolves. Like a grey shroud, they covered the helpless hospital casualties, eating away their skin. It was the most dreadful death. I had to feed up Nikolai Orlov, to give him a chance to recover and save him from hospital. And in fact, my situation was also grave: for several days in a row I'd been sleeping next to Nikolai, so I knew that in a couple of weeks I would be sick with typhus too.

At the time my business was not bad. I was drawing portraits of the Germans and sometimes receiving a scrap of bread or some leftovers in return. But the day before, I had felt offended. I'd drawn a miniature portrait of one officer and got from him a new sealed cigarette pack: I could have swapped something like that for a full loaf of bread. But I found only cigarette butts in the pack – what an operator! Luckily I hadn't tried to swap the pack for something, for I would have got it in the neck!

In the morning we were escorted to work again. We trudged over snow that had fallen in the night. The sun broke through the wall of pine trees, dazzling us, and illuminating the forest, as it should in February. If there had been no barbed wire by the sides of the road, we might have fancied we were free men and not POWs.

Our team workers were assigned a job each. Tolya, Nikolai Goutiev and I were taken to the office again. Willi ran in, breathless, saying that Major Menz was calling us. This time Menz allocated twenty-five minutes to finish off the portraits. I wasn't as strained as before and felt the portrait was coming out all right: chalk and charcoal went well with the grey colour of the paper, and the Major's image was life-like and handsome. That day he cooperated with us a little more, holding the poses we needed much longer. But at eleven o'clock Menz raised his hand over the desk. Tolya interpreted: 'Herr Major cannot pose any longer and requests you to show him the work done.' The Baron looked attentively at my work and said something, of which I only understood the words 'family portrait'. Tolya interpreted again: 'Herr Menz reckons that this work deserves a place in his family portrait gallery.' Heinrich was called in. The Hauptmann was pleased, for it was he who had found 'the artist'.

Next morning, I returned at nine o'clock prompt. There was only Hauptmann Heinrich in the reception office. When we were alone with him he would always fart, and it would be done loudly, like a trumpet issuing a challenge. I had never been able to get used to it. Perhaps he wanted to demonstrate that we were not really there; that we didn't really exist? But who knows? Maybe he would have done it at home as well! The Hauptmann came up to me. Then, silently – as if he were preparing some kind of revelation – pulled out a tattered magazine illustration from his pocket. It was the worst, most vulgar pornography possible. He put it in front of me and announced: 'Gut!' I moved his dirty sheet of paper aside: 'Nichts gut!' Heinrich was surprised and upset: 'Warum, Nikolai?' – 'Why, Nikolai?' But then he brightened up, smiling sagely, as if with great understanding, and pointing at my skinniness. He suggested I reproduce the illustration on a larger scale, so he could hang it on the wall of his room, and promised to pay me for it. I was disgusted with the fact that I, a staggering skeleton, had to sketch to ignite the lust of this well-fed, balding captain. But I remembered Kol'ka, who urgently needed food, put away my shame, and promised to do it. Heinrich whistled and walked to his desk very pleased.

I immediately began drawing, hoping that the sooner I got the job done, the sooner they'd let me go. A Polizei came around with a bundle of newspapers and leaflets dropped from our aircraft: 'Sir, a plane dropped this and I've picked it all up.' And by gestures, he showed how he had done it. 'Sir' gave him a pack of Makhorka. It was normal payment for this kind of 'feat'. Capturing an escaped POW – two packs of tobacco. And there were those who liked smoking this Makhorka and did their best to earn it. It flashed through my mind that there still existed the Soviet Union and Moscow, where people walked freely, fought and bore the proud name of 'Russian': and here I was, sketching porn for this baboon – an enemy of my country – to enjoy. It was impossible to bear! The Polizei bowed and left. Hauptmann Heinrich took the papers and leaflets to the interpreters' office. But I noticed that one paper was left under his desk, so I grabbed it, hiding it under my blouse, although I knew the order: capital punishment for keeping newspapers or leaflets. But what was the point of taking that into account?

I had already forgotten how many times I should have died – one time more or one time less . . .

I finished the drawing, tinting it with chalk and coloured pencils. It had turned out spectacularly well, and I expected to get no less than two pieces of bread for it and maybe something else. Heinrich came back and seeing the work I had done, snapped his fingers, clicked his tongue, took the picture and thanked me. Then he pulled three cigarettes from a pack and handed them to me: 'Bitte . . .' ('Please . . .'). I did not hold out my hand for the cigarettes, and there was probably a look of unhidden astonishment on my face. Anger was simmering inside me. I pulled out my home-made tin cigarette case, took out five of my cigarettes and handed them over to Heinrich. This time he was astonished and indignant. He threw the picture on the desk and yelled: 'Wenig?!' – 'Enough?!' He ran out of the room. I sat down and tried to pull myself together and not think about the consequences. Half an hour went by and the Hauptmann appeared again. He held a freshly slaughtered and plucked hen by its leg! It was marvellous, with a yellowish tint! He twirled it in front of my eyes, repeating triumphantly: 'Wenig? Wenig?' I agreed it was enough and took the hen from him.

I couldn't believe my luck, already tasting the cooked meat in my mouth. I wanted to run straightaway – not in formation, under no command – to cook the chicken and eat my fill. But I had to wait. Eventually, we walked home in formation. But I was elated, my mind racing, thinking how I would cheer Nikolai up by cooking chicken broth, and giving him a whole chicken leg. He would recover immediately, for sure!

The command to disperse rang out unexpectedly. I ran to my room, which I shared with Nikolai. The room was small, it barely fit two, but – what the hell?! – someone was lying on my bed fully covered. It turned out that Vanyushka [a diminutive of Ivan – Trans.] had fallen ill with typhus and they had decided to hide him in my room. I received this news with little enthusiasm, as it made my falling ill inevitable: I would have to sleep between two typhus patients and cook two chicken legs today – and what would I feed them with later? I cooked the head, neck and giblets, and though I feared I would lose control of myself, I didn't eat – not even a taste.

When everyone had calmed down and my patients were napping, I pulled out the paper and began reading. It was the *Pravda* newspaper containing Sovinformbureau communiqués [Soviet Information Bureau – Trans.]. It was almost incredible to read the truth about ongoing events, and the small piece about the oath sworn on bended knees by our commanders heading off to the front. I dropped a tear and hurriedly wiped the moisture off the paper. I never thought that a paper – something we used to handle so thoughtlessly, for packing food and without even reading – would one day become the most important thing in my life, inspiring faith. And why were we not there, on Red Square? Again these thousands of 'whys?'! Because we had not done our duty – it was obvious – and I had less and less justification for my presence here: but I knew that hatred had been building up inside me. To hate didn't mean to be angry and to curse. The hatred was resolution and determination, it was a struggle, and it meant you knew what was what – now and forever. It was a struggle, not just against your personal enemy, but the enemy of your people, of your Motherland. And avenging the desecration of your Motherland was a sacred mission.

Suddenly I saw Nikolai's shining eyes looking at me. He asked me in a hoarse, whispering voice, what was wrong with me? He saw the paper, and although I didn't want give it to him – for one shouldn't disturb a man with a high temperature – I couldn't refuse, and began quietly reading it aloud. When I reached the line describing the oath, Nikolai cried: first silently, swallowing tears, then burying his head in the pillow, unable to hold his sobbing. Vanya was delirious. I touched his head and sensed he was feverish. I gave him water and he opened his eyes, but I saw that he didn't recognize me – he called me Lena and whispered something.

Then I crawled to my sleeping place – a chair and three stools – but couldn't fall asleep for a long time. I thought about whom I might show the paper to, and how to do it so as not to get caught ...

Next morning I awoke with a headache. My knees and calves were hurting and I began to feel feverish. Yet I managed to drag myself up for roll-call. Bormann was in a bad mood, yelling at us that from today the whole camp would be under quarantine.

Orlov had already risen to his feet. Vanya was still at the height of his illness and not enduring it well: he kept crying and asking me to stay with him. Kolya Goutiev fell ill too. Actually, he'd been ill for a while, but had stayed on his feet, and when he was raving from high temperature, everyone thought he was clowning around. My condition went from bad to worse. Eventually, the day came when I failed to get up for work. Vasili called for a POW doctor he knew, who wouldn't give me away. He examined my chest, looked at me and said: 'It's typhus.' The news didn't surprise me at all, for I'd known that I would fall ill and my temperature was about forty degrees. Then I lost consciousness.

Later, I found out I'd been shouting in delirium, writhing and jumping to my feet. No matter how much they tried to persuade me to keep quiet, it was no use. On the third day, when they heard of an imminent inspection of the working team, they decided to hide me. They wrapped me in a trench coat and groundsheet and took me up to the attic. They tied the bundle up with belts, in order to restrain me and prevent me from revealing my whereabouts, and put flasks of hot water near my feet, chest and wherever it was feasible.

I lay in the attic near the flue, semi-conscious, and saw a strange vision: I saw a group of POWs break out of camp, running across snowdrifts. They entered a forest, dragging me on pine branches, feet forward, my head dangling. I was choking with snow. But then car lights came through the trees and motor vehicles appeared – they were our vehicles with Red Army soldiers! All began kissing each other, rejoicing in the liberation. And then my turn came. I was allocated a clean vehicle, into which I was pulled on stretchers, and some caring female hands – probably a medical nurse's – began tending me. She lifted my head with loving care, gave me warm milk, placed me by a warm stove, and I recognized my Galochka! She was the nurse! She took me to Kharkov in the vehicle and we arrived at my kinfolk's place. My father dug a cellar and they hid me in it from the Germans ...

My liberation-dream returned several times, and I feared to lose it, for in a corner of my consciousness I felt it was true – and how I wanted to believe this truth!

I regained consciousness. I was in a small room at the top of the building, under the roof. Smoke from a home-made stove was blinding my eyes, as the stove had no chimney. The window – which had no glass – was curtained with a groundsheet. Volod'ka [a diminutive of Vladimir – Trans.] – the light-haired guy from the Volga billeted in our building – lay next to me, also sick. He was being looked after by Kol'ka Orlov, still weak himself. It was he that I had called 'Galochka' in delirium; it was his hands that I had taken for tender female ones. But there had been no milk: only boiled water, which Kol'ka had been treating me with, for I'd got badly chilled in the attic while the inspection was on – it was nearly thirty below outside. Then my mates found a room to move us into.

Our bread rations were brought up, but I couldn't eat, for the sawdust in it crunched between my teeth, making it difficult to swallow. I was dreaming about white bread. It seemed to me that it was the tastiest stuff on earth – a piece of white bread! But in spite of all efforts, my mates couldn't get any. Instead, Nikolai Orlov got a mug of cranberries. It was hard to get something from outside, but now we had the chance to drink a refreshing, sour compote – even if from just a few berries. And so these smoky, frosty days of temperature and delirium, tinged with the tiny pleasure of sour cranberries, slipped by. We were already recovering, and lying on our beds, began to tell stories or read aloud. We read Chekhov, for it somehow soothed us, or we would recall something from the past, separated from us by barbed wire and the blasts of war ...

Kolya Goutiev stood in the door smiling and spreading his hands wide: 'My namesake, matey, how are you finding it – like a resort?!' He hugged me and we laughed. Kolya had already recovered and managed to draw a portrait of a German, for which he'd got a piece of fish. 'Here it is!' said Kolya, unwrapping the paper and handing me a tail of boiled fish. It was the first bit of food I had tasted with pleasure for a long time. I didn't know fish was so tasty! It turned out that I had eaten hardly anything during the two weeks of sickness and now my appetite had woken up. Kolya told me of his sickness: that he had withstood it on his feet, no one realizing he was ill; that the Germans fell sick with typhus too, but didn't endure it well – out of sixteen sick, only two survived. The Germans didn't stand up to typhus and for this reason were saying: 'The Russians are breeding special lice that only wipe out Germans.' Kolya told me that Hauptmann Heinrich – the office manager – had been stricken by typhus too and he, Kolya, had seen him get bitten by a louse that had crawled from him, Kolya, over to Heinrich's armchair: 'See! Our Russian lice are Partisans too!' I laughed and assured him that mine had been there as well. The excitement was replaced by tiredness and I fell asleep. Next day I waited for Nikolai to come again.

Several days went by, I was still in bed and it was hard to get up. Kolya brought me a German's photograph to draw from, but I had no strength to do anything. Nevertheless, I tried to sketch, drawing my wife's portrait from a photo, for I wanted so much to revitalize her in my memory, to make a portrait of Galochka sitting amidst flowers, with flowers in her hands, during our first date in Sorochintsy, far in the sunny Ukraine. But my vision grew worse and worse. Everything was blurred, and when I tried to focus, all I could see was a purplish haze with light and dark circles floating before me. I closed my eyes and lay down for a rest. But as soon as I tried work, everything began to blur again. Obviously my end was not far away. Already, my hair had stopped growing – my head was bald, as if shaved – and my toenails had fallen off.

Day after day I lay with my eyes shut. Nikolai Goutiev grew weak too, and there was not enough work to enable him to feed us both. And without food, there was no chance of getting my eyesight back. So I had to make a decision. I didn't want to drag it out any longer and decided to throw myself out of the window of our third floor. But at this hardest moment of my life, help came unexpectedly. A fellow-countryman had been looking for me, and in the evening, came to our room. I could only recognize him by his voice. In the past, we'd seen each other a few times during the camp roll-calls. He was from the Poltava Region and even knew the village my father was born in. Nikifor Vasilievich – such was his name – was a calm *Khokhol* [a typical nickname for the Ukrainians in Russia – Trans.]. Stubborn as a Ukrainian should be, if Nikifor Vasilievich got an idea into his head, it was impossible to beat it out of him. 'Eh, brother,' he began, 'what an awful thing for you that you can't see. There's something that concerns you as well, and it's so delicate I can only talk it over with a fellow-countryman.' I said he was too late, as it seemed I was beyond any kind of business. 'Eh, Mikola [a Ukrainian version of the name Nikolai – Trans.], if only you had known I was a cutter in the working team for the Germans. I don't wanna talk business yet 'cause now we're gonna give you a treat. You stay in bed, I'll go to your kitchen ...'

Some time passed. I assumed he'd gone for good and submerged into my drowsy condition. But the door opened and Nikifor Vasilievich came back. An appetizing smell of boiled soup filled the room. He sat next to me in a businesslike way, pulled me up on the pillow and began to feed me with his wooden spoon. The broth was rich and hot, we blew together on the spoon, and I gulped it down. He gave me a piece of meat – it was heart (the Fritzes had been leaving the offal for the kitchen hands after butchering) – and pouring the leftovers into my mess-tin, left it with Nikolai Orlov so that he could feed me up later. Feeling warm, I fell asleep, comforted by hopes of seeing the bright world and the shining sun once more.

Nikifor Vasilievich was lodged on the ground floor of our workers' quarters. He began to visit me every night. He brought around a POW doctor who examined me and said: 'Everything will be all right, his sight will come back if he's fed well. His toenails will grow out again.' Nikifor Vasilievich took me on as a dependant, and in a week I could see again, though only dimly.

One day Nikifor Vasilievich brought me passports wrapped in a rag. I hid them in my lair and only then did he tell me he and his mates had decided to escape. But in order to get through Belorussian territory one needed a passport with a special note, declaring that you were not subject to call-up. For that photographs were needed: in other words, forged photos had to be drawn in the passports – photos looking like each man's face, stamped with the word 'gesehen' ('checked'). The passports had belonged to dead POW civilians. Now I had something to do. I had been ready to throw my life away, now it was a great thing to be needed!

I cheered up and set about this laborious task. The job required a lot of effort and thoroughness. I would have to paint from life a portrait of each escapee, then draw up a matching 'photo'. Then these 'photos' – miniature portraits – would have to be put in their final form. This could be done by scraping up white emulsion from unnecessary photos, dissolving it in hot water, and dipping the tiny drawings in. When the emulsion hardened, the portrait had to be wet down again, stuck to clean glass, and then rubbed with petrol. A glossy 'photograph' would be the result. Then it was to be stuck into a passport, the missing part of a round stamp would be drawn on it, and a rectangular German stamp – 'gesehen' – added. And all this was to be done so that no one noticed! And so I could only do the work furtively, when I had a chance to be alone in the room.

In a month the passports were ready and the group made its escape. Suspicion immediately fell on me, for all of them had been coming to me to pose. In my room they began to give me black looks: 'If everyone is gonna pose for you and then go on the run, maybe you'll draw our portraits too?' Vas'ka – the working camp commandant – called me up and began to talk about the same stuff: 'We've been looking after you (as if it had been him doing it!) and the result is you're drawing suspicion on us. You see, the Polizei are saying it's fishy that Nikifor used to feed you up . . .'

I watched silently as this ex-railroad clerk pretended to be a big boss in front of me, and it was not pleasant. I understood I had to do something to stop him from blabbing. I reminded him that I had drawn his portrait many times: so might a suspicion fall on him too? After all, when I showed these portraits to the German interpreters, they were impressed and wanted to know what he needed so many portraits for? Fright flashed in Vas'ka's eyes and although he was still fooling around, I could see he had begun to fear me. Speaking casually, I said this was all folly and it would be better for us to part: I would live with the interpreters upstairs, since it would be quieter for us both. I added that it would be better for him not to mention the portraits I had drawn of him. That same evening I was already upstairs ...

Kolya Orlov and I came out of the Commandant's office and bumped into the kitchen chef Kuntzel, who was walking from the 'starvation' guardhouse, where he'd spent two weeks. Kuntzel was wasted and miserable, he greeted us as kinfolk and quickly told us how the Russians had destroyed the Germans near Moscow: 'My brother wrote a letter – he ran 40 kilometres over snow in just his socks – so fast were they retreating. The jackboots were bad – they let the snow in.' He showed us his jackboots with broad tops – just like those his brother lost in the snows of Moscow. His brother was now in hospital with frostbitten legs. Kuntzel finished his speech: 'Hitler nichts gut! Stalin – gross!' Thus we found out about the destruction of the Germans near Moscow.

We knew what Kuntzel had been in the guardhouse for. His fellow-countryman and friend had betrayed him. Kuntzel had gone to a village near the camp, stayed overnight at one of the housewife's, returning to the camp next morning blind drunk. He had a pillow in his hands and was hammering it with his fist, the down was bursting out of it, flying like white snow, and Kuntzel was plastered with it from head to foot. Nikolai Orlov had noticed Kuntzel from afar (he had a pass to the village) and went out past the gates to meet him, for Kuntzel might be detained by guards as he entered the camp and face trouble. Kuntzel was delighted to meet Kolya, who couldn't get him under control straightaway. The man kept beating the pillow, saying again and again: 'Hitler kaputt! Stalin gut!' and wouldn't give up the pillow at any price. Eventually, Kolya managed to snatch the pillow and throw it away. He shook the down off Kuntzel's uniform, calmed him down, and walked him to the guard-post. A friend of Kuntzel's was on guard but that didn't save him. He was detained for being late, and because his uniform was peppered with down. Kuntzel was sentenced to two weeks of 'starvation' detention. Had they heard him shouting 'Hitler kaputt!' who knows what would have happened ...?

Kuntzel was kind to the POWs and had been reprimanded for it more than once. We knew about his conversation with the Camp Commandant. Major Menz had been informed that Kuntzel was socializing with the POWs and generally being friendly to them. Menz summoned him, asking why he had broached discipline with this kind of infringement? Kuntzel could find nothing better to say than: 'It's more interesting for me with them.' Then we discussed Kuntzel's behaviour and decided it had been thoughtless, for his open-heartedness might have brought about the worst possible backlash, both for him and for us.

There was another German who commanded respect and sympathy among the POWs. Unfortunately I don't remember his name. He was a fat and kind-hearted man who served as a procurement officer in the kitchen. He would voluntarily go on his own to the nearby villages, to scrounge potatoes from the peasants for the POWs. And it was dangerous! Partisans and locals might not know the reason for his errands or what motivated him. And yet, despite the risks, he continued with his mission for the sake of others.

CHAPTER FIFTEEN

The Blonde Betrayer

March 1942 arrived. The frosts were still keen from time to time, but the days were sunny with dark-blue shadows and clear skies. The quarantine in camp ended and suddenly Nikolai and I were called to see Major Mentzel – Menz's deputy. Mentzel was a short, plump, square-faced man of about fifty years, with a pince-nez on his nose. He lacked the military bearing and aristocratic manners typical of Baron Menz, being a teacher and gymnasium [i.e. grammar school – Trans.] director before the war. He spoke calmly and quietly, raising his hand in the 'Hitler' salute with some hesitation, and pronouncing 'Heil, Hitler!' a little uncertainly. Mentzel said he recognized us as artists and considered it necessary to help us out: 'I'll walk with you to look at the landscape. The weather is fine today, maybe something will encourage you to paint.' Nikolai Orlov went out with us but the Major didn't use the interpreter, walking in silence and not dropping a word on the way.

We left the camp for the first time in many months. We passed through the gates, giving way to a couple of two-wheeled carts, loaded with the corpses of POWs who'd died over the last day. The carts were covered with old groundsheets, from under which, stiffened yellow legs stuck out. The carts were pushed by POWs looking like the very same dead bodies, but revived for a moment to carry their comrades to a common grave.

We walked further and were stricken by a heavy putrid smell as we passed the huge pits into which the corpses were dumped. Some 300 to 400 people had been dying in the camp daily, and they were carted here, to these pits. When a pit was full – perhaps holding 3,000 corpses – it would be covered with earth. Legs, arms and heads were sticking out everywhere. Fresh corpses were casually dumped near half-filled graves like firewood. All the corpses were naked. The Major walked in silence and we followed him. I made a sketch of the graves and the carts on the way.

We entered a forest. Our working team was there, labouring, and two-wheeled carts were scattered around. When the POWs were unharnessed from the carts, they were ordered to cut firewood, German soldiers and Polizei standing guard. The Major stopped and we began to draw. Here two POWs were cutting wood, jerking the saw with small pushes. The loading of logs followed slowly and painfully, everyone having chilled hands. I saw one POW fall to the ground and fail to get up. A German patrol set off to investigate, but his mates stood him up before the soldiers arrived. Meanwhile, a worker who had just urinated couldn't fasten up his pants, his hands were so cold and raw. It looked like he was being deliberately clumsy, but his nerves were strained to the limit and his hands wouldn't obey him.

We returned to the camp. The distribution of gruel had already started and a long queue stretched towards the cauldron. And again the camp Polizei were yelling, using their whips to keep order. I watched the Germans and their lackeys beat a POW who had attempted to escape, to prevent the Gestapo men from accusing them of being too soft and lacking true Nazi spirit. We had gone through purgatory and hell, Mentzel escorting us as Virgil had guided Dante.

We couldn't understand this 'walkabout', which according to the Major, we so badly needed. Mentzel had baffled us. But I decided to draw what I'd seen on bigger sheets and show it to him. A whole series of pictures was produced: the horrible scenes we had witnessed, tinted with watercolours to create the impression of landscapes, rather than detailed records of atrocities. I was wary of depicting the horrors and yet I wanted to check Mentzel's reaction. When everything was ready Nikolai and I asked Willi to escort us to the Major.

Mentzel lived on the ground floor of the Commandant's building. He received us well. I handed him a bundle of pictures, he carefully examined each one, and then asked if I had shown them to anyone else. 'No, no one has seen them,' I said. He offered us cigarettes and asked if I were going to give the pictures to him. I answered in the affirmative. He opened a locked trunk and put the pictures under some clothes. 'From tomorrow,' said Mentzel – his words interpreted by Boris Levin – 'the Lance Corporal will be selecting people to be sent to Germany, to the Ruhr mines. They are bombed by the English. Being on the mines will be no good for you, being dispatched to the Ruhr Province means no way back to life. At six o'clock I'll come to the camp and pick you up – you'll carry the road sign lying next to the gates.' We had already seen the motorway sign, on which an inscription 'Borovukha-2' was to be made. It had been knocked together out of three thick 6-metre-long planks, with the thoroughness peculiar to the Germans. 'I'll be around before roll-call,' Mentzel continued, 'because if you are selected by the Lance Corporal I'll be unable to keep you in camp.' We explained to Mentzel that we would be unable to lift the board: 'Why not take our mates along with us?' Mentzel agreed: 'Bitte, bitte, gut . . .'

In the morning we gathered to wait for Mentzel. We decided that the board would be carried by Tolya Vedeneev, Tolya Kharlamov, Grisha Tretiak, Asmodey, Kolya Goutiev and me. We warned the others who might be selected during the roll-call that they would have to lie low: but then we were told the 'Little Lance Corporal' made a thorough search of the whole camp, looking for hideaways. Next morning, everything was repeated. Mentzel came about quarter to six, we took the huge board upon our shoulders and carried it to the Commandant's office, the Major following. We placed the wooden shield against the wall of the entrance hall and began bustling about, drawing lines with chalk, making sketches, trying to place letters the best way. The necessary hour and a half went by: then it was safe to return to camp. We carried the board out to the wire fence and Willi escorted us home. This went on for six days, while the selection of POWs was on, and each day Mentzel would come around quarter to six, to take us up to the Commandant's office. On the last day, when the POWs bound for Germany were lined up prior to departure, we waited in his room.

Lisitsky, Nikolai Goutiev, myself and some Fritzes were in a room of the Commandant's office. Vas'ka was writing village names on wooden boards, Nikolai was quietly sitting and drawing a portrait of a German officer from a photograph. Germans were working at their desks: Hauptmann Heinrich – the office chief, senior officer Krems and a small, puny clerk. The clock struck twelve – a holy hour for the Fritzes – and they got up like clockwork, straightened their uniforms, and went off to lunch. I had a walk around the room. In a corner near the bookcase was the clerk's carbine. I imagined how good it would be to make some noise – to slay the Germans with the carbine! But it probably had no rounds in it and there was no way out of here with barbed wire all around. Anyway, it was not the right time to die. I knew escape was impossible, but it remained my dream, one scene after another rushing through my mind ...

I noticed an open bookcase: usually the clerk would lock it up before leaving the room. Inside were piles of blank *Ausweis* identity papers. Before I had chance to come to my senses, I grabbed a bundle of clean, new forms, rolled it up, and hid it in my blouse. I closed the bookcase. None of the other guys even noticed. But walking past the clerk's desk I saw an Ausweis on it and became certain that the forms were numbered. The Germans would be back soon, and when issuing a regular pass would notice the shortage. At best, the gallows would be a punishment for me, but since I had stolen a whole bundle, I would undoubtedly be joined by many more gallows-birds. I had to admit to Nikolai and Lisitsky that I'd taken the blank forms but hadn't known they were numbered: now they would have to be put back. Only a few minutes remained till the end of lunch, after which the Germans, punctual as they were, would be back. I feverishly smoothed out the creases on the passes. Anya – a marvellous golden-haired girl, also a POW, who worked as a cleaner in the Commandant's office – entered the room. I hurriedly explained the situation to her and she stood behind the door. She would cough if someone walked along the corridor; if a German came up to the door, she'd try to delay him. If this did not work, she would cough again and then Nikolai – keeping watch on my side of the door – would thrust it open, knock the German as if by accident, and begin apologizing profusely. Lisitsky would open the bookcase and I would put the passes back. The minutes were passing inexorably. We heard Anya talking to someone in the corridor. Nikolai was a bag of nerves, holding the door handle. Beads of sweat formed on Lisitsky's forehead. The whole procedure failed several times because of Fritzes walking along the corridor – Anya would cough and we would leap away from the bookcase to the middle of the room. At long last Vas'ka threw the bookcase open and I put the blank forms back. But again, without thinking – in fact, to my surprise and Lisitsky's – I pulled out another bundle of papers from the bottom shelf, which I hid under my blouse as before. We took two steps back and heard Anya cough in the corridor. Then Hauptmann Heinrich entered, cheered by the attention Anya paid him. Nikolai was shuffling around by the door explaining: 'Ich wollen Toilette!' The German was laughing.

We were especially happy that day when the guard walked us back to the camp and it was all behind us. I'd manage to work something out before my number was up. But it was only a small piece of luck on the way to freedom. Kol'ka was grumbling that I should have watched out before taking anything, but he always grumbled. But when I told Grisha about it he smiled and said: 'It was a good thing to do.' We examined the bundle of blank identity papers and realized we had another task before us: to produce authentic passes, they would have to be certified with a seal and signatures. Grisha asked if I could do it, hinting at my work in the Commandant's office. I said I would think it over. We hid the forms behind a heating radiator under a window-sill – we couldn't afford to let them get too dry or soaked with water. Now I began to wait for drawing sessions in the office with impatience . . .

I told Grisha how Anya had helped us. He wasn't surprised. 'I've heard about her. I know her sister – she fell in love with me.' He spoke these words simply, without boasting, and I felt sorry for her. The female POWs were sometimes sent to the kitchen to peel potatoes and wash dishes – thus Anya's sister met Grisha. The female POWs lived in a separate building and marched in separate columns. They often sang songs when marching, changing the lyrics. For example: 'When we are sent to fight by Comrade Tanya . . .' – instead of 'Comrade Stalin' – but everyone knew the real lyrics, and felt cheered, for that sort of thing was felt keenly here.

In fact, two girls were walked to the Commandant's office every day – they worked as cleaners and both were named Anya: that's why we called them Anya 'Tall' and Anya 'Small'. Anya Guseva (Anya 'Small'), who had helped us, made an impression on everyone with her long golden hair and her cheerful character. Anya was from Sverdlovsk, a student of medicine, and came to the front as a medical orderly before being captured. The other Anya was tall and slim. She reminded me of Galochka in some way and I always enjoyed seeing her. To tell the truth, the Germans didn't touch the female POWs in our camp, and our POWs were not allowed to talk or mix with them, so in Bormann's working quarters they were as if in a monastery.

That day I was drawing a Russian landscape by order of Hauptmann Heinrich. Several pine trees and a shack could be seen from the office window. I developed the theme and a picture came out of it: a forest edge with trees covered in snow, a village far away, smoke rising from the chimneys. The office clerk returned from his leave. We'd been waiting impatiently for him, for he'd promised to bring us watercolours. He entered the room with much pomp, and with great import placed an aluminium box of colours before Kolya and I, one for each of us. How much would be done with these colours – both in camp and later, when we had escaped to the Partisans ...

The interpreters came in. There were four of them: Fuchs, Olszewsky, Hans and another man – an old fellow. Fuchs and the old man were Russians from Lithuania, Olszewsky was a pure Lithuanian and Hans was a German from Dnepropetrovsk [a city in the Ukraine – Trans.], although in looks there was nothing German about him. He had been a spy for eight years. He was recruited when he lived in a German colony in the Volga region, then he moved to Dnepropetrovsk, where he worked at a steel plant while performing spy duties. This time Hans came in swearing. There was a woman with him, about thirty-five years old, with dyed-blonde hair, finely frizzled, and rouged lips. She was wrapped in a Russian shawl. Hans addressed Heinrich straightaway, in a disaffected manner: 'This one wanna talk to you.' The woman smiled coquettishly, winking an eye. 'She wanna talk to the master face-to-face.' Heinrich stared at her. One-eyed Hans explained: 'She's brought some info.' The Hauptmann asked us to leave. The clerk left too, and we smoked and waited in the corridor.

A frenzied Hans appeared after some time, the blonde woman following, and bowing her head, she quickly sneaked out of the office. Hans was cursing: 'What a bitch of bitches! Even the Hauptmann was scared!' We tried to find out more. Hans continued: 'So many traitors I've seen on your side but I've never seen anything like this!' Hans swore again. 'She came to rat on her husband. He's a political officer, escaped from the Polotsk camp, wounded in the leg and hand. How did he manage to get here? Now he's hiding in her attic. His wound is so bad he'll remain a cripple, but she came to give him away. She even wanted to choose a new man for herself in the camp – a fit one! The Hauptmann said to her: "You're a viper! You should be in the camp instead of your husband!" But she told him: "Don't even try! I'll complain that you're trying to hide a *politruk*!" [political kommissar – Trans.] And then Heinrich got scared. Now she's gonna lead them to arrest the husband.' Hans couldn't calm down and kept cursing the blonde bitch: 'I'd hate to have to put up with her ...'

We felt bad too. We were ashamed of the Russians, ashamed of the women. But this was an isolated incident: how many others took risks to protect or just feed someone? We kept talking – both Russians and Germans – trying to regain our composure. The man had crawled back home to his wife and she wanted to swap him for a fit bloke with no love at all, just like livestock, just to have one with legs and arms! This event shook everyone. Its cruelty horrified even the Fritzes. Later, Menz ordered that the guy be taken up to a hospital.

Having returned to the office, all picked up their jobs again. The clerk stamped a seal and began filling in an Ausweis: but he made an error and threw it into a bin under the desk before taking a new one. Now I only had to wait till lunch and not be called off anywhere else! When the Germans went out I rushed to the bin. The Ausweis was filled for the blonde betrayer, and perhaps due to nervousness the clerk had made many mistakes. I hid the crumpled paper in my pocket and it calmed me down a bit. Anya 'Small' came around to clean up and carried away the bin with other papers. I asked her to burn everything straightaway, in case the Germans decided to look for the spoilt pass.

That evening I was already drawing a seal with an eagle on an Ausweis form. My art was to determine one's fate, one's way to life or death, and it was taking my breath away, as if I were standing on a high ledge with vertigo. Grisha said that someone was being readied for escape and they'd tell me his name later, so I could add it to the Ausweis. Escapes from the camp had been happening but nearly all of them had failed.

At last the seal was ready and they told me the name. Tolya Vedeneev filled the form in German. Later, Grisha told me that a colonel escaped with this pass. First, they'd set him up with a job sawing and transporting firewood, feeding him up to give him strength for the escape. The crew of woodcutters consisted of twenty-six men and they were called 'horses'. They dragged firewood out of the forest, harnessed up to huge carts like beasts of burden: but unlike horses, they had to saw the wood themselves. The crew consisted of tried and trusted people, and they took part in the preparation of the escape. The escort Polizei for the 'horses' was Vanya Gousentsev nicknamed Vanya the Gypsy – also one of our men. There was a pass for twenty-six men on the gate guard post, but they had to lead through one more than that, and it was skilfully done by the crew and its escort. On the day of escape, Vanya escorted out of the camp not twenty-six but twenty-seven POWs. He created a mêlée at the gates, yelled at the POWs, muddled up a German guard, and walked through an extra man. Then the German guards led the crew into the forest. When they scattered to saw wood, the guards couldn't keep an eye on everyone. Vanya caught a moment and handed the Ausweis to the Colonel. The Ausweis authorized the holder to move about the district up to the village of Beloye. There was one of our men there: the escapee would change clothes at his place and be transferred across the front line or to the Partisans.

Thus the clandestine work for liberation from the camp began – and so did the agonizing suspense after each escape. If someone was caught there would be no difficulty in pinpointing the man who'd stolen passes and who'd been filling them in and drawing the seals. Then it would be all over for us. But a man always hopes for the best and I would begin to draw seals again: and again the tormenting suspense and counting of days would begin. Currently I was preparing documents for a night flight airman ...

CHAPTER SIXTEEN

Violin Wrapped in a Bedsheet

I was proud that I'd managed to get Vanya a violin. The story began when Kolya Goutiev had been singing tunes to Vanya, who lamented: 'If I had a violin I would play!' Before the war he'd played in an orchestra. One day, Vasili – the former commandant of the working crew – visited us. He'd just got married and lived in a village near the camp. I began explaining to him that we needed a violin and he suddenly blurted out: 'I know how to get it! I will! And you, Nikolai, paint a carpet for me: I wanna give my wife a present.' I agreed straightaway: 'I will paint a carpet, you only have to find a blanket or a bedsheet.' Vasili, a hot-headed chap, got fired up: 'I'll bring you a blanket tomorrow!'

He actually brought a bedspread with a light pink pattern. I immediately stretched it on the wall and scrawled a picture with chalk: a seashore with palm trees, a reclining beauty dressed in white with a wide-brimmed hat, a young man sitting next to her against a background of sea and surf. Vas'ka lost his mind! I dissolved some chalk, added some blueing powder (he brought all that himself) and began to draw the blue sea, and the golden sand of the beach. I liked the picture myself, and everyone who popped in stopped and looked at it silently for a long while. I never dreamt it would have such effect on the prisoners, who felt as if they'd broken out through the web of barbed wire into a different life: a life in which everyone has his moments of happiness. The carpet came out so well that my mates asked me to keep it, at least for a day. Vasili agreed, but early next morning he came with a violin wrapped in a bedsheet and asked me to give him the carpet. He hadn't been able to keep the gift a secret and now his wife was waiting. Thus I bartered my work for a violin for Vanya Gousentsev.

When we got the violin, Dimka the violin player and former conservatory student, couldn't play it! He explained that he needed sheet music. But Vanya had perfect pitch: Nikolai would sing and Vanya would immediately improvise on the violin. Nikolai's mother was a piano player and he remembered how she'd played Tchaikovsky's 'Francesca da Rimini'. So he and Vanya decided to prepare a performance.

Kuntzel was lenient towards us, that's why we had a chance to gather in this huge hall of the former dry mess, where officers once held parties and concerts, and now our Vanya the Gypsy stood in the middle of the hall and played 'Francesca da Rimini'. More and more people were coming, leaning against the walls or lying on the concrete floor. Nearly the whole working crew came: there were about 200 people, but the silence was complete, for everyone was overwhelmed by this dramatic music. Many of the guys were crying. It was getting darker and darker, but Vanya kept playing. And in this semi-darkness the music sounded more and more emotional, more and more intense; and his emaciated, ragged listeners seemed like resurrected shades come back from the nether world. It was heartbreakingly sorrowful ...

CHAPTER SEVENTEEN

Chain of Conspiracy

It was spring 1942. On the parade ground prisoners lay spreadeagled, their bodies a yellowish-white. Others sat with bent backs, bony spines sticking out, covered with dead lice. Food was scarce and people crawled about on all fours, devouring the new-grown grass – despite eating their fill, most died within two weeks.

One day, Fuchs the interpreter found me and invited me to come to the guardhouse with him. Fuchs was an ageing man of about fifty (maybe more), but still able-bodied. He had been telling me how he used to serve in one of Mamontov's punitive detachments [Mamontov was a Russian general in the counter-revolutionary or 'White' forces of the Russian Civil War – Trans.], showing a photo from those years: three officers in black uniforms posing next to a black banner with the emblem of Mamontov's Army – a skull and crossbones. Their armbands had the same pirate emblem as the banner. Fuchs was intoxicated by his own stories of how they used to make their way through lands engulfed by peasants' rebellions with fire and sword. He was amused by the fact he could tell about his atrocities with impunity. At the beginning of the war he returned to his estate in Lithuania, but embarked on a career as an interpreter in order to receive a grant of land in the eastern part of 'Greater Germany' – that is to say, Russia.

In the guardhouse, Fuchs sat down and seated me in front of him. I was curious as to what kind of talk he had prepared for me: 'The camp awaits replenishment,' Fuchs began, 'if you engage in collecting information and rumours from POWs it will be very useful for the German Command.' Without batting an eyelid I replied that I would be very happy to fulfil the wishes of the German Command. 'Remember,' Fuchs went on, 'that we're interested in what's been happening in the Russian rear. The newcomers may be talking about it. When I call you up, you'll report.' Fuchs called the guard and sent me to continue working in the theatre.

I couldn't wait to tell Grisha the whole lot. We talked the matter over, obtained advice on what I should report – what sort of 'rumours' I should inform Fuchs about. The discussion lasted a long time, but eventually all the 'rumours' were worked out. The camp was full of new POWs and they stood out, for the novices were not yet reduced to the pitiful condition of the old-timers. But still, the camp Police dragged the boots off the new POWs, taking the leather belts along with them. A queue formed to get wooden clogs – no one would be able to run away in them.

A week passed and the death rate rose sharply. The German announcer shouted into the loud-speaker: 'The Russians are not used to eating honey and butter! That's why they can't stand it! They're used to rotten potatoes!' Meanwhile, the soap we were issued turned out to be made of sand. The new brushes and powder were ersatz as well. A surprising contempt for human dignity was behind all this: a desire to humiliate the Russians, to prove the semi-bestial level of their development. The same announcer shouted that lice were the brood of the Russians and they propagated from Russian bodies.

One morning an escort came to pick me up from the Commandant's office and walked me to the guardhouse to see Fuchs. He greeted me amiably. And I – continuing to fake simplicity and credulity – told him straightaway that I'd managed to collect very interesting information for the German Command. Fuchs pricked up his ears: 'What have the newcomers been talking about?' 'They're madly outraged with the conduct of our Command!' I began to jabber. 'Ours issue 800 grams of bread for each German POW and we are issued with nothing here. They've been cursing ours for feeding the German POWs. They've been saying that Voroshilov had built up a 6 million-man army and would drive the Germans back to Berlin.' Fuchs was wincing. He was muddled by my artless looks, but when I said: 'a drive to leave no single German on our land . . .' He stopped me: 'Enough! Don't collect any more rumours for now.' I understood that I'd overdone it a bit, and in the evening I got my share from Grisha. Fuchs wouldn't call me up any more. Thus my career as an informer came to an end.

A few days later, Grisha was taken to the Gestapo. They drove him away with two other POWs, not even letting them collect their meagre belongings. It foreshadowed nothing good. A thought struck me: is it possible that someone out of the twenty-eight men for whom escapes had been organized had been captured with our fake passes? There were too many reasons to suspect that Grisha had been arrested because of the escapes. We'd been making passes for people needed at the front: in other words, for the senior officers and night flight airmen.

We couldn't pull ourselves together after Grisha's arrest. Each hour we expected to be arrested too. Obviously the chain of conspiracy had snapped somewhere. An agonizing suspense hung over us. Then, suddenly, the head of the camp Polizeitruppe came to the room we worked in: 'So, artists, you'll be going to Polotsk, you've been called up.' He ordered us to make ready for the journey. Anything might be expected from such an invitation, but the fact we had to gather our gear made us hopeful – maybe we would have to draw something? Our preparations were quick. Sasha Lapshin and Volodya Shipulya were already waiting for us near the kitchen door: it appeared they would be going as well, by the Commandant's order ...

CHAPTER EIGHTEEN

Sister Lizabeth

We climbed into the back of a *Trekhtonka*, a military vehicle of ours valued by the Fritzes for its good cross-country ability [a Soviet-made 3-ton lorry – Trans.]. Two German guards climbed in after us. Two men were already lying on the floor in the back: one old and one young. They looked at us apathetically. I asked: 'Where are they driving you to?' The old one said: 'They're gonna shoot us. But for some reason in Polotsk. First they wanted to do it here but then decided that it would be better to do it up there.' He fell silent and then asked: 'Are you being taken up to be shot or something else?' I couldn't look him in the eye, ashamed to express my hope for a better personal outcome, so I replied a little uncertainly: 'Don't know, they haven't told us yet.' The younger of the two guards noticed we were talking and smacked the old man on the hip with his rifle butt, shouting in a fearsome voice: 'Jude – kaputt!' And then he rocked with laughter, letting us know it had been a joke. The other guard sat on the plank next to his comrade with his back to the cab, the better to keep an eye on us all. The truck was running down the road and it was odd to be conscious that at least two of us were on the way to the spot where life would end, that it was their final journey, and their escorts were two cheerful Fritzes laughing and gladdened by the spring day.

The fields were replaced by a fir tree forest. We looked at it longingly, imagining ourselves on the run – or even better, Partisans dashing out of it. But there were no Partisans around and we didn't fall upon our guards. Eventually the road got busy: we were approaching Polotsk. We were driven to the centre of town and ordered to get out near the German Commandant's office. Our guards handed us over and the vehicle with the old man and the young guy sped off. We stood in the street and waited. Thirty minutes later the Commandant himself came out, announcing that we were to decorate the German soldiers' hostel, the 'Soldatenheim'. Immediately after this, two guards escorted us to a neighbouring house.

The renovation of this building, which had been damaged by shelling, was in progress. There had been a *raikom* [a district Communist Party committee – Trans.] here before the war: now Germans were walking about, Russian POWs were dismantling scaffolding and carrying away construction litter, and house-painters were whitening walls and ceilings. We were escorted into a big half-whitened hall, its floor covered with rubbish and sawdust. One of the guards went away to look for the hostel manager, and we looked around, wondering what to expect from this encounter. A young woman in the grey uniform of a nurse emerged from a dark doorway and approached us. I noticed her dazzling-white apron, and headband stitched with a large red cross. The guard announced: 'This is *Schwester* Lizabeth, the hostel manager.' Schwester – 'Sister' – Lizabeth nodded and her whole face blushed. There was no interpreter around and we had her to ourselves. We gave our names and asked what we had to do. Schwester subdued her initial embarrassment and began speaking in short phrases: 'This hall needs its walls decorated.' We moved to another hall – a squarer one. 'It needs to be decorated too,' said the Schwester, 'soldiers will dine here and drink beer.' The third room was small – the Sister wanted to make a leisure and library lounge out of it. We immediately decided this room would be our workshop, for the time being, and arranged it with the Sister. Putting our bags down, we asked for some time to talk over the forthcoming work. Sister Lizabeth departed, leaving us with the guards, who had made themselves comfortable in a couple of old armchairs.

Although ready for anything, the last thing we'd expected to find at Polotsk was a female nurse for a boss, and the dream job of decorating white walls! We began to suggest themes, vying with each other. But then we were also thinking – this is for the Fritzes! One thing was clear: while the themes could not openly oppose fascism, they must at least express humane ideas. Kolya and I agreed to decorate the big hall, reproducing engravings by the Medieval German artist Albrecht Dürer. This would enable us to make something artistic, while the Germans would not be able to reject 'their' artist. We decided to decorate the rest with ornaments and human figures. We made sketches. I asked the guards to provide us with German magazines: one of them readily went to see Sister Lizabeth and brought us a whole bundle. We scanned them avidly: for the first time German life was laid bare before us. We were curious to know what was happening on their side. We feverishly searched for confirmation that the war had no 'taste of honey' for them either, scrutinizing photographs of their destroyed houses and streets. I found what I needed for the wall decoration amongst the commercial photographs: we didn't want to draw Russian faces for the Fritzes.

A Russian girl came in with a saucepan of stuff that didn't smell like gruel. Instead we found soup with peeled potatoes and macaroni in it. The girl had a white apron and headband: she worked as a waitress. Her name was

Lyuba and she had a scornful look: 'Here is soup for you and the guards. Do your best work for the Germans and we'll feed you.' She looked at us with irony. We were supposed to answer, to hurl something in reply to the ambiguous challenge, but it was already clear that it wasn't just a challenge, but a bridge over which we might establish a mutual understanding. By that time we had already got used to this kind of ambiguity and I replied in kind: 'And we've been doing our best for them all the time, we're even sitting in camp for them.' Lyuba glanced towards me, trying to search into my eyes. Then she said artlessly: 'Well, they'll teach you a thing or two, maybe something will come out of you.' We were delighted by Lyuba but feared for her: she was a rash girl, taking chances from the first encounter – what if we turned out to be rascals?

In the meantime, the guards poured soup into their mess-tins and sat down, pulling out spoons and laying bread on a table. The taller of the two was a Czech from Prague; the other was a German from Berlin. His name was Hans and he had been foreman of a gang of road menders before the war. The Czech – his name was Henryk – even tried to say some Russian words. Hans was sitting quietly and smiling shyly. 'Now stop chatting,' Lyuba began to bustle, 'eat your soup quicker! I have to serve the second course now, or the *Nemki* [plural of *Nemka* – a German female in Russian – Trans.] will shout at me. Oh, how furious the Nemki in the kitchen are! They are not like Lizabeth, even she's afraid of them.' Lyuba rumbled the saucepan lid and disappeared behind the door. Everyone became absorbed in eating, rarely exchanging impressions. It was hard to imagine how lucky we were! We hadn't been taken to the Gestapo but had been brought here to decorate walls. And the soup was superb! We couldn't remember when we'd eaten stuff like this.

Lyuba turned up again, but this time she was not alone. There was a young girl with her, perhaps sixteen or seventeen years old. She was a waitress too. We understood at once that she'd latched onto Lyuba to have a look at us. Her face – framed by two braids under the white waitress's headband – was still childlike. My soul was filled with a wrenching pity and fear for her fate: front-line soldiers would be staying here, and they were not the same as the rear echelon Germans, who lived by the norms of semi-civilian life. Her name was Naden'ka. She looked at us guardedly with black eyes and was shy of talking. But Lyuba seemed relaxed, even speaking to the guards in German. Having happily given them rissoles with macaroni, she began serving us with the second course, asking the most unexpected questions and answering ours unexpectedly as well. Well, we wouldn't get bored with her! It was clear she was 'one of ours', but fate had made these marvellous girls come here to the 'Soldatenheim' to work as waitresses.

Having cheered up after the food – and the meeting with our girls – we returned to our measurements and designs, becoming increasingly keen on the work. We were glad they had not made us draw a portrait of Hitler or any patriotic scenes, letting us work out what we wanted ourselves.

And so the day imperceptibly slid into night. Schwester Lizabeth came around and we tried to show her what we'd thought up. She liked everything and kept nodding, giving her approval. Then she said something to the guards and left us in the big hall. All the Germans had already left, the workers had been escorted back to the camp, and only our group was still in the building. Lizabeth returned and looking a little perplexed, said we should come to a neighbouring room to have dinner. We opened the door and froze: a long table stood in the middle of the room, covered with a white tablecloth. Plates, cups, coffee pots, a milk jar, dishes with ham and cheese, saucers with cubes of butter and sugar were lined up on it. No one was in the room. Having approached the table we were still looking at it in disbelief: had we been invited to sit down, take cutlery in our hands, eat from plates and saucers things that had long since vanished from reality to haunt our sleep and daydreams? The white tablecloth with ironed creases, the snow-white serviettes: it was as if all had been prepared for welcome guests, not men degraded by imprisonment in a POW camp. When we recovered from our stupor we decided to behave as if we'd been having such dinners every day. In other words, not to stuff our bags with everything we could not eat, but just to take a few pieces of butter and sugar and leave the rest on the table: when received in such a way, one had to act properly. But our guards were as bewildered as us: obviously they hadn't had such a windfall too often. I saw Hans take a piece of ham from the plate and put it into his mess-tin. Then he nonchalantly chewed on some bread, pretending nothing had happened – he had done the same thing at lunch, hiding his rissoles. The sugar and butter from his saucer also disappeared into the same place. I couldn't understand why he was collecting everything into his mess-tin, and doing it so surreptitiously, casting down his eyes as if he wasn't hungry at all and bread was better than ham and cheese. Henryk, on the other hand, was clearly enjoying himself, saying that the ham was as good as in Prague.

The dinner came to an end. The guards escorted us to camp through the town. The Polotsk camp was situated on the territory of a former military station. Five- and three-storey barracks stood in the distance, the parade ground trampled down by thousands of feet – not a green blade of grass to be seen. A strange construction 30 or 40 metres long stretched out in the middle of the complex. It consisted of high poles joined by crossbars, two planks were laid across, forming a flimsy scaffold. A ladder was set against it. Under the scaffold, on the ground, was a row of huge drums. We were puzzled. What could it be for? As we stood gazing, an emaciated prisoner climbed up the ladder and shuffled onto the swaying planks, barely shifting his feet, while holding onto the handrails so as not to fall down. He began fumbling about with his trouser belt and we suddenly understood. The parade ground was huge, capable of holding thousands of people: but we realized that prisoners were forced to do in public, in front of everyone – over their heads, in fact – what should be done in private! And what if it were windy, raining or snowing? What if the planks were frosted over? And a man had to hit the drum, otherwise he would be beaten and made to clean up his faeces with bare hands. We'd seen a lot of horrors in our camp, but to hit upon an idea to mock people in such a way! How simple it is to crush human dignity, to drive people down to a swinish condition. Was that what they'd been trying to achieve? All had been pondered by their scientists and intelligentsia in order to annihilate us physically and morally: to leave a space on the earth only for the 'master' Aryan race.

In the morning a Polizei ran up to our guards, pointing at us. Soon we were cheerfully striding towards the gates. We walked through the streets, leaving behind the horrors of the camp. It was still early – freshness filled the air – and as we walked, we dreamed that we would be fed shortly. We entered our workshop and received a saucepan of soup with macaroni, meat with gravy. Our guards sat down next to us, and I noticed that once again, Hans put his meat into his mess-tin and shut the lid . . .

Schwester Lizabeth came in, freshly starched in a white dress with thin grey stripes. It was the uniform of the German nurses, but it looked solemnly elegant on her. Lizabeth asked if we needed anything for our work and we could make a start? Volodya was the best German-speaker among us, but we had all learned to manage without interpreters: if something was unclear I made a quick sketch – soon everyone understood and things fell into place. We explained our plan to draw on the walls: we needed dry pigments, chalk and glue for this. I showed sketches of figures for the smaller hall. Lizabeth liked them: she nodded and smiled. We told her what kind of ornamentation we were going to apply to the doors, to make them the same style as the decorations, and suddenly, of my own accord, I offered to draw the Sister's portrait. I didn't expect my proposal to embarrass Lizabeth, but she blushed all over her face – right up to the white headband on her forehead. She shyly said that she had no authority to divert me from my job. I explained that a portrait might be made during a lunch break or after hours and that I had a piece of paper and watercolours for it. The Sister relaxed and said: 'Well, later on.'

We were busy with our work till evening, when once again there was the white table with plenty of food. Henryk explained to us that Lizabeth didn't want to reveal to the other workers, labouring during the day, how we were fed. That evening we strode in the streets of Polotsk, already in a good mood. We established friendly relations with our guards and were not afraid of the camp wire any more. Thus day after day went by.

CHAPTER NINETEEN

Back to Reality

In five days we began to decorate the walls. Schwester Lizabeth came to the room where we were drawing and said she wanted to ask us something. Blushing, she began to explain how inconvenient it was for us to spend several hours each day commuting between the camp and the hostel. She'd discussed the situation with the Polotsk Commandant, and he had allowed her to take responsibility for us: we could live here in the 'Soldatenheim' with our guards, but we must give our word of honour not to escape. 'You think it over,' she concluded, 'and tell me can you give me your word of honour.' Lizabeth was completely flustered, her speech was long and full of significance. We understood that she didn't care too much about the work itself, she simply felt sorry for us having to head back behind the wire each day.

Left alone, we began discussing Lizabeth's offer. Of course it was tempting to give our word of honour and remain in the hostel, under guard but as good as free. Then, if a chance came, we could seize the moment and escape. After all, although Lizabeth was a kind-hearted girl, she served in the German Army! But I said that once our word of honour had been given we could not escape, for a man could have but one word of honour and it didn't matter to whom it was given, friend or foe. Nikolai supported me and we all came to the decision that we would work at the Sister's place for the time being, postpone our escape, but continue to make preparations.

Hans and Henryk came in. They already knew what the Sister had told us and were concerned: they were our guards and would be responsible if we escaped. Henryk began explaining how good it would be to live at the hostel and not have to trek back to camp each night, but we could see he was tormented by one thought: would we escape or not? Henryk said he was a pacifist and if we tried to escape he would be incapable of shooting. Hans, meanwhile, was an Evangelist. He wouldn't take up his rifle either: but they would both be court-martialled for it. We tried to assure them that once we had given our word, we would keep it.

Henryk told how he had been called up to the Commandant of Polotsk and asked in front of a Czech colonel: 'When did you live better: before the Germans came or after?' Henryk saluted and clicked with his heels: 'Before!' The Commandant swung around and gave him a blow on his temple, almost knocking him over. Then, acting as if nothing had happened, the Commandant repeated: 'So when did you live better – before they came or after?' 'After!' The Commandant told the Colonel joyfully: 'You see how happy the Czechs are with our arrival?' But Henryk's behaviour had marked him out, and as he told us, 'The Colonel made a note of my name.' Hans had also been blacklisted. According to Henryk – who usually spoke on behalf of his shy comrade – 'He's in Polotsk for two reasons: his age and because he's an Evangelist. He has no use for war.' Hans nodded. Hans had met a Russian woman in Polotsk – she worked as a cleaner in the Commandant's office. Her name was Liza, and she had a small daughter. Hans loved them very much and it turned out he didn't eat anything tasty because he collected food for them. Hans had written a memorandum to his superior, stating that his house in Germany had been bombed and his family killed: consequently, he requested to live in Russia and work as a road foreman. But the German Command discovered that his house was still standing and his wife alive and well. He was punished with ten days in the 'starvation' guardhouse. But he was happy that he had not been moved from Polotsk and could still see his Liza.

After these disclosures, our guards' behaviour became understandable: the Fritzes were not all the same. Schwester Lizabeth came around and asked if we were going to give her our word? We all replied in the affirmative. Lizabeth smiled cheerfully and said we could go for dinner. Later, we would be escorted upstairs to sleep where the German soldiers lodged. Our guards would collect us in the morning, as there was no room for them up there. We couldn't comprehend the kindness and humanity that had befallen us. After our supper we remained at the table for a long time. Then, when darkness fell, we went upstairs to the second floor and entered a huge hall.

The floor wasn't ready yet but gymnastics bars had already been set up. Henryk knocked on the door and a loud voice yelled 'Ja?' Henryk reported that he'd brought the Russian artists for the night. Then we heard curses, followed by: 'What have you brought those lice-ridden swine for?' and 'That's a bit too much to sleep next to them! If they snore I'll stick a cork in their throats!' We heard everything and understood it all, despite a poor knowledge of German. Hans told us we would have to go in quietly and lie down straightaway – there were vacant beds by the window. Then our guards left.

We opened the door and entered the semi-darkness of a huge irregularly shaped room with a high ceiling. In the middle of the room was a candle on the floor. The Germans – there were seven of them – were lying on the beds blowing on the candle, for they didn't feel like getting up. We would have to cross the whole room. We walked quietly but the soldiers suddenly stopped blowing and began yelling that we were lousy pigs, and if it entered our heads to walk to the lavatory in the middle of the night they'd shoot us dead! Every one of them was yelling out every insult imaginable. After the kindness of Sister Lizabeth, the candour of our guards, and a good supper, we had entered this room relaxed: but now we wanted to forget our promise and fall upon these creatures and wipe the half-beasts out. All the sufferings that had befallen us emerged in our memories, all the horrible scenes. But we calmly threw off our boots and lay down.

The Germans continued blowing on the candle for a while. The flame was flickering, tilting but didn't want to die down. Then one of them threw his jackboot: the candle fell over, a spurt of smoke went up, and a guffaw resounded, for the jackboot's owner had to get up and retrieve it. Then he jumped back into bed and everyone fell silent, as if under orders. But we couldn't fall asleep. We lay in silence as we couldn't talk. But what could we talk about? Each of us probably had the same bitter thoughts and feelings. We were back to reality. The soldiers slept noisily: snoring, tossing and turning. Gradually we began to doze, comforted by the thought that in due time we'd be on the run and have our revenge on these ones from the 'master race' . . .

Suddenly morning came. One of the Fritzes announced its arrival by rapping on a helmet and yelling: 'Good morning!' A couple of pillows and curses were hurled in his direction. He was laughing and kept drumming on the helmet with a dagger. The soldiers woke up, scratching. One took off his shirt, spread it out, and began pressing over the stitches with a spoon: lice were crunching. The others were laughing and pulling off their shirts too. The one who had woken everybody up grabbed a helmet and began to smash lice with it. Yesterday they yelled that we were lousy creatures, but now we feared getting lice from them, for we'd managed to get rid of ours.

Henryk came in. The soldier who had thrown his jackboot at the candle told him: 'We shoot each other in the trenches and now they've put these lousy Russians right next to us!' Henryk replied that it was the Commandant's order. The soldiers began to laugh: 'Thank God, we weren't herded into their camp to sleep there!' Henryk escorted us out of the room, marching somewhat quicker than when he'd entered. While walking downstairs, he told us that these soldiers were on their way home for vacation – they were front-liners, returning only yesterday from the trenches and because of that were noisy and angry. Then we understood how they felt being in one room with their foes! We washed in the yard at a water-pump, which gave out cold, clear water. Then we had a shave. Now this operation was easy, for Henryk had given us a pack of razor blades.

Lizabeth agreed to pose and I drew her portrait on a piece of silk stretched out on plywood. From the first touches of the brush I saw that the portrait would come out well. Lizabeth liked it. I showed her the watercolour landscape pictures I made in Borovukha. She was delighted by them and I decided to copy some works for her. After 3 pm the hostel would be empty – only we would be left. Lizabeth would pose.

On one such day, during a break in a drawing session, I saw Lizabeth through an open door. She walked across the hall dragging something rumbling on a string. Entering our room she pulled the string up and the item swung in the air: it was a portrait of Hitler. As usual, Lizabeth blushed before speaking: 'It has to be hung on a wall in the officers' room. I know Nikolai would hang it this way with pleasure,' and she passed her hand across her neck, 'but this time it has to be fixed on a wall, otherwise the officers will be displeased.' We were dumbfounded by such trust.

It was four o'clock when Lizabeth suddenly suggested: 'It's a nice evening, why don't we all go for a walk by the riverside?' The guards remained behind and we accompanied Lizabeth to the banks of the Dvina and the walls of a monastery. Lizabeth's red setter dog was running about – sometimes ahead of us, sometimes alongside – in astounding harmony with her red hair. I said that if oil paints could be found I'd like to paint a large portrait of her with her dog. Lizabeth replied that she would ask the Commandant to allow her to go Riga, where she would try to get hold of some paints. I was happy with that: I would be able to paint in oils again! I began to explain what else I needed for the portrait: that a sack would do instead of canvas and a stretcher would be needed. She kept nodding: 'Gut, gut, Nikolai.' Next morning I ordered a stretcher from a POW cabinet-maker and began making a palette and knocking together a makeshift easel.

I liked Lizabeth. Initially I had been conquered by her kindness, independence and courage: now I realized I was feasting my eyes on her. I knew that Lizabeth treated me in a special way too. Once, Henryk – on the second or third day after our arrival – asked me: 'Nach Haus, Nikolai, Frau ist?' ('At home Nikolai, there is a wife?'). I answered in the affirmative and asked why he was interested? 'It's not me, it's Schwester who wants to know,' Henryk replied. Then I added sternly: 'Tell her I'm married.' What I had noticed in my attitude towards Lizabeth seemed impermissible to me; and to give her hope would be a betrayal of my wife.

Lizabeth went to Riga. We were left in the care of the German women subordinate to her. They decided to capitalize on her absence and asked us to draw them Vasnetsov's 'Tri Bogatyrya' ['Three Knights' – a celebrated picture by a famous Russian artist of the nineteenth century – Trans.]. I had to do it, so as not to spoil relations with them.

Lyuba and Naden'ka came around at noon and brought lunch. Hans had stopped being shy about hiding his portion in his mess-tin. I went out behind the door with Naden'ka to find out what was new in town: 'The seaman is going to take off some day soon,' she told me in a whisper. A man had been hiding in the attic of their house and now he was about to join the Partisans in the forest. Damn enviable! Yes, we had to escape. We couldn't remain here for the whole war, decorating 'Soldatenheims'.

After lunch we set off to a metalworker's with Henryk to order small tubes for brushes. Oh God, how much I expected just of a simple walk in the streets! I would be able to view the town a bit – maybe something would turn up? Maybe the metalworker would tell me something new? In the metalwork shop – a wooden shack with a signboard in Russian and German: 'Surovkin and Co. Metalwork shop' – an old Jewish craftsman stood up to meet us. Surprised at this, I couldn't hold back and blurted out: 'How come you're the workshop owner?' He silently pulled out a shabby but neatly folded newspaper. A whole page was filled with portraits, the headline contained the following: 'German Jews-patriots working for the welfare of the Greater Germany.' The shop owner pointed at the portrait of some bearded man: 'You see, this is Shapiro – I am Shapiro too. They haven't touched me yet. I keep saying he's one of my kinfolk.' There were already Jews working for Germany ...

Lizabeth was absent for several days, but one morning a car suddenly ran up to the front steps of the hostel. Henryk and Hans brought in two trunks, Lizabeth followed, happy and shining. She brought paints: now I could begin to draw her portrait.

CHAPTER TWENTY

A New Twist of Fate

One morning in June 1942, Lizabeth came around, anxious and alarmed. It turned out that the German women under her had informed the Commandant that the POWs had been drawing portraits of her instead of working in the 'Soldatenheim'. Still, the day went along as usual: from morning till noon I painted figures of dancers, using the colours the Sister had brought from Riga. Kolya was finishing off his drawings in the hall, based on Dürer's etchings.

After lunch, as always, I set an armchair on the catwalk and seated Lizabeth in it, arranging the dog beside her. The red setter, Vesta – which willingly cooperated – stood out nicely against the background of Lizabeth's green dress. But Lizabeth said she was afraid of a possible inspection arranged by the Administrative Headquarters of the Occupied Territories of Belorussia, for they'd learned there was a portrait-painter in Polotsk.

About five o'clock we heard the sound of a vehicle pulling up outside. I looked out of the window and saw an Opel convertible in front of the doorway. I quickly took the portrait off the easel, placing its face against the wall, and left the room. Having closed the door behind me, I blocked it with a table and piled paints on it. I was just about to disappear into a neighbouring hall when an *Oberst* – a colonel – appeared, a smart young *Oberleutnant* following him. The Colonel confidently strode across the hall. I stood before the closed door: 'It's a working room. We prepare paints for decorating the hall in it . . .' The Colonel moved me aside with his hand like a mere object, giving a sign to the Oberleutnant, his aide-de-camp: 'Ich wollen . . .' ('I want . . .'). The aide pushed the table aside and opened the door, revealing Lizabeth, who stiffened in the armchair as Vesta jumped to her feet. The Colonel immediately spotted the canvas leaning face down against the wall. I leaped forward and pushed the picture away – this was unheard-of! The Colonel flushed with anger, the Oberleutnant lunged towards me, preparing to grasp my arm. I said as quietly as I could: 'Herr

Colonel, it's the Madam's portrait – her permission should be asked.' Suddenly, the Colonel understood he'd been caught displaying bad manners, and in front of a woman who was also his subordinate. Suppressing his anger he spun round, approached Lizabeth, took her hand, kissed it, and asked: 'May I, Madam?' Lizabeth nodded hastily: 'Bitte, bitte ...' I turned the portrait around and showed it, tilting it so there would be no glare. The Colonel kissed her hand once again and said: 'The portrait is superb! I didn't know that there was such a portraitist here. The General will be very pleased with it, we should send the artist to Headquarters straight away.' I understood everything without interpretation but asked Volodya to translate: 'I need some time to finish the portrait.' But Lizabeth translated it for the Colonel herself and he nodded, 'Ja, ja ...' and briskly exited the room, his aide in tow.

We stood frozen for a while, unable to say a word, then moved to a neighbouring room so the German female staff couldn't overhear us. A new twist of fate was before us. Once again we didn't know what would happen on the morrow: the Colonel's politeness could not conceal the harshness of his order, for at any moment we might be taken away at the request of an unknown German General. Lizabeth said she had already heard of the General's wish to have a portrait of himself. If he liked it, he would take the artist to Munich, for he wanted to have his own portraitist – the General would provide the artist with a studio and the means of living. 'I live in Munich too,' Lizabeth said, 'it will be nice if Nikolai goes to Munich with the General.' I felt that Lizabeth was in love with me. Unable to lie to her, I replied: 'I don't want to go to Munich with the General. And I will come to Lizabeth together with the Red Army.' Lizabeth flushed and left somewhat hesitantly.

And here the outrage of my comrades erupted. Sasha and Volodya, barely restraining themselves, hissed: 'How could you tell her about your romantic ravings?! What was this show with the Colonel for? And now with Lizabeth? Did you think about us? What if she's scared and tells the Commandant? She vouched for us, didn't she? Who the hell made you say all that? Who asked you to refuse to go to Munich? Maybe it's worth going! Maybe he'll take us out of here – isn't it a way out? We could wait and then see how it goes ...'

I said that I felt Lizabeth was in love with me and for this reason would not give us away. Again there was outrage over my 'romanticism' and 'fantasies'. When the Sister did not return the guys' anger boiled over. My belief in her love aggravated the situation even more: I had almost become a traitor in their eyes! Everyone was talking in whispers, the suspense becoming tighter and tighter. As for me, I didn't know what to think. It was impossible to unsay all I had said.

A pause ensued, everyone fell silent and began smoking. In the stillness came a knock at the door – I stood up and went to open it. Lizabeth stood in the dark doorway, embarrassed yet animated, clutching some kind of bundle close to her chest. Brushing past, she dumped some stuff on a bed: boxes, cans, packs, chocolate, tobacco, toothbrushes, razor blades. She had also brought woollen socks, gloves and warm clothes. She simply said: 'There is a large forest next to General's Headquarters. Keep this stuff aside for now: you'll need it in the forest – none of it in there.' We were shaken! It wasn't my 'fantasies' any more! It meant the Schwester had been collecting stuff for our escape to the forest for a while. Her actions impressed us ...

Our presentiment didn't trick us: next morning we found out the Commandant of Polotsk had ordered us sent to the Administrative Headquarters of the Occupied Territories of Belorussia. We were still finishing off our work in the halls and after lunch Kolya drew a seaside scene: he wanted to leave the Sister something as a souvenir. Meanwhile, I finished Lizabeth's portrait. In the evening we all went to the banks of the Dvina: graceful Lizabeth in front, we following her, and the two guards closing up the strange procession from the rear – tall, sturdy Henryk and slender Hans, whose submachinegun seemed unnaturally huge.

Lizabeth invited me to her room to look at some pictures in frames. The room was light and large. On an antique wooden bed there was the portrait of Lizabeth with Vesta, leaning against the wall. Against another wall were mine and Kolya's landscapes, and nearby some odd items obviously bartered for bread. Well, our pictures, if one thought about it, had been bartered for bread as well. Lizabeth approached a desk, pulled out a photo from a drawer and showed it to me: it was a young woman in an embroidered nightdress, standing in the middle of a room with nice décor. Lizabeth pointed at the woman, then at herself: 'It's me. Munich, my house, my room. I made the dress myself.' She showed how she'd embroidered the dress, to make it clear. On the underside of the photo was Lizabeth's dedicatory inscription and her address in Munich.

I kissed her hand and left. I had to prepare myself for departure.

The cabinetmaker brought me a crate that could serve as a trunk and I gave him some crackers and sugar. The upcoming events were full of uncertainty. The table in our room was laid, Lyuba and Naden'ka were arranging the settings. Nadia was so sad I thought she'd shed tears. Lizabeth served the wine herself. We raised the glasses saying: 'Thank you! See you again!'

At four in the morning Lyuba ran up, gave us our clean, laundered underwear, then she and Naden'ka brought us food. Knocking on the door, Lizabeth came in exactly at five. We were prepared and waiting. A German cab with plank benches in the back was already standing near the entrance – it was time to come down. We kissed Lyuba and Naden'ka (my heart was aching for their fate), hugged Henryk and Hans.

It was noisy at the railway station. Lizabeth walked along the train and addressed an orderly. He showed her to a freight car with an open door. The car was rocking steadily as if lulling us to sleep and hundreds of situations were crossing our minds: what if we jump out? What if Partisans blow up the train? All the time I was calculating the odds of escape, but a thought would always return: what about our obligation to Lizabeth? And another haunting thought was tormenting me: how come that I – who loved Galochka so strongly and passionately – could fall in love with Lizabeth? I was tortured by remorse ...

The guys continued sleeping but I sat next to Lizabeth, holding her hand. I wanted to kiss her but drove this desire away from me, for it would have been unfaithful to Galka, and I wouldn't have been able to look my comrades in the eyes. Huts on hillocks, poles with wires drifted past the car. Many poles had been cut down, replaced by temporary crosspieces holding wires: it meant there were people who had been cutting down poles at night, making German signallers yell into silent receivers.

We entered Vitebsk, got off the train, and shouldered our way to the bombed and burned-out railway station building. A huge German banner hung over the street: we had reached the Commandant's office. It was busy inside – lots of soldiers and drivers – but all courteously let our patroness pass through. A captain was sitting at a desk. When he realized we were travelling by order of the General, he respectfully said 'Ja, Ja,' and immediately called a driver and a guard. We went outside. We said goodbye to Lizabeth, each of us carefully pronouncing 'Auf wiedersehen!' We sat on benches inside a small vehicle sheltered by tarpaulin. A soldier sat inside with us. Swinging his submachinegun, he happily showed us how he would shoot Partisans ...

CHAPTER TWENTY-ONE

Holding Our Breath

The vehicle sped off through the bumpy streets of Vitebsk. Time and again we saw German flags, German posters, German road signs. The road ran into fields with hillocks, sometimes with huts on them, sometimes with small groves. We had joined a column of military vehicles, some ahead of us and some behind. Our guard said we would have a halt shortly. The vehicle turned off the road and stopped by some brushwood. A half-buried water tank lay nearby and we all quenched our thirst. The driver turned on the engine and we climbed up on our benches. Thick pine tree trunks flashed past us. Behind the trees I noticed figures in dark-green uniforms and black coats with red armbands – Polizei. It turned out that the road was guarded for several kilometres. The vehicle stopped in front of a turnpike. A guard checked our passes and glanced into the back. Our guard explained: 'Kunstmaler, zeichnen General portrait' – 'Artist to draw the General's portrait.'

We drove up to a barbed wire gate, exactly the same as in the Borovukha camp. To the right of us stood a watchtower: machinegun barrels stuck out from an upper platform enclosed by a wooden barrier. The guard at the turnpike shouted something to a guard on the watchtower and we came through. This was 'Borovka', a former military sanatorium, now the Administrative Headquarters of the Occupied Territories of Belorussia. It was surrounded by several rows of barbed wire fence, about 3.5 metres high and shaped like a wide cone. Trees had been cleared around the compound, which was protected by belts of wire and watchtowers. Our vehicle made a sharp turn around a one-storey building and stopped near a shack, knocked together from fresh planks. Next door was a stable. It was here that we jumped out. The guard picked up a bag of letters and set off towards a big building. We were escorted into the shack by a lance corporal – obviously a Pole, for he talked in Ukrainian but with a Polish accent: 'Well, *panowie* ['gentlemen' in Polish – Trans.], an apartment built for you.' It really was a luxury. Everything was fresh: sand on the floor, the planks of the walls smelling of resin, a wooden table alongside a two-storey plank bed. 'That's a stable nearby,' the Lance Corporal said, 'there are horses in it, and it's a lounge for you.' We were happy. In a corner there was even a bucket with fresh water and an aluminium mug. The Lance Corporal said that further down the backyard there were auxiliary services: kitchen, workshop, garages and stables. The workforce here consisted of POWs who lived in a one-storey building next to the gates. Also there was a Polizei barracks, which guarded the Headquarters and the barracks of the off-duty German guards. 'Maybe, panowie wanna swim?' The Lance Corporal continued, 'you can do it – me show you where.' We walked past the stable and down to a lake between pine trees. Our guide explained: 'Cannot go further. Barbed wire over there and guard will shoot.' We took off our clothes and began washing with a small, rock-hard piece of soap. If we could wait till night-time, sitting in the reeds, we could try to swim to the opposite bank – although it wouldn't be easy to cross such a wide lake, especially if there were boats patrolling it, and most likely it would be lit by flares. Sasha Lapshin said in irritation: 'Would have been so simple if we'd gone to Munich! We would have been all right and not shot up ...' Volodya Shipulya supported him: 'He's right, what's the point in taking chances?' Well, for all that, two courses were taking shape: one was to look for a way to join the Partisans and the other – to sit the war out. When Nikolai and I stood face-to-face we decided not to come out in favour of anything but wait till the moment came.

A tall, sturdy figure in the green uniform of the Lithuanian Polizei appeared in the doorway. But as he was also one of us POWs, we invited him in and two others like him followed. In captivity, one learns to become a good judge of people, recognizing friend from foe by instinct. We asked what units they were from? They asked us why we were going to paint a German General?! We replied that we were seeking a quiet place, free from Partisans and were hoping to have a rest at the Headquarters. One of them pulled a funny face: 'You can feel safe here! You've already been provided with guards and even at night your sleep will be taken care of.' This guy's name was Yurka. We briefly told our story and they told theirs: where and when they were captured, in which camp they were held. It turned out there was a small POW camp nearby, from where they'd been recruited to work at the Headquarters in the garage, stables, and so on. They had been issued with the Lithuanian Polizei uniform: a dark-green army jacket with green buttons, turn-down collar – like a civilian suit – and field caps of the same colour. We agreed to see each other next morning. One of the visitors, Nikolai Klochko, was from Moscow and this quickly brought us close together. I also liked Ivan Artemenko from Donbass. He spoke slowly, weightily, and would fall silent after uttering a short phrase – as if listening to his own words.

Later, we ate our dinner with German soldiers at a long table. The dinner action was going energetically, for soldiers are always hungry! Two women from the kitchen came in: an older one and a young girl of about seventeen with short blonde hair. Her name was Lyuba. Everyone piped up: 'Lyuba, another spoon of porridge. Another helping!' holding out empty plates. Lyuba gave us some more and took away the empty saucepans. Later we found out that Lyuba and her mother were evacuees from Leningrad who had been brought from a civilian prison camp to work in the Headquarters' kitchen.

After dinner, a soldier came up and said he was our guard and would escort us to our room. I felt tormented and couldn't fall asleep. On top of being a prisoner of the Fascists, I had to draw their general's portrait: moreover, I was in love with Lizabeth! In the morning, we were roused by a brisk 'Guten Morgen!' from our guard, standing in the doorway. We jumped up and began washing ourselves. Soon we were ready for whatever Fate had in store.

The guard led us to the central building. We arrived on the third floor and turned into a corridor. The guard knocked on the second door. We heard: 'Ja, ja.' We entered and stood before a desk, at which the smart Oberleutnant – the General's aide-de-camp – was sitting. He gave us a friendly greeting and a ceremony of introduction followed it: 'I would like to talk to you on what is to be done at Headquarters – what you are here for.' Schultz – the officer's surname – smiled as if softening the last phrase. He was speaking a mixture of German and Russian, supplementing his words with gestures. Schultz explained that we had been brought to make a frieze in the soldiers' dry mess, and a series of pictures of gallant German fighters for several other rooms – depicting their struggle and hardships at the front and how they were awaited back home. We gladly replied 'Ja, ja, gut.' We were relieved, for we were afraid they'd make us paint a portrait of Hitler or something political. Pointing at me, Schultz said: 'Nikolai is a portraitist, he will be working on a portrait of the General. Tomorrow you will tell me which pictures you intend to draw, and what is needed for the work.'

During the very first chat we found out that Schultz 'lived in Paris a long time' – he was there with the occupation forces – and that his father was a businessman. Schultz himself had a factory and a country estate. Schultz was doing his best to give us the idea that he wasn't alien to the interests and habits of French Bohemia. We liked him for his relative democracy, but despite his exclamations – 'Oh, Paris! Montmartre! The Louvre!' – he didn't invite us to sit down. The Oberleutnant pressed a button. We heard the sound of hobnailed jackboots. A soldier appeared at the door, a submachinegun across his chest. We said goodbye and left.

Arguments about the proposed pictures' themes seethed in the shack: though no one mentioned the General's portrait, for all knew I would be doing it. Lapshin suggested two themes: 'Workers in a mine' – symbolizing hard work in the homeland, and 'Hardships at the front' – German soldiers rolling out a cannon from the snow during a blizzard. Nikolai Klochko and I began to discuss my part of the work, and I suggested drawing a series of pictures about life in the German homeland to touch a soldier's heart and make him less willing to fight. For example, an old woman sits, holding on her knees a photo of her son – a German soldier – in a frame with a black bow, a young woman with a child stands next to her, sobbing. Alternatively: the biting blizzards of the Russian winter, with German soldiers stranded in deep snow. We also might depict the homecoming of a one-legged soldier: his wife rushes to him and his sick mum lies on a bed ...

We were afraid that Schultz, on seeing these themes, would realize we were peddling propaganda, and at best send us back to the camp. But after perusing some preliminary sketches and hearing our explanations, the Oberleutnant seemed pleased. We were astounded. If our political officer had seen them, he wouldn't have allowed the work to go ahead. Furthermore, he would have sent us as far away as possible, to prevent us from undermining the fighting spirit of the soldiers! But Schultz was touched so deeply, we were astonished at his simple-mindedness.

Having obtained Schultz's enthusiastic approval, I went with Nikolai (escorted by an out-guard) to a cabinetmaker to order stretchers. A German cabinetmaker ran the workshop and auxiliary work was done by our POWs. When we arrived the German was alone. We got to talking and he told us that the German Army had already reached the Volga; that Stalingrad had been captured – the Caucasus too – and soon they would reach the Urals. He added that Japan would strike Siberia and the Bolsheviks would have nothing to hold on to. At this point we couldn't restrain ourselves. I turned over one of the draft sketches I was carrying and drew a map of the Soviet Union. I outlined the Urals and the Volga, explaining that provinces fertile in grain were situated beyond the Volga – there was bread over there, steelworks, and 6 million soldiers. These were the very same semi-myths we used to make up in Borovukha. They would come back to us with embellished details and we would begin to believe in them too. The cabinetmaker became thoughtful and said heavily: 'The war is very bad for soldiers and German families.' He was staring at me as if being magnetized by my map comparing distances from Berlin to the Volga, at Siberia stretching out to the ocean, and no longer rejoicing in the reports that the Führer's army had reached the Volga.

We left, pleased with the conversation, and told our comrades of our successful 'agitation work'. But Sashka became angry again: 'You can't take such risks! And Siberia won't be that unassailable if the Japs press on ...' He had already plunged into his artistic quest and was annoyed by our attitude towards the pictures, which we wanted to be our weapons and not merely pictures to please German soldiers. In the evening we went for a swim.

Nikolai and I were training ourselves, holding our breath under water, breathing through reed stems. We were pulled out of the water completely exhausted.

One day we came across Klochko, Yura [a diminutive of Yuri – Trans.] Smolyak and Artemenko. We got into a general conversation, but I had a feeling the guys were waiting for a moment to talk face-to-face. We already knew that Klochko was familiar with a woman – one of the locals – who had been telling him what was heard from the other side of the wire. She worked as a kitchen hand at the Headquarters, and after hours would walk home beyond the wire. Yurka invited us to the old guardhouse to have a look at their billets. Iron beds with grey blankets stood close to each other and it was filled with smoking fumes. Mates of theirs came up to us, I produced a pack of tobacco Sister Lizabeth had supplied us with, and everyone began rolling cigarettes from bits of German newspaper. Smoke rose above our heads, we were introducing ourselves, and already felt mates with them. A feeling of breaking away from old pals, with whom I'd gone through so much, came on imperceptibly: followed by a desire to join with the new people who had recently entered my life – one with a hope for the future. Klochko – speaking frankly in front of his mates – said he'd found out about a Partisan detachment. He had sent word to them, asking them to get in touch: perhaps they could help us out? Or perhaps we could be of some use to them? Now we had to wait till next week for a response ...

One evening, Schultz called me and warned: 'Tomorrow Nikolai will have to draw the General's portrait.' I knew that I would have to portrait the General but felt somewhat uneasy deep inside. A session might last for an hour from eleven o'clock till noon, and after that the General would be busy: then he would have a break and lunch at two.

In the morning, I presented myself to Schultz with a map-case containing paints, a plate for a palette, and a jug of water. The Oberleutnant stood up, glancing at his watch, and stepped towards the door, courteously held ajar by a soldier. We strode along the corridor towards the General's office. Two guards with submachineguns stood by the office. Schultz knocked on the door. Hearing 'Bitte!' a soldier opened the door and let Schultz, me and the guard in. The door behind us closed silently. We entered a big room with huge windows – the General's office. Left of the centre was a huge antique desk, on which stood a lamp with a green shade. Behind the desk, a big man with grey hair was sitting. He had a fat nose, tight lips, and dingy grey-green eyes. His glance was heavy and one felt uneasy under it. I laid out my gear on a chess table in front of the General's desk. Then, in the strained and unpleasant silence, I began to work. The General's silence and the straightened figure of Schultz behind my back were oppressive. But even worse, the eyes of a black dog, sitting next to the General, tenaciously held me in their glare: what if the beast leaped upon me?! Time passed. The General made some movement with his hand and the Oberleutnant asked:

Nikolai Obryn'ba, Kiev 1937.

2. Galochka, August 1939. This photo was with me throughout the whole war.

Kamenka, summer 1940.

4. August 1941,
Opolchenie trainin

5. August 1941,
Opolchenie training.

6. POWs on the march
October 1941. Durin
marches, POWs
rushed to the corpse
of horses, tearing m
off them, while the
guards shot. To the
right, a ditch with th
bodies of POWs in t
Borovukha-1 camp.
(picture drawn on th
underside of a
German postcard).

On the road, October 1941. The POWs are flaying a horse's carcass (picture drawn on the underside of a German postcard).

8. Punishment – the Polizei at work, April 1942 (picture drawn on the underside of a German postcard).

'Free' passage beyond the barbed wire, February 1942. Corpses were driven out of the camp this way (picture drawn on the underside of a German postcard).

10. Working team trar porting firewood, March 1942 (pictu drawn on the underside of a German postcard).

11. Sunday in the Borovukha-1 POW camp, April 1942. When spring arrived, starving POWs ate the grass growing on the parade ground. Beyond the barbed wire everything was green, but the parade ground was grey (picture drawn on the underside of a German postcard).

12. Kombrig Fedor Fomich Dubrovsk and Kommissar Vladimir Eliseevic Lobanok, Decemb 1942. I took this photo on the same day I started work on their portrait.

. The scout, Fedya Moshev, October 1942. Aged only 13, everyone looked after him and fitted him out: a blouse was adjusted for him, breeches hemmed and jackboots found in his size.

14. Dmitri Timofeevich Korolenko, December 1942. Commander of the 3rd Detachment of our brigade, he was killed by a mine explosion after 20 hours of combat, in April 1944.

. Three friends: Mikhail Didenko (left), Vasili Nikiforov (centre) and Boris Zvonov, November 1942.

16. A leaflet, January 1943.

17. N. I. Obryn'ba, February 1943.

18. 'Echelons on Fire' – a sketch for the picture of the same name, February 1943.

N. I. Obryn'ba (left) and N. Goutiev, February 1943. I sent this picture home, with the inscription: 'To my dearest and closest. I am happy that I'm here and you don't have to blush for me.'

20. Stepan Borodavkin, February 1943. The brigade was built of people like him, and I wanted to preserve the memory of the brigade founders in portraits.

Construction of the staff dugout, February 1943.

22. Ivan Chernov and Misha Chaikin (right) test a kite designed to scatter leaflets, March 1943. Misha is in his early 20s, and in a month he would become a cavalry squadron commander.

23. Spring 1943 in our camp – everyone enjoys the first warmth and sunshine. On th left, platoon commander Nikolai Klochko; on the right Misha Chaikin; second right Vanya Chernov; next to him Nikolai Goutiev.

4. The last tribute to the machinegunner, Lepik, April 1943.

5. F. F. Dubrovsky on his horse, 'Grey', April 1943.

26. Our girls Lena Sharaeva (centre) and Vera Ladik (right) embroider the brigade banner.

27. Spring in the Partisan area, April 1943. On approaching Pyshno I was astounded by this scene. The Partisans were expecting a German advance and had set up a gun in the old woman's yard – undaunted, she was sowing potatoes around it!

28. Mounted reconnaissance, May 1943.

. In N. Safonov's detachment, Staisk, 17 May 1943. Poznyakov (standing) delivers information about the V Plenum of the Communist Party Central Committee. Nikolai Safonov is on the right, sitting on a bench.

30. Dmitri Bourko, May 1943. This photo was taken when Dmitri was leaving the camp to join his detachment at Veselovo. It was half–manned by Polizei men who had crossed the lines to join our side.

.. The 'Unsubdued', 17 May 1943, the first day of the blockade. Forty years later the picture I called 'Unsubdued' was created.

32. Our way, 17 May 1943. The cannon was pulled by a team of six horses.

33. Mikhail Chaikin's cavalry squadron enters Staisk, May 1943. On the right, Misha rides his horse, 'Orlik'.

. A gun crew, Staisk, 19 or 20 May 1943. The German blockade was tightening; there was no chance to save the gun which had to be buried. Left, crew commander Ivan Artemchenko; third from right, artillery commander Sergei Markin who would be wounded in 1944.

. A group of Partisans from Safonov's detachment take off to the German rear for a sabotage action, Staisk, 19–20 May 1943. Left – the platoon commander gives the order. Front row, second from the right, is a former POW who later became a section, then platoon, commander.

36. An ambush on the road to Ushachi, July 1943. At this time around 40,000 Germar troops confronted 5,000 of ours. Blocking roads was a priority. This photo shows group of anti–tank riflemen from Didenko's detachment.

37. I took this photo during an encounter with a detachment marching to rescue me Pyshno, June 1943. In the centre, Vera Margevich and Andrei Korolevich. On the right, Nastya Boulakh – a marvellous medical orderly of fabulous kindness and attentiveness.

. Mikhail Didenko's detachment on the march, June 1943.

. The first days of the blockade, an ambush, end of May 1943. The machine gun had been taken from a burnt-out aircraft and repaired.

40. Doctor F. Salnikov (last on the right) tastes a meal at the kitchen of V. Zvonov's platoon, August 1943.

41. N. I. Obryn'ba, August 1943.

42. Petro Litvin, Starinka, July 1942.

'Stop him?' The General, slightly raising his hand above the desk stopped Schultz, and he in turn passed over to me: 'Zeichnen, zeichnen!' – 'Draw, draw!'

I saw the portrait gain lifelikeness and now switched to details. I drew with a brush the medals, orders, and the white enamel cross – received from the hands of the Führer himself, as Schultz had told me. Suddenly the tuneful chime of a clock sounded, announcing it was about to strike twelve. I felt much easier, as if a noose on my squeezed throat had been slackened. 'Enough for today,' the Oberleutnant said quietly, 'Nikolai is dismissed.' Everyone except for the General began to move like mechanical children's toys. The guard came up, stooped and took the jug, holding back his submachinegun. I took the plate, paints and brushes. Schultz picked up the map-case. The dog's eyes followed our every motion. We went out through the corridor and one of the guards quietly shut the doors behind us.

Schultz was silent in the corridor but when we entered his office he said: 'Sehr gut, Nikolai. Tomorrow at eleven – be here.' The guys were waiting for me and as soon as I got home I realized how tired I was and how much I'd been strained. I lay on Kolya's plank bed, having no strength to climb up on mine. After some time the guys began to question me. I told them briefly, but how could I tell them everything I'd been through? Kolya, Klochko and Yurka knocked on the door and came in: 'Chaps, we've come to invite Nikolai to our place, our mates liked his tobacco very much.' Everything tensed inside me: Nikolai wouldn't have invited me for no reason! But I shouldn't let the rest sense that we had secrets from them. I searched my box and pulled out the tobacco. 'Eh-h, there is only a half here, it won't be enough for all. Maybe, you've got some?' I said to Goutiev, 'then let's go and have a smoke.' We walked out and when outside I threw out: 'Pity we haven't had a swim ...' Yurka reacted straightaway: 'Well, let's go down and have one.'

We had a swim, came in, wiped our faces with one towel, put our clothes on, and lay on the grass. We took out tobacco and began to smoke. We were waiting for what Klochko would say. I couldn't contain myself for long: 'What's up? Have you seen or spoken?' 'Yes,' Nikolai began leisurely, 'but the Commander said: "We can't help them, let them escape themselves. They got themselves into captivity – let them find a way out. I'll give no people for it."' We began to confer again: what if we asked them to pass us explosives – maybe we would blow up the Headquarters? But we took it no further. Instead we walked back, and agreed to say nothing about our negotiations with the Partisans to anyone: any careless talk might come back on the messenger-girl – the girl Nikolai Klochko was in love with.

CHAPTER TWENTY-TWO

Russian Pig – Run Away!

July 1942 came. Issued with passes, the guys went out of the Headquarters' compound to mow grass and rake hay into stacks. Once out of the gate, they turned right towards Vitebsk and a couple of kilometres later, came to a meadow. Further away, up on a hill, was a Polizei barrack. Sometimes they harnessed up our huge gelding, which couldn't understand a word of Russian, and brought back hay to the Headquarters' stables.

One morning I sat and waited for eleven o'clock. Moments later, I was before the dog and his master again, trying to paint a portrait of the man and his white enamel cross. Such crosses were not awarded for kindness and humanity . . .

In the opinion of the German soldiers, to be entrusted with the job of painting the General's portrait was a great honour. I was outlining the General's eyes, and it seemed to me that everything was going well, when Schultz whispered behind me: 'Nikolai, Mars! More like Mars . . .' And so I was to make the General more like the Roman god of war! With a sinking heart, I tried to add more fire to the eyes. Then I tried to tighten the sagging lips and give an energetic knit to the brows. Now there was belligerence! But the portrait lost its likeness and this was immediately confirmed by Schultz: 'It's not the General . . .' But on the other hand, what a warlike glitter shone in the dog's eyes when he looked at me! And hypnotized by the beast's stare, I unintentionally copied it onto the face of the lacklustre General. Suddenly he acquired the features of brutality.

The clock struck a liberating twelve. The General wouldn't sit a minute longer – I knew his punctuality. Schultz took the map-case from me and I understood that he would show the portrait to the General. The guard came up on his signal. I handed him the jug and the plate of diluted paints and left under escort. I was weary, but in a different way from the first time. We crossed the yard, caught in the stares of the soldiers: for them I was a special person, for I had just seen the big man.

A day came when the guard walked me to Schultz once more. Having heard his sprightly 'Ja, ja!' I entered his office. Schultz was excited: 'The General said the portrait is good, Kunstmaler Nikolai – gut! The General will take Nikolai to Munich! Nikolai will have a studio in the Kunstakademie …' His speech ended with an ecstatic exclamation: 'Sehr gut!' 'Ja, ja, sehr gut …' I echoed. I was surprised that the brutal expression of the face in the portrait had not enraged the General and that he actually liked it. Schultz asked if I were going to do more work on the portrait. I replied in the affirmative. Schultz added: 'Tomorrow a Gestapo Hauptmann will come around for a portrait. The Hauptmann is keen that you paint him. He has already rung three times!' Then, as if apologizing, Schultz added: 'I suppose I could say no …'

At three o'clock, straight after lunch, the Hauptmann rode up on his motorbike. I saw him drive up the alley into the Headquarters' compound, throw off his black oilskin raincoat, and run up the stairs. The guard came to pick me up immediately after, escorting me to the administration office. The Hauptmann was strolling along the corridor. A red armband with a black Swastika in a white circle was on his sleeve, and his jackboots were polished to a shine. He addressed me in broken Russian: 'Want ya make my picture.' The Hauptmann's manner was cold and stiff. But I set to work and he began to talk. Occasionally, he even laughed – though his mirth was more spiteful than cheerful. 'You did General's portrait,' he said, waving his hand towards the General's office, 'now you do Hauptmann Gestapo!'

I worked intensely, wishing to finish sooner rather than later. Gradually, the Hauptmann became more talkative and asked when I became a POW and what my name was. 'Nikolai, where did you live?' 'In Moscow.' He nodded approvingly, then slumped into boredom again. After a while, he decided to continue with the 'polite' conversation: 'Soon Germany cross the Volga, end of war come. Kaputt Stalin, Kaputt Moskau!' I simply said: 'The General is going to take me to Munich.' The Hauptmann became animated: 'Nikolai see all Europe! I was in all Europe, Africa, Egypt, France, Holland. I had all kinda women …'

He kept talking, but I couldn't concentrate and feared my feelings would find reflection in the portrait. He began to recall Egypt, showing with his hand how women did belly dancing. Then he switched to Paris and his mouth broke into a lustful smirk: 'Women very good, can do everything.' After a moment's reflection, he added, 'Rus women sehr gut! Best women in Europe!' He was smiling, as if calling to mind some particularly amusing adventure. I began to loathe his red mug with the plum-like nose, and was already drawing close to reality, trying to reproduce all the unpleasant features of this Fascist. He began again: 'Moskau will soon be ours – all will be German!' Anticipating a good time in Moscow, the Hauptmann warmed to the topic of Russian women and the beneficial consequences of mass rape: 'Oh, Rus women and Deutsch Soldaten will make good Nazis! Better Nazis!'

I'd foreseen that drawing a Gestapo officer would be an unpleasant task, but had not expected it to be unbearable. What made it worse was the realization that he'd picked up his meagre Russian by interrogating our men. With all the composure I could muster, I innocently asked: 'And what will happen to the Russian children and menfolk?' The Hauptmann was delighted. Clenching his hand into a fist, he stuck out his thumb before jabbing it downwards: 'Kaputt! Kaputt!' Now I had caught him. Speaking in broken German, I explained that Russian women were the best in Europe because Russian men had fathered them: if they were replaced by Germans all the kids would be red-haired! At first the Fascist Hauptmann laughed, lewdly licking his lips till wet. But then the significance of my words hit home: he realized he had denounced Nazi ideology by suggesting mixing German blood with a 'lower' race. Now his expression changed, his face flushing with fury till it reached crimson. His hand convulsively flicked towards his holster and thrusting his head forward he screamed: 'Rußische Schwein – Russian pig – run away!'

In place of fear I felt relief, as if I had become weightless: only a slight nausea rose to my throat. I looked straight into his flaming eyes, saliva flying from his mouth. But as the Hauptmann raised his pistol, he was illuminated by a beam of light shining from behind me: Schultz was standing in the open doorway, accompanied by several guards. A shadow of fear flit across Schultz's face, but he feigned a cheerful smile: 'Gut portrait, Nikolai! Sehr gut!' The Gestapo Hauptmann was letting forth a stream of oaths, but he couldn't shoot, for Schultz was standing right behind me. Schultz asked him to explain what was happening: 'Russian bastard!' the Hauptmann yelled. Schultz abruptly ordered the guard to escort me to his office. Then he calmly asked the Hauptmann what he was displeased with? In a tirade of foul language, the Hauptmann began telling what had passed between us, but then thought better of it, realizing the nature of his admission. Catching a final scowl of malice from the Hauptmann, I was escorted along the corridor to Schultz's office.

I stood before the desk in Schultz's empty office, shaking with humiliation. The Oberleutnant entered. It was obvious he was alarmed. He sat down but left me standing: 'Herr Hauptmann gone. He took his portrait – sehr gut portrait.' Schultz leaned back and looked at me, framing the obvious question: 'Why was Herr Hauptmann angry?' 'I did bad – schlecht,' I said in broken German. 'Gut, Nikolai,' said the Oberleutnant, apparently dropping the subject, 'now I want Nikolai to draw big Führer portrait.' I hadn't expected such a proposal. I stared into his eyes, searching for a plausible reason why I couldn't agree to his request. Back in Borovukha, when we artists had to draw Germans, we agreed that if any one of us drew Hitler's portrait, he would be considered a traitor: 'Perhaps I could draw a picture for the Oberleutnant?' But Schultz repeated his demand: 'Nein, Ich wollen portrait Führer! – No, I want a portrait of the Führer!' Then suddenly, a slow smile of comprehension spread across Schultz's face: 'Ah, Nikolai doesn't want to draw a portrait of Führer!' I saw no point denying it: 'No, I don't.' 'If I were a POW of the Russians,' said Schultz pointing at himself, 'I would not want to draw Stalin portrait. Yes, Nikolai, I understand that.' But before I could relax, a new question was fired at me: 'Nikolai is POW – why? He doesn't wanna be free?' Again I feigned simple-mindedness, explaining I wanted to become free and hoped I would be released one day. The Oberleutnant agreed: 'Yes, you'll be released. Nikolai is free today! He puts on German uniform and will be free German soldier!' He stared directly at me, a little bit above my eyes. I had to reply immediately, for I understood he was cornering me, like a chess player who had calculated a forced checkmate. I began to explain that I couldn't become a German soldier: 'I swore my allegiance, I can't fight against my countrymen ...' 'Yes,' said Schultz, 'I see, one can't fight against his own army.' Then, brightening, he added: 'but Nikolai will fight against the bandit-Partisans!' Anticipating this move, I bluffed good humour too: 'Long ago I wanted to tell the Oberleutnant that he's been deceived – they're not bandits or Partisans but Red Army paratroopers. They're soldiers too and I can't fight against them.'

Schultz stood up, came up to me, and tapped on my shoulder: 'Good man, Nikolai! I hate those Russians that were Reds yesterday, are Germans today, and hell knows what they'll be tomorrow!' He summoned the guard and I was escorted back to my billet. I felt such emptiness, such fatigue – as if I'd been squeezed out – I couldn't say a word and lay on my back, my gaze fixed on the ceiling.

CHAPTER TWENTY-THREE

A Surprise for the General

August 1942. It had been nearly a month since we moved to Borovka, but the summer was still in full swing: warm with rains and thunderstorms. Our plan to escape to the Partisans was taking shape, as was the list of escapees. There would be ten men in all, but Shipulya and Lapshin were not among them. Relations with Volodya and Sasha had become more and more strained. The fact that Nikolai and I were supportive of each other and often stuck together apparently irritated Sasha and Volodya.

One day Oberleutnant Schultz called me up. It turned out the General's birthday was imminent. 'Would be nice to make him a gift, to paint a Russian landscape,' Schultz said. I promised to do my best to draw a big forest. Schultz approved: 'Gut' and 'Prima' poured down upon me, as if from a horn of plenty. At that moment a thought struck me: if something happened – if they caught me during the escape – I could tell them I was making a drawing as a surprise gift for the General. In order to cultivate this seed in Schultz's mind, I repeated that I would be very happy to draw a forest for the General. When I told Klochko about my talk with Schultz, he nodded in approval, saying that it might come in handy ...

We were already asleep when our guard came in: 'Schnell, schnell. Herr Oberleutnant is calling you.' It was eleven o'clock. We quickly got ready and the guard escorted us – not to Schultz's office – but the General's, up on the second floor. Schultz emerged and announced that we had a female visitor. Through the General's open door we could see a carefully laid table – judging from the sounds, a regular banquet was going on in there. A moment later, Sister Lizabeth appeared. Greeting us, she said she was glad to see us all in good health and wanted to present us with souvenirs. Producing some small paper bags, she gave sweets to Sasha, Volodya and Nikolai. Then she addressed me, Volodya translating: 'I have just spoken with the General: he'll be leaving for Munich soon and is taking Nikolai with him. Does Nikolai stick to his original decision?' 'All's the same,' I replied. Lizabeth produced a pipe and a pack of tobacco and handed them to me: 'A souvenir for Nikolai.' I kissed her hand: 'Auf wiedersehen ...'

Lizabeth had found an opportunity to warn me that it was time to make a decision. Now I had to escape! We knew we were parting for good.

Several days passed, when Yurka popped in and announced: 'On the run tomorrow. In the evening, everyone be at our place.'

In the evening, Kolya and I were in the barrack. Kolya Klochko told us the escape time would be two o'clock in the afternoon – our passes were ready. He, Smolyak, Artemenko and five others – plus the two of us, making ten in all – would go to the hayfield beyond the compound. Kolya and I would come to the stables when they were harnessing the horse, and tell the stableman that Oberleutnant Schultz had allowed us to ride with them, to draw a Russian landscape for the General's birthday. We decided not to take Shipulya and Lapshin and to tell them nothing.

Sunday morning came, cloudy but warm – there was a touch of mist, as if before rain. Nikolai and I had dressed carefully, meticulously wrapping our feet in white foot rags. We didn't know what would happen on this long-awaited day, but from soldierly habit we put on clean clothes. I took the watercolours and the map-case with me. It was time to see the Fritzes, to have breakfast with them, and to do the General's portrait. But the whole affair ran into complications when the General shifted the drawing session from its usual eleven o'clock slot to noon. This would give me less than two hours to finish the portrait. 'After the session, come over to pick me up straightaway,' said Nikolai, 'we will have to hide our gear in the cart ...'

Nikolai went to the workroom and I went to the General's office. The Oberleutnant greeted me amiably, saying: 'Nikolai must finish the portrait today. The General can't pose any longer.' I worked hard, straining to the limit. I had to complete the portrait to avoid any delays. By the time the clock struck half-past one, I had already finished. Schultz himself confirmed this: 'Gut, it is complete.' The General asked Schultz to show him the portrait – the first time in my presence. I moved my chair away from the General's desk, leaning the portrait against its back. The picture was lit as well as possible and I could see that it looked like the General. But my priority was to get out of the office as soon as possible. The Fritzes didn't work after two o'clock on Sundays, so we had to make our getaway on time. But Schultz was lingering in silence, scared of being the first to venture an opinion on the picture. At last the General said quietly: 'A good portrait.' The General was touched. He loved his dog and – strange to say – did not spot the resemblance between his own countenance and that of his familiar. He gazed at the picture: an angry old man with tightly pursed lips glared back.

Suddenly, the General announced: 'I'll be somewhat free after lunch and will be able to give the artist a bit more time.' I hadn't expected this! It was an unheard-of favour: the General freely offering precious minutes from his after-lunch siesta. I felt a lump in my throat. To me, the General's favour sounded like a life sentence. There was only half an hour before the escape: the guys would be looking for me and any delay would frustrate the whole effort. I pulled myself up: 'Herr General, it's very kind of you, but I have to decline the honour with regret, for after lunch the lighting will be different.' Schultz immediately chipped in: 'Nikolai, it's overcast today!' But I persisted, repeating my argument and showing with gestures that the outdoor light was changing. Morning light was one thing, I explained, but afternoon light another: shadows would fall on the face in a new way, and I did not want to ruin a good piece of work. Schultz did his best to smooth the situation over: he moved the portrait towards the wall, examined it from a distance, then came closer, studying and appraising the details. After the application of a bit more pressure he eventually succumbed, saying in a respectful tone: 'Yes, Nikolai has done a great job today and managed to achieve a complete resemblance ...'

I fully understood the extent of my audacity. The General was looking at me – a POW and his personal serf-artist – from above. He had honoured me by offering to pose and I had refused! I stood petrified, awaiting the verdict on my artwork: if the General was not satisfied with the painting and wanted me to do more, escape would be impossible. Schultz was silent too. He had his own reasons for hoping the General was satisfied with the portrait: for having recommended me, he hoped to recoup favour from his superior. And so, both Schultz and I anxiously awaited the General's judgement. Eventually, the tension reached its limit. The General slowly rose in silence. The dog leaped to its feet but was restrained by a gesture from the master, freezing like a statue. The General walked up to the portrait, leaning over it to examine its details. He paid particular attention to the white cross. At long last he spoke, his words falling heavily, like a stack of gold coins: 'I suppose my family will like this portrait. I'll take it with me to Germany and find a place for it in my office.' I could have jumped for joy! But restraining myself, I simply said: 'I am happy, Herr General, that I managed to complete this portrait. I appreciate the responsibility and confidence vested in me.' Schultz interpreted my words for the General: then we picked up our gear and left. I spoke again about a souvenir for the General, so as to smooth things over ...

Having had lunch, I went with Nikolai to the stable. We took the sugar, candies and tobacco earned by making portraits, and the things presented to us by the Schwester. Having packed everything into a groundsheet, I took the paints and map-case and carried everything to the stable, where the horse was already being harnessed to drive to the hayfield. A German handed over the reins to the guys, asking us why we were going with the workers. I launched into my tale about painting a Russian landscape as a souvenir for the General, adding that the idea had been approved by Herr Oberleutnant Schultz. The German nodded gladly, fumbling with the harness.

The horse was harnessed up and all ten escapees – eight workers plus Kolya and me – were waiting for permission to drive off. There were passes waiting beyond the gates for the eight workers, but my story about a surprise for the General would move any German and I was confident of getting through. Suddenly, a lieutenant from the guard turned up, asking the groom where the artists were heading to, and who had authorized it? We explained that we had an arrangement with Oberleutenant Schultz about a souvenir for the General, now we were on our way to make a landscape drawing from nature. The Lieutenant was unmoved. At this moment Schultz appeared, returning from the lake. The Lieutenant sent me over to get things clarified. Schultz had been swimming and was out of uniform, a trench coat thrown over his pyjamas. I quickly approached him, to prevent his coming too close to the cart and seeing the bulging groundsheet containing our stock of food. I reminded Schultz that he had agreed to let me draw a Russian landscape as a surprise for the General. The Oberleutnant objected that we hadn't understood each other: he'd meant that I should make the drawing from the Headquarters' yard, not from beyond the wire. He protested that, as it was Sunday, no guards were available to escort us out of the compound and 'his heart would be worrying much' – he put his hand on his chest, showing how it would be beating. Acting casually, nonchalantly, we feigned indifference, walking beside the cart so as to carry our stuff back to the stables unnoticed.

Nikolai and I decided to act as follows. We'd go to the main building, where the Germans had their canteen, and where the barman owed me a glass of Schnapps for a portrait. We'd have a drink, then go for a swim. We'd swim out to the middle of the lake, then, taking our chances, we'd try to push on to the other side. If we were held back, let it be: but we couldn't stay here any longer. In less than an hour it would become clear that eight people were on the run and the whole story about the 'Russian landscape' would crumble. Then no one would believe our concern for the General's birthday and we would be in dire straits. At best they would send us back to the camp . . .

We came up to the bar. I asked the German – the canteen supervisor – to give me a glass of Schnapps. The Schnapps went down well but didn't bring any relief. We drank to the unanimous guffaw of the Fritzes sitting in the canteen. Well, it was all to the good, now we had an alibi: if they caught us we would say we were drunk and the soldiers and barman would confirm it. Then we walked down to the lake with the paints and map-case – we were allowed to swim there, where the horses were watered. When we arrived we saw – to our astonishment – seven of our comrades from the escape team!

We rejoiced at seeing each other, but what had happened? It turned out that the guys – all eight of them – had been stripped of their passes at the gate, as if the Germans had a list of who was going to escape. And where was the eighth man? He wasn't among us, which meant only one thing: he was an informer.

To our right was a high wire fence, climbing up the hill to a watchtower overlooking the approaches from the lakeside. It was normally manned by a machinegunner. Beyond the wire was a clearing about 10 metres wide, then a wide strip of coned wire. Everyone was looking in that direction. I saw my mates' eyes slide over the wire, sensing a new, unspoken scheme. A glance was enough and Yurka began to walk up the hillock. Without exchanging a word we understood his plan: to find out what the sentry was doing – he was not in the watchtower! Yurka made a reconnaissance and reported: the Fritz was speaking with an old woman bartering eggs for his cigarettes. This meant the lower part of the hollow wasn't in his view: by moving quickly and quietly there was a chance we might get through the fence. The main thing was not to rattle the empty tins hung on the wire – we knew the Fritzes had been turning off the electric current in the daytime.

Klochko and Yurka were already pulling apart the dense lines of wire just above the ground, and Ivan was digging the earth with his hands. A gap we could sneak through appeared and Yurka was the first to slip under the wire. I saw him reach the strip of coned wire, stepping on small posts, balancing like a rope-walker in a circus, so as not to fall into the dense spiky web. The others followed. It all went like a dream – silently, not a word or a sound. I was the rearguard, Nikolai and Klochko were ahead of me. Everyone crossed the wide strip of coned wire his own way. Some walked on the posts – stepping on spikes so sharp they could pierce your boots – and holding onto sticks stuck in the ground on both sides of the coned wire. Others were making their way on all fours, leaning on posts and sticks with hands and feet. Nikolai dropped his spectacles. They fell into the grass and I was trying to pick them up with a fallen tree branch, for Nikolai was blind without them. Six guys had already disappeared into the woods, leaving three of us still next to the wire. At any moment the sentry might climb the watchtower – and we were still messing about trying to fish out these glasses, which, as if on purpose, were caught in the grass. At long last I managed to hook them. Klochko was holding me by the belt, and aided by Nikolai, pulled me out and I regained my feet. An instant more and we were in the woods.

CHAPTER TWENTY-FOUR

The Night Forest

As soon as we came out on the main road a vehicle emerged from behind a bend: the German driver asked me why 'the Kunstmaler' was walking about? I prattled on about a souvenir for the General. The German was ecstatic and let us go, wishing us good luck. A little farther and we found ourselves in a meadow full of Polizei and workers serving the Headquarters. But the Polizei, having noticed me and Nikolai, offered to entertain us with Schnapps. They were trying to suck up to us: after all, we made paintings for the General and even spoke to him, so they wanted to make a good impression (what if I complained about them?). I said we would come around with pleasure, but first we must paint a Russian landscape for the General. Off we all went up the hill: Nikolai, me, and the other escapees. But what the hell? Suddenly there were ten of us! Leshka – who hadn't been involved in our preparations – had decided to accompany us. But as soon as we passed the first clump of bushes our file switched to a line and everyone broke into a sprint. Leshka, somewhat surprised, was looking over his shoulder: 'Hey, guys, why are we running? What about the drawing?' Stopping to catch our breath, we looked at each other with the same question in our eyes: what to do with Leshka? His presence in our effort had not been anticipated. A thought flashed around our minds – tie him up! But Leshka immediately understood the situation and smiled: 'Could it be you're on the run? Then I'll join you!' And again, with no delay and no discussion, we pushed him into the middle and continued our run. The map-case containing paper for landscape-drawing got in my way, so I threw it into the bushes, but I kept the paints close to my chest and stuffed the pencils into my pockets.

We had to bear towards a triangulation post to reach the Partisans' village – Klochko knew which one – but at the moment we saw neither the horizon nor the post. Tree branches whipped our faces and we heard only the tramping and gasping of running people. Suddenly, a clearing appeared in front of us: behind it – far away – a forest loomed. Pink and yellow circles blurred my vision – a bit more effort and we were on the other side. But beyond the scrub we came across a railway track with two Polizei guarding the crossing. No time to deliberate: we threw ourselves forward and they dropped into a ditch without shooting. Several leaps and we raced past them: we had no time to deal with them and they, apparently, had no stomach to deal with us.

We ran into the forest without slowing down. Water squelched under our feet as we splashed into sodden ground. The sound of barking of dogs came from afar. Everybody stopped for a second, listening, aware of how the guards pursued runaways with dogs. We knew the guards would be chasing us on horseback with a pack of dogs. First they would unleash a pair of German Shepherds, taught to outflank an escapee from both sides – they would knock him over and keep him pinned. On hearing the commotion, the guards would unleash another German Shepherd and a huge black cur, before riding over themselves. Finally, they would tie up the runaway and the dogs would keep watch over the captured fugitive. But we had stumbled into a bog, something all runaways hoped to find: for mounted guards cannot ride across a marsh and their dogs lose the scent. But we could not remain in the bog, as the guards would eventually work their way around it. Our only hope was to push on and hope to find a road that would lead us away from the pursuers. Eventually – after much thrashing about in the swamp – we reached a dry spot. The barking remained in the distance and we strained every nerve to get across the wood quickly.

We'd been on the run for two, perhaps three, hours. Our bodies burned but nothing mattered. We didn't speak and we had no leader. I was in a small group ahead of the rest. I glanced back and saw saliva foaming in the corner of someone's mouth. Crimson bubbles frothed in the mouth of another. Well, this was the way exhausted horses died, but we had to keep going – just keep going! But my chest and throat were burning as though scalded. I had no strength to inhale, so I swallowed air in small gulps, gasping loudly. My legs seemed filled with something heavy – it was becoming harder and harder to get them off the ground. Wiping my mouth, I saw the same drops of blood on my hand. I noticed a red cluster of rowanberries. I bent a branch down, tore off the berries with my teeth and chewed them while running. The other guys snatched berries as well. The sharp, stinging juice tightened my throat with its acid and brought me to my senses. I heard the barking of the dogs more clearly now. The sound no longer came from our rear, but from our flanks: this meant the riders had managed to skirt the bog and bring the dogs back onto our tracks.

We lunged forward as if pushed – the barking and yelping getting closer and closer. Ahead of us the ground grew boggy again and we lurched on towards life-saving water. Behind me, one of the guys dropped with a faint cry. I turned back and found him stretched awkwardly, face down. I turned him over but he was dead.

Meanwhile, the dogs were closing in. We heard their cries as the riders broke through the forest, undergrowth snapping and cracking under advancing hoofs. Suddenly I came upon a creek – the bog began a little further on – and I splashed into the water, which came up to my waist. Skulking among the reeds, I felt completely indifferent: I no longer cared if they caught me or killed me – nothing mattered. I had lost contact with the guys ahead of me, but a nearby voice hissed out: 'Drop down! Pull the reeds over yourself!' I squatted in the water, doing my best to catch my breath and camouflage myself. Remaining motionless, I heard the pursuers draw near, dogs panting and yelping as they ran. Up to the water's edge they came, horses foaming and dogs drooling. Through the reeds and alders I saw the search party stop. The horses and dogs were straining to enter the water, but the Germans restrained them, preferring to shoot aimlessly – spraying everything with bullets. But they didn't see us. One of them told his comrades that it was getting late; that there might be Partisans about; that it was time to get back as soon as possible. The dogs were pulled back and the horses turned around, retreating in fear of the night forest.

Several minutes passed and everyone emerged from the water around me. A mist was descending on the marsh and I had no will to move, not even to stir. But we couldn't afford to rest: we had to get as far away as possible under cover of night. But where to? After thrashing through the forest and blundering around the bog, we didn't even know where east and west were, never mind the triangulation mast. Only now did Klochko tell us that our rendezvous with the Partisans was to take place at midnight, in the village of Pounishe. The password was: 'Seventy men and three girls. Valya from Moscow.'

We checked our food. I found a piece of sugar and a little tobacco – others produced wet matches or lighters. I was relieved that my pictures had apparently survived the soaking, sealed in a rubber pack, though there was no time to check on them. But what about the paints? Pouring water out of the paintbox, I hoped for the best. Then my turn came for three quick puffs on a half-soaked cigarette. We spoke of the man who died: a young guy from the Donbass – he had a heart attack.

It showed ten o'clock on Leshka's watch – we'd been on the run for a full seven hours. And again we had to gather strength for a new spurt. Yurka encouraged us with anecdotes. I found that my boots felt surprisingly tight. Meanwhile, my left leg was badly scraped at the back. A discussion about where we were, and where the mast could be, was in progress. At last we decided we just had to get up and go. We walked, squelching and constantly sinking in the slough.

Exiting the wood, we came upon a ploughed field. A peasant shack loomed in the dark of the night. A pair of lovers darted away from us into the bushes and we rushed for cover. We had found a village. Sneaking into the settlement, we approached one of the outermost huts and quietly tapped on the window. A small window to the side of it opened and an old woman peered out. We asked her the name of the village and those roundabout, not letting on we were looking for Pounishe. At last, the old woman pronounced the name 'Pounishe', adding that it was: 'About 12 *versts* [8 miles – Trans.] from here, right of Sedovo.' We headed off into the night, sometimes stumbling upon a vegetable patch, sometimes a country track. Already late into the night, we entered a forest, where we were caught by heavy rain. We were exhausted. Piling one upon the other, we collapsed into sleep.

By dawn the rain had become stronger: it poured from the branches of the slender spruce we were lying under, so we found a thicker one. Then a buzz of vehicles was heard. We thought this might be our troops moving towards the Carpathians. Why the Carpathians? It was rumoured in the POW camps that our Command had ordered all Partisans and escaped prisoners to make for the Carpathians, to organize a second front. We heard that aircraft were sent there to drop paratroopers and supplies. We used to ascribe this plan to Stalin. And so we decided that if we couldn't find a Partisan detachment, we would have to move through the forests – without compass or map – to the Carpathians! Generally speaking, we had the most heroic and resolute plans! It seemed to us that a real struggle was beginning – the sentiments of those joining the fight, and who believed in its cause. How long we had been cut off from the outside world – and now we could go wherever we wanted! In fact we didn't know where to go. How glad we were of the rain, which washed away our footprints; and of the spruces that had hidden us – Freedom!

We set off, and moving through more marshy ground, approached the edge of a wood. A village on a hilltop appeared before us. To the left, a granary with a sentry beside it loomed through the fog. We had to communicate with the locals to find out where we were, and if any Partisans were near. We stood, wet and hungry, each one of us waiting for someone else to volunteer for a reconnaissance. Finally, everyone's eyes rested on me: only I had a Red Army uniform, the others wore the German-issued uniform of the 'Lithuanian Nationalists.' I removed my belt, rolled it up to make it look like a revolver, and stuffing it into my pocket, moved off – looking as menacing as possible. Nikolai walked about 100 metres behind, to make things more secure.

I walked up the hill towards the first shack, close to which stood a small group of elderly men and women. Straightaway I said: 'Good day!' They replied somewhat apprehensively. I asked what the village was called, and to my great surprise they said, 'Pounishe'! Well, astonishing things can happen sometimes! Without blinking, I shot out another question: 'Do you have a Burgomaster here?' Then, addressing the youngest-looking one, 'take me to him!' And I jabbed forward the improvised 'pistol' in my pocket. 'No, he's in Pyshno,' came the reply, 'you see, this is just a village – what would he be here for?' But I was not about to give up: 'Then take me to a Polizei! We're gonna finish him off now!' 'What's with you?' came the response, 'there's no Polizei around here!' Finally, I said: 'Well then, take me to the *Starosta* – the village elder.' The old folk, shifting from one foot to the other, began talking all at once. I caught the words: 'He's ours ... no point shooting him!' With the word 'ours' the tension relaxed and everyone agreed there was no need to shoot. 'Well, then,' said I, 'give us some food!' Nikolai came up and we were taken into a shack. The hostess gave us half a loaf of rye bread, a field-cap full of potatoes, and several pickled cucumbers. We mentioned the Partisans and were told that a detachment came around last night. No one knew where it had gone, but it turned out that Germans were camped nearby at Pyshno. We said goodbye and returned to the woods.

It may seem ordinary, but that morning of our first encounter with the world, that first talk with people on the other side of the wire, required a particular effort from us. For nearly a year, we POWs had been shut away, unable to communicate with civilians. We didn't know what was happening in the world, in the country. In the camp, the Germans used to say that Stalingrad had fallen and the whole of Russia was in their hands! We didn't know what to expect beyond the wire, or how we ex-POWs would be treated by our people. And were they really ours – the people we came across? After all, there might be Polizei around as well ...

On our third evening of freedom, we approached another village perched on a hill. We decided to split into three-man groups, entering the village from three different sides for security's sake. The place was quiet – no barking of dogs – and a blanket of fog was falling, muffling sounds. Walking towards a shack, I lightly tapped on a window. A woman in white opened up and I asked: 'Do you have milk?' 'Got some in a pot,' she replied, 'will you take some?' Suppressing my joy, I continued, coolly: 'No, we are just hungry – others will come later to take some.' The woman disappeared, but a moment later she handed us a jug of milk and a piece of bread.

At that moment, a warning whistle sounded in the dark. Kolya and I ran towards the sound and bumped into our breathless comrades. Klochko began to talk quickly: 'There are Polizei over there! We were drinking milk and there they were, on bicycles, two of them. One leaped off his bike and pulled out a Nagan [Belgian revolver, used widely in Russia – Trans.]: "Who are you?" We said: "Lithuanians." "What are you doing here?" I said: "Ambushing Partisans." "How many of you?" I said: "Forty men." The one with the Nagan asked all that, the other – a tall one – stood to the side, aiming his submachinegun at us. Then they asked: "Have the Partisans passed through here?" We said "No." They got on their bikes and said: "We are from the Commandant's office, checking on Polizei outposts." Time to bolt,' concluded Nikolai, 'they might have dashed for help!' But I said it was clear they were the Partisans: 'What kind of patrol could it be if the Partisans get their milk here?!'

Now we feared the Partisans would wipe us out in the night, having mistaken us for Lithuanian Polizei. But Nikolai had had no choice: how could he say that we were looking for Partisans – what if they were Polizei? And having said 'forty men,' he probably saved us from both Polizei and Partisans. All the same, we remained alert, hiding in foxholes unable to sleep.

At dawn we made our way towards the forest. We followed the tracks of bicycle wheels, clearly visible on the dewy grass. Then we saw the remains of a burnt-out farmstead. A peasant was picking up what remained of his belongings. The guys hid in the bushes so as not to scare him, and I spent an hour persuading him to say where the Partisans were. At last he gave in: 'I'm scared of you and sorry for you. Go straight ahead and you'll see a forester's shack in a clearing. To the right, there's a trail to Istopishe, to the Partisans . . .'

We took off in that direction and soon the clearing opened before us, a fenced shack in the middle of it. A boy, aged about thirteen or fourteen, was flattening the field around it with a roller. Again I went forward, leaving the guys in the bushes. I approached the kid and began asking him where the Istopishensky Forest was? But the boy skilfully pulled away from me, back to the fence, pretending he didn't understand. I was about 15 or 20 metres from the fence when suddenly, from behind it, I saw angry eyes staring at me down the barrel of a levelled rifle. Then came the words: 'Halt! Hands up! Who are you?' Reacting instantly, I said: 'You are just the man I need – I'm looking for the Partisans.' At that, everything came to life: Partisans hiding behind the fence popped up, surrounded me, and escorted me to the farmstead. I noticed a group of people behind the shack with a heavy machinegun on a cart: everything was ready to meet the 'Lithuanians'. Everyone was tense.

Part Two

Red Partisan

CHAPTER TWENTY-FIVE

Drawing a Line Between the Past and the Present: August 1942

We'd been on the run for three days. For three days we had not removed our boots, walking through forests and marshes, avoiding tracks, driven by the fear of pursuit. Now, having finally met the Partisans, I was so happy that I sat on the ground and began pulling off my soggy footwear. But one boot would not budge: my foot was swollen and the sodden bootleg was cutting into flesh. Inside, blood had oozed from a wound that had opened while I was on the run. The Partisans looked at me with concern, but I kept fiddling about with the boot, recounting the events of the previous night: how they'd taken us for Lithuanians and we'd taken them for Polizei – that was why we'd said there were forty of us, and that we were ambushing Partisans. A young guy came up and took hold of my boot: 'Hold tight.' He jerked my leg and the jackboot came off.

A stocky man, wearing blue breeches and an officer's woollen blouse, suddenly spoke: 'So that's the way it was!' He grinned and turned to a tall, stooping Partisan: 'That was great, Pasha [a diminutive of Pavel – Trans.] how we frightened them – nine turned into forty straightaway!' 'And we turned into Polizei!' Pasha rejoined. But the Partisan boss suddenly became stern: 'And where are your "Lithuanians" now?' I explained that I'd left them in the bushes, behind the clearing, for we were afraid to move in a group – after all, they might have gunned us down. 'Let me go back and get them,' I said. But this aroused suspicion rather than approval. Fortunately, Nikolai Goutiev's figure appeared in the clearing and I rejoiced: 'Here comes my friend, he's in the Lithuanian uniform issued in Borovka.' Then, waving at Nikolai, I yelled: 'Kolya, come back quickly, get the guys here!' But the stocky guy cut across me: 'Let your Kolya come here. We'll see what kind of a bird he is.' Nikolai came up, staring at me – standing in my bare feet – with astonishment. The Partisans scrutinized him in silence, as he stood adjusting his spectacles. Then the Partisan chief piped up: 'Why are you walking one at a time? Get the rest over here – and quickly!'

As Nikolai left to fetch the others, I began explaining that we were both artists: I from Moscow and he from Rostov; that we'd been transported to Borovka from Polotsk to draw a German general; and that we'd been brought to Polotsk from a camp in Borovukha. But the more I talked, the more confused the Partisans became. Suddenly, a thought flashed: perhaps they're not impressed with my story? Perhaps they're thinking something along the lines of: 'We've been fighting the German bastards down here and these artists turn up, who've been pandering to one of their generals!' I felt uneasy. At last the guys appeared. Wearing their Lithuanian uniforms, the eight men looked more like a military section than escapees. Pasha and his chief recognized Klochko straightaway – it was him they'd spoken to last night. Meanwhile, Nikolai recognized yesterday's cyclists.

A man appeared from a nearby shack, tall and sturdy. Approaching us, it was clear he was the Partisans' Commander-in-Chief. His manner was straightforward. In a clear, calm voice, he said: 'Serezha [a diminutive of Sergei – Trans.], line up the newcomers, I want to talk to them.' We formed up: tall Klochko took the right flank, then came Ivan Artemenko – another athlete – and the others followed. Finally, Smolyak and I completed the line. We looked an impressive bunch – real Red Army fighters – except for me, that is! Only I spoiled the formation: standing without boots, my foot badly swollen. The Commander examined us with curiosity, greeting us in army style: 'Welcome, Comrade fighters.' The word 'Comrade' touched our hearts and we replied simultaneously, as was common in the army: 'Good morning, Comrade Commander!' He slowly walked along our line and said: 'Congratulations on your arrival at the Partisan detachment.' We immediately liked this cool-headed man with the calm voice. He asked: 'Has every one of you been in service before?' We answered all at once: 'We all have!' 'We'll get introduced shortly,' the Commander said, 'my second-in-command, Sergei Markevich, will write down who is specialized in what.'

Markevich – the stocky guy who had questioned us before – pulled a notepad from his map-case and began writing down our surnames and military professions. First, he addressed Kolya Klochko, who answered laconically: 'Muscovite. Worker. Drafted in 1939. Platoon commander, artilleryman. Fought in Finland.' [The war between USSR and Finland 1939–40, known in the West as the Winter War – Trans.] Next came Artemenko: 'Coal miner from Donbass, from Gorlovka. Drafted in 1939. Graduated from an artillery school. Battery commander.' Markevich laughed: 'If it goes on like this we'll never have enough cannons for you!' Then came the turn of Nikolai Goutiev – he introduced himself as a machinegunner: 'Took part in the Finnish War and the liberation of the Western Ukraine.' [The autumn campaign of 1939, when the Soviet Army entered Polish territory, known in Russia as the Western Ukraine – Trans.] These answers totally dismayed me – what I could say? That I was a final year student of the Institute of Arts and used to be a medical orderly? That I was captured because I had slept through a retreat? No! No way could I say all this! I started to panic. Perhaps I could say that I'd made Ausweis passes, that some of our officers and night flight airmen had used them to escape captivity? Perhaps I could say how I'd saved wounded men at the front? But all this would have made a long story and would have to be proved. Yurka Smolyak, a machinegunner, came next. He reported: 'My profession is shooting Germans, either with a machinegun or a rifle!' Now it was my turn. Bracing myself, I said: 'Muscovite. Private in the army, from the Opolchenie, student of the Surikov Institute of Arts.' I thought: why mention Surikov – do they really know who he was? Then I added: 'I drew a German general's portrait in Borovka. Escaped with the group of POWs.' Markevich, who was writing everything down, asked again: 'So you're a civilian with no military profession?' I resolved to say that I used to be a medical orderly in the army. 'At ease,' said Markevich, 'wait here till the big shots decide what to do with you.'

Markevich and the Commander went back to the shack. But no sooner had they disappeared inside, when another Partisan officer opened the door and walked down the steps. Big and broad-shouldered, we judged by his bearing that he must be a Regular Army man. He even made more of an impression than our own mighty Artemenko. He introduced himself: 'I am Zhukov, Commander of the 2nd Detachment.' He proceeded to question us: who was who, where we had fought, and how we were captured. Again I was dismayed: what to tell? Zhukov came up to me. Glancing at my bandaged foot, he said: 'You haven't been in combat yet but already you are wounded! Where are you from? Where did you fight?' I answered that I had been in the Opolchenie, adding once more that I used to be a student of the Surikov Institute of Arts. Zhukov simply asked: 'Want to beat the Fascists?' 'Yes, I do. That's why I've escaped.' 'Was it you who drew a German general?' 'Yes, I had to ...'

At this point, a cart entered the farmstead, carrying three more commanders. They went straight to the forester's shack, accompanied by Zhukov. Something was up – that much was obvious – but we couldn't ask what: so we stood and waited. It seemed to us that the men in the shack were talking about us, preoccupied with our fate. It was the hardest moment of my life: for I understood that all the facts were against me, and I would have to make up a lot of ground for people to trust me. Suddenly, the soft-spoken Commander emerged from the shack. It was only then I heard his name for the first time. He said: 'My name is Fedor Fomich Dubrovsky, I am Commander of the 1st Detachment.' Producing a list, he read aloud which detachment each of us was to go to. It so happened that when we joined the Partisans, two independent detachments were merging into one brigade. Two days later, Dubrovsky became the *Kombrig* or Brigade Commander, Zhukov, the Chief of Staff, and Sergei Markevich, Chief of Intelligence. That was why we had seen so many commanders at once.

Sergei Markevich came up to me: 'Artist, I've put you in the reconnaissance group. Now you'll kill generals instead of drawing them!' Zhukov led forward a small, chubby girl and introduced her: 'Lena Sharaeva – Political Officer of the 2nd Detachment.' Then he asked jovially: 'So, chaps, tired of waiting? Let's go and have lunch – I guess you got hungry on the run?' We cheerfully agreed. Zhukov turned to the girl: 'So, Lena, walk them to our detachment for lunch.'

The day was already far advanced when we walked down a forest trail, dodging hazel bushes and birch trees, yellowing in anticipation of autumn. Although things appeared to be working out, we'd never dreamed that we – POWs who had served at a German Headquarters – would be accepted by the Partisans so easily; that they would just jot down our names in a school notepad and congratulate us on joining. And as it happened, a real induction with a military oath followed later. Meanwhile, we reached a small clearing, in the middle of which a fire was crackling. Above the fire, suspended on a wire, was a cauldron. Soon, instead of the expected coolness and mistrust, a cook poured hot soup for us. And bread was given, as if restoring our human rights. Again, there was an emotional shock – followed by happiness. At last we were eating our own food, given to us by right, and not begged for, or thrown off a table! We exchanged glances of delight and gave the thumbs up. Lena sat nearby. She treated us with sympathy, trying not to ask too many questions. On the contrary, we talked non-stop. We wanted to tell everything, and as quickly as possible, drawing a line between the past and the present. But more than that, we wanted to ask questions, and while telling of the camps and captivity, we also asked about events at the front. That was how our first lunch with the Partisans took place, after which, Lena walked us back to the camp.

The camp was located in a birch forest. The Partisans lived in shelters made from the branches of trees. We were introduced to the Kommissar of the 1st Detachment, whose name was Mikhail Karaban: 'At dawn, the detachment will set off for an ambush,' he said, 'Klochko and Goutiev from your group will be there.' After some small chit-chat, I sensed that Karaban wanted to ask me something: the attack I'd been expecting was coming. 'Let's take a seat,' Karaban suggested. We sat down and he immediately launched his offensive: 'How come you agreed to draw the German general?' I understood that the Kommissar was concerned about my motivation for joining the Partisans, so I told him in detail about the camp at Borovukha, about the Ausweis passes, about Polotsk, and how we had been transported to Borovka to paint the General's portrait and decorate the canteen. I told him about the conditions we'd lived in. Had we escaped from a camp where people were dying of hunger, where we'd been beaten and threatened with death, everything would have been clear and understandable: but I told Karaban how we'd been given bread and chocolate in Borovka, and that the General wanted to take me to Munich and make me his personal artist. I didn't want to appeal to Karaban's compassion or belittle my own faults: and for this reason I told him about the chocolate, although it had only been given to us once, by Lizabeth. Karaban spoke with some reserve: 'How come you've escaped from chocolate?' Certainly, it was hard to comprehend why one would have risked death escaping from an enemy who treated you with sympathy, and even valued your talent. I understood that all these considerations were in the Kommissar's mind, and that I had to break through his mistrust. And so I put it to him plainly: 'So, is it a case of, "if they harm you – run, if they help you – stay"? If I'd been selling myself for chocolate, I would have stayed there!' 'Well, well ...' said Karaban, caving in, 'I didn't want to offend you. Let's go, we need to find somewhere for you to sleep.' And off we went.

Karaban said: 'Until you have your own tent, crawl into the machinegunner's, as he'll be out on the ambush.' Then turning to Nikolai Goutiev, he said: 'And you will go with the machinegunner as his number two.' At this point, Kolya Klochko came up to ask how we were settling in – one could see he was nervous about combat. We said goodbye and they departed. Looking at the machinegunner's tent, I noticed a gun barrel sticking out of it, and a muffled figure curled up inside. The tent was small, though two men could easily fit inside. But the figure didn't budge. I said cheerfully: 'Let me into your shack for a night's sleep.' The man squinted over his upturned collar: 'Well, fugitive, crawl in, let's get some sleep before dawn.' I noted his Ukrainian accent [the author was from the Ukraine – Trans.], but disliked the word 'fugitive'. My countryman fidgeted a bit, moved over, and I crawled in to lay beside him. The introductory chat began: 'What's your name?' I answered and asked his. He told me his name and asked where I was from. I began telling him about the camp at Borovka, but he interrupted me: 'I asked where you were from?' 'From the Ukraine.' 'So, you're Ukrainian ...' 'Used to be, but turned Russian in captivity.' 'Why did you sell your identity then?' 'It wasn't like that – I didn't give my nationality in the camp. They used to form Ukrainian units there and give them extra gruel. There were a lot of traitors among our countrymen ...' My neighbour said nothing and turned his back on me, obviously preparing to sleep. And so I stuffed a bundle of grass under my head and shut my eyes. But my neighbour spoke out again: 'So you noticed there were many traitors amongst the Ukrainians. Who do they betray?' The question was snide and unfriendly, and I replied without hesitation: 'Obviously, not the German Polizei ...' He fell silent, as if digesting my words, then suddenly rose and swore in my face: 'Bastard from Moscow! Get out of my tent! And you got under my trench coat, you scum!' Realizing communication was at an end, I slid out and sloped off. It was a shame I'd been so sincere: he was a Partisan of sorts, but probably a Ukrainian Nationalist. I didn't dare discuss the matter with anyone, for I hadn't been among the Partisans long – only a few hours. Deciding that it was best to stay away from him, I crept into the weeds and soon fell asleep.

I was woken by the cold. The air was misty, everything dripping with dew. I crept out of my shelter and saw Dubrovsky several steps away from me. A young Partisan – just a boy – poured water on his hands. Dubrovsky noticed me crawling out of the weeds and laughed: 'How did you sleep, Artist? And where did you sleep, on what kind of feather bed?' I was plastered all over with rose-bay down. 'Come and have a wash!' I joined him with pleasure. The young Partisan lectured me: 'Why don't you have a branch tent? You've got to build one so as not to sleep in the weeds.' The camp was waking up. It was chilly and I stood near the bonfire to warm up. Karaban was already up and greeted me cheerfully. Although it was unpleasant to recall, I told him about my 'chat' with the machinegunner: 'You reckon he's a Nationalist? He joined us not long ago, his surname is Statsyuk. When he comes back from the ambush we'll talk to him together.'

The Partisans soon returned from the ambush mission, supporting Kolya Klochko under the arms. His head was bandaged – he'd been wounded in the jaw. A medical orderly named Stasya walked beside him – it was she who'd dressed his wound during combat. He was immediately laid on a wooden bed. Our medic, Fedor Salnikov, deftly cleaned up his wound, removing splinters of teeth, and bandaged him. It turned out that Nikolai had leaped out on the road, and shooting from an upright position, had slammed his bullets into an oncoming truck packed with troops. He killed the driver straightaway, but the Germans in the back returned fire and hit him. A bullet pierced both cheeks and struck his jaw, damaging the teeth. When they retreated, the Partisans wanted to carry Nikolai, for he'd lost a lot of blood, but he refused, indicating that they should support him under the arms. The wound was serious and difficult to dress, and there was no way Nikolai could talk, eat or drink. And yet he was lucky: a little higher or lower and the wound would have been fatal.

Kolya Goutiev came up with a heavy machinegun. He looked perplexed. It turned out that his number one – the Ukrainian who had driven me out of his tent – had fled. They hid together for the ambush and then the machinegunner had said: 'I'll go see the Commander and ask if he needs us to move to another spot. You stay here with the machinegun.' Kolya aimed at the road and awaited the Ukrainian's return. Ten minutes later, Zhukov came up and asked Kolya where the number one was? Nikolai answered that he'd gone to see the Commander. The combat commenced, the truck with the Fritzes was hit straight away, and the action never reached the spot where Kolya was. When pulling back, they searched the bushes but couldn't find the machinegunner. Karaban swore: 'He's gone!' Then he told Markevich about my talk with Statsyuk. Markevich got angry too: 'You really screwed up, scout! You should have reported it to the Kommissar.' I felt guilty and uneasy: why had I not acted immediately?! 'Trust but check,' Karaban concluded, 'we might have been left without a machinegun because of that skunk!' Sergei gave a wink and said, as if to console me: 'Doesn't matter, we lost one man – that bastard who ran away – but nine men joined us, including some who've been fed with chocolate by a general!'

This case of betrayal on my first day with the Partisans illustrated the difficulty of their situation. There was no rear echelon down here: the enemy might sneak in through any chink, and one couldn't afford to become the weakest link in the chain. Meanwhile, I built myself a tent, light and small. I could sneak into it, as into a bag, and when sitting outside, I could put a board on a tree stump and draw. I took a liking to a young Partisan in a peaked cap with a red star on it. I asked to him to sit and pose and drew his portrait. It was the first picture I made when I was with the Partisans and I still keep it. There is a date on it: 27 August 1942.

The affair with the deserter influenced us greatly – it was as if a shadow had passed over us. People were tested only by combat: only your enemy's death proved your loyalty. There would be a lot more talk about the turncoat. Markevich gathered our group and warned that spies were being sent to the camp, the forms of their subversion were subtle, and everyone should be on the alert. He told us that recently, two people had joined the detachment: a young fellow had brought a Jewish girl with him, saving her from execution, as there had been rumours that a massacre of Jews was about to take place. But the detachment Kommissar ordered him searched and sachets of poison were found sewn into his clothes. During interrogation it was discovered that he had been set the task of pouring poison into the cauldron at the Partisans' kitchen, and so as to worm himself into the Partisans' confidence, he had resorted to the trick of saving the Jewish girl.

The following spring, Statsyuk would come back to our brigade. He'd come cap in hand, with a promise to execute a bold operation: to kill the Commandant of the German garrison in Lepel. He would be trusted, given two young Partisans for assistance, and sent out to do it. Three days later, a peasant related the terrible sequel. Statsyuk's group stayed overnight at his place before the sabotage and liquor appeared on the table – Statsyuk was entertaining the young guys. During the night he slaughtered them with a knife and disappeared. He would turn up again later, as an instructor of the sabotage school in Lepel, in which wreckers were trained for provocations, scouting, mining roads, poisoning wells and assassinating Partisan commanders.

In the occupied territory surprises lay in wait all over the place. It was natural that our arrival raised caution: the group was large, and if a mistake had been made in accepting us, it would have caused a lot of damage. Dubrovsky later told me the top brass had disagreed about what to do with us – one of them was even in favour of shooting us! The brigade was only just forming and there were nine of us, all military men: good news if we really were soldiers, but what if we were traitors? Perhaps the commanders' concerns were caused by the nervousness we ourselves had raised, when posing as Polizei during the encounter with the Partisan scouts? Moreover, the guys were wearing uniforms typical of the Lithuanian Polizei. And of course, everyone was taken aback by our stories – especially mine and Nikolai's: artists, painting a German general's portrait! But apparently, Zhukov stepped in: 'I am ready to give these people arms and will go on an ambush with them. I will lead them into combat and check what kind of people they are. But if they stand the test they will all be mine – I'll take them into my detachment.' At this moment everyone was engrossed in their thoughts. The list of our group was on the desk and a comment on our military skills was placed against each name. Suddenly, the commanders realized Zhukov had got one over on them, having reinforced his detachment with nine fighters in one go. Envious of Zhukov, they decided to distribute us among the different detachments and battle-test us in the first operations to occur.

CHAPTER TWENTY-SIX

Singing and Dancing in Sight of the Enemy: September 1942

The bullock-cart was jolting, bouncing up and down on a rough track, and we were jolting and bouncing along with it. We were on our way to block the path of a German tankette [small reconnaissance tank – Trans.], which had broken through a Partisans' outpost. We rode upright, holding on to the handrails. I had a small pistol in my breast pocket: I pulled it out from time to time, showing off that I was armed, and the boy who owned the cart kept whining: 'Guvnor, let me hold it for a while.' The boy was the driver and I generously let him hold the weapon for some time. The pistol could just about kill a fly – and only then at point-blank range. I had coaxed it from Olga, our *komsorg*, before the operation began, as Markevich didn't want to take me along unarmed. Sergei had a submachinegun, and at the other end of the cart stood Fimka with a heavy machinegun. Sergei was gesticulating wildly, explaining the plan of operation – he was passionate about being in command, and didn't care who was in his unit, as long as he was in charge. On this occasion, having snatched an order from Dubrovsky in passing, he'd dashed out of the shack, noticed Fimka the machinegunner, grabbed a Maxim [Soviet machinegun used in the Second World War – Trans.], and off they went into action! When they came across me, I asked them to take me along: 'If you can find a weapon, catch up with us!' Markevich yelled. I caught up with them when they were already out in the field, where Sergei found the bullock-cart and ordered the hay thrown off it. We placed the machinegun in the cart and then raced off ...

Thus we reached the hamlet of Dvor-Zhury. The main road went by the hamlet and we hoped to take a position by it and stop the tankette. Before the farmstead we split: Fimka took the machinegun and took up a position on the left of the road, near a shack; the boy was sent away into some bushes beyond a hillock with his cart; and Sergei and I crawled towards Dvor-Zhury. We needed to find out if the Fritzes had already passed through, and this proved to be the case. We heard German voices from afar, then spotted three trucks. Germans were everywhere, and judging from the number of vehicles, there were no less than 100 of them: but there was no sign of a tankette. 'Let's crawl closer,' Sergei whispered, 'let's listen to what they're talking about.' Sergei knew German pretty well.

We crawled across a cemetery, perched on a hillock. To our horror, the clouds cleared, and the bright moon illuminated our position: strung out over high ground and in full view of the Germans about 100 metres from us. Ducking for cover, we pulled ourselves together, straining our ears for signs of the enemy's movements. Sergei whispered: 'They're gonna stay here overnight.' There was no point even thinking about action – we would be lucky just to get out alive! But it was impossible to creep back over the crest of the hill in the bright moonlight. And so we stayed put: pressing ourselves into the ground and watching the Germans as if entranced. Several submachinegun bursts shot into the darkness: the Fritzes were firing at random, but sooner or later, they might hit us by sheer luck. Fortunately, a big black cloud came over and screened the moon. We quickly crawled back, cursing ourselves for our carelessness.

We inched our way over the hillock and ran, stumbling, into the darkness of the night. I glanced back, saw the inky skies, clouds enveloped in silver halos, and suddenly I was gripped by delight: 'Sergei! Look how beautiful it is!' Sergei waved me off and kept running. We reached Fimka, then the cart, climbed in, and dashed towards the forest, giving thanks that the full moon had returned.

Back in camp, Sergei immediately went to see Dubrovsky. I began looking for Olga, to return her pistol, but Fimka caught up with me: 'Let's go quickly, the Kombrig is calling for you.' It turned out that Sergei had reported to Dubrovsky: 'It's possible Nikolai has lost his senses. We were running and he was looking at the skies and yelling: "How beautiful it is!" ' This is how my first combat action ended up! Of course, it was unskilful and somewhat childish warfare: Sergei, the boy, and me – we were still playing at Partisans, influenced by ideas we'd picked up from books and movies. Nevertheless, our reconnaissance wasn't useless. That night, Nikitin's brigade arrived in our Istopishensky Forest. They were seasoned men, who always fought boldly. It was decided to wipe out the Fritzes in Dvor-Zhury.

Again a group of Partisans left for an operation: a detachment of about twenty people lined up along a trail screened by birches and spruces. Sergei Markevich was in command. Our scouts were in the formation: Pasha Logvinenko, a tall and skinny man, stooping and with a hoarse voice; Mikhail Chaikin, a young Cossack from Kuban, with a pug-nose and hazel eyes (it was he who had poured water on mine and Dubrovsky's hands after my first night with the Partisans); a Kazakh called Zebik, broad-cheek-boned and calm; Vali, also a Kazakh, but a tiny and very lively man; Ivanov, a broad-shouldered bumpkin; and other fighters. The first guys had sub-machineguns and rifles, the other ten had whips and thick coils of rope tied around their belts.

Dubrovsky set a task: 'The Fascists have collected livestock, commandeered from the locals, in Ushachi. The herd is large – up to 100 cows and more than 150 sheep. They are afraid of driving the animals to the station and are holding them in Ushachi, awaiting reinforcements. There is a 600-strong garrison there, made up of Germans and Polizei. Your task is to snatch the cattle and drive them to the forest, avoiding combat. The detachment is provided with ten herders who will drive the cattle. The rest will be their cover.' Again I asked Dubrovsky to allow to me to take part in the operation. Dubrovsky refused: 'Later.' Markevich asked: 'Is everyone ready? All in order?' But it turned out that one scout was sick with fever. Sergei ordered: 'Hand your rifle to Obryn'ba, and yourself to the doctor.' Rejoicing, I took the guy's German rifle, and a small stock of ammo, and joined the formation. Sergei clarified the task: 'The herd is in pens on the outskirts. We have to sneak up quietly, so as not to let the Germans – or anyone else – notice. We'll tie up the watchman, drive the cattle out, and the herd is ours! We'll be far away before they find out about it in the barrack, and they won't be chasing us: they don't stick their noses out at night.'

We were quickly striding through the evening forest. I was happy to have a rifle again, and to be lucky enough to join a combat group. Having passed through the forest, we walked down by a lake. Dusk had already descended, silhouettes of men serenely drifting in the fog. 'Have a rest,' Sergei's quiet voice was heard. A main road was in front of us, wires were making noise against the poles. 'Who can climb poles?' the Commander asked. 'I can!' Misha Chaikin volunteered. He even had clippers for wire-cutting on him. We lay in the wet grass, watching and listening. Mishka's silhouette appeared against the background of the night sky. Grabbing a post with his hands, he began to climb. He got up, pulled out the clippers and began to tinker. Clank! The sound of snapped wire resounded. Clank! Clank! Others fell, coiling, and it seemed to us the Germans would appear shortly and begin shooting. But everything was quiet: I imagined the face of a German distorting when his telephone receiver fell silent. May they know that the Partisans are everywhere – always close, like shadows! All began to whisper, glad the work was done. Mishka had already climbed down and was telling how difficult it had been, cutting the wire with one hand. Zebik rolled up a cigarette, and screening himself, lit up. We crept up in turn and everyone inhaled twice from his roll-up.

Now we were walking on one side of the main road. The atmosphere was tense, for most of us were on the way to the enemy's stronghold for the first time. When approaching the village, Sergei explained: 'When you get to the pens wait for me there. I'll have a sniff if everything is quiet near the houses. Some people may have "guests" here. I know all those who've been receiving "guests". Don't come close to the huts – move along the roads, and at intervals.' Sergei disappeared in the dark and we stretched out, nervily treading the edge of a cobblestone road past huts with dark windows, scared by sunflower heads bobbing behind fences. We were alert, ready for any surprises. We tried to walk quietly, but there were twenty of us – some with iron-shod heels, others with steel toecaps – making for a heavy footfall. Of course, we were not supposed to enter the village in one group, and on top of that, to walk down the main street on a cobblestone pavement, but we were inexperienced, including our commander, a former chemistry student. We didn't know how to behave, each of us expected an order, not knowing our rights or obligations. For example, were we permitted to drop to the ground to seek cover, without this being taken for cowardice? We were unsure even of this: so we obeyed Markevich like God Almighty. It seemed to us that he was the man who knew everything – all the tricks of warfare!

Having reached the pens, we settled under the trees to wait. Sergei appeared from behind a corner and began cursing us: 'Who waits like this, eh? You should have dropped on the ground and aimed your weapons at the bell tower, because a machinegun may strafe us from up there.' Again, it was folly! What could we have done against a machinegun with our weapons? If it struck from above, we'd have no chance of hitting it. Meanwhile, the cattle pens appeared to be located in the centre of the village, not on the outskirts, so we should have prepared for action while still on the road: then, if the Fritzes dashed from their barracks, or the Polizei from their huts, we could have taken cover in scattered groups. Now we were bunched up on flat ground like sitting ducks. But the confidence of our commander was inspiring. We believed that everything was going the way it should – the way he was telling us. After cursing us, Sergei announced: 'I've passed by the huts, all was quiet. We're gonna start now.'

We came up to a barn, where some of the animals were penned. A watchman sat by the gate. While we were opening it, Sergei spelled things out to the old man: 'We're Partisans and we've come to take the cattle from the Germans. We're gonna tie you up so they don't think that you've given us the cattle yourself.' Skilled herdsmen, who knew how to handle cattle quickly, began driving the livestock out of the pens, but one particular cow started bellowing and fussing about all over the place, while one of the rams obstinately refused to budge. The herdsmen had already set the other beasts in motion, but we were still grappling with the recalcitrant cow and the rebellious ram. Finally, Sergei ordered: 'Nikolai, let's drive them back.' We quickly drove the cow back into the barn, then rushed over to the ram, and aided by Zebik, grabbed the beast's horns from both sides and dragged him to the door. The watchman, tied up with rope and lying on a patch of straw in a corner, began lecturing us: 'You men come here, taking livestock without permission, but you can't see that the cow is blind and the ram is lame in his front leg! How do you expect to drive them out?' We shut the door of the barn and replaced the bar, leaving the old man grumbling inside, and ran off to catch up with our mates.

The herd stretched out along the road, the cattlemen keeping it in order with whips, while we used our rifle butts. We walked quickly, half running, and the herd soon switched to a lively trot. For us, it was important to quit the village as soon as possible. Once the huts lay behind us, a machinegun opened fire from the bell tower. To our relief, the tracer bursts fell away from us, strafing the forest track: the Germans seemingly oblivious that we were driving the cattle along the main road. But suddenly I noticed sparks: bullets were striking the cobblestones. Then something jabbed me in the left leg. I felt no pain, and kept running, but I soon began limping slightly. We were already far away when the banging bursts of mortar shells resounded, but once again, the Fritzes were targeting the wrong sector. Sergei was running beside us. Puffing, he ordered: 'Move it! We'll stop shortly.' This gave us strength and everyone ran faster. At last, the herdsmen turned the cattle onto a forest track and we slowed to a walk, trying to catch our breath. My leg was examined – it turned out that a bullet had hit the back of my jackboot, tearing off the heel.

It was clear we were not being chased, so Sergei halted the combat team, while the herdsmen continued driving the cattle and sheep to the camp. It was time for us fighters to accomplish the second part of our mission: 'We will do agitation,' Sergei announced. We headed off around the Ushachi lake and approached a village, late into the night. Sergei tapped on the window of a shack and a man – perhaps forty years old – came out on the porch, a raincoat thrown over a white nightshirt. Sergei greeted him by name and asked: 'Any Fritzes in the village?' 'No, thank God, none have been here since the evening . . .' They went into the shack. Five minutes later they reappeared and Sergei said: 'We're gonna stay overnight. Tell us, Pavel Mikhailovich, where are you going to quarter us?' Pavel Mikhailovich led us to a shack, apologizing: 'You will please forgive me, I've got no bed sheets . . .' He realized the absurdity of his mortification, but couldn't quite abandon peacetime notions: it seemed to him that we were his guests and he, being the host, was supposed to take care of us. The guys laughed. 'You keep quiet!' hissed Sergei, 'and forget about smoking for the night. You, Zebik, and you, Vali, will stay outside as watchmen. I'll sleep in the shack.'

We entered the dark barn, fragrant with the scent of fresh hay, but failed to sleep. The strain of the night's adventures had not left us, and everyone was ready to exchange details. We were nervous but cheerful, elated and inspired by our fortunes. The door creaked and Zebik's angry voice sounded in the dark: 'Sleep! Stop chatting. You talk too much, it carries a long way.' We calmed down but soon began whispering again. Ten inexperienced men had sneaked into the very middle of the German garrison and driven a herd of cattle down the street, as if we were on a collective farm! Had we been seasoned fighters, we might not have dared do this.

In the morning, Pavel Mikhailovich warned: 'If possible, observe secrecy and come out for a wash one or two at a time. I've brought you water and towels.' We were quickly putting ourselves in order. Sergei was explaining what we were going to do now: 'This village is a suburb of Ushachi. Partisans have never been here, you'll be the first representatives of the brigade. We need to introduce ourselves to the locals and make a good impression. We need to show them we are cultured, humane and educated – not beasts and mobsters like the Germans say. I have a guitar, I'll play and sing. Mishka is a good dancer, let him dance with all the girls. You, Nikolai will be drawing portraits to let everyone see and tell others that the Partisans even have an artist.' It turned out to be more difficult with Ivanov: he was a clumsy guy. Sergei warned him: 'Don't sing on your own! You'll be singing in a choir when all the others sing along.' It was arranged with Zebik, who didn't speak Russian well, that he would tell a fairy tale in the Kazakh language and Sergei would interpret it.

Having distributed the duties, we walked to an area where the local youths had been partying. Bearing in mind that on the opposite side of the lake there was a German garrison, with 300 soldiers in barracks and the same number of Polizei billeted in quarters, we had to be very careful not to let anyone give us away. Pavel Mikhailovich took it in hand. It turned out he used to be a teacher before the war: now he did underground work for the Partisans, aided by his schoolkids (three of his students had gone off on an ambush). First, about eight guys came over to the party ground, summoned by Pavel Mikhailovich and his schoolkids. Serezha took up his guitar, struck the strings, and in an impressive baritone, launched into his favourite song – the rest of us joined in. Then he played a waltz and Mishka set about his task of inviting the local girls to dance. But the village maidens stubbornly refused our Kuban Cossack. Eventually, Mishka grabbed a boy for a partner, spinning him round in such style – and revealing such skill – the girls thought better of their rebuffs and eagerly stretched out their hands. Mishka danced with ease and grace, his breeches fastened tightly with a belt sporting a Belgian-made Nagan pistol.

More and more people arrived, including an accordion-player, who began improvising to Sergei's guitar. Meanwhile, I was wary of the success of my mission, but to my surprise, while presenting someone with my first picture, I discovered a group of three girls in a queue – ideal subjects for portraits! Conversations were starting, and we were trying to appear carefree, to show we weren't afraid of quitting the forest within sight of the enemy. We were telling jokes and the girls' laughter rang out time and again. The village guys told us the Germans had distributed call-up papers and would be conducting mobilization on the other side of the lake today.

We already knew this. In fact, it was the real reason we had come: to let those who'd received call-up papers see us and make the vital decision whether to submit to the Fritzes or join the Partisans.

When it was time to say goodbye, someone said: 'Girls, bring up what you have – we must feed the Partisans!' The meals were organized near the forest. The girls laid out towels, then all of a sudden, potato and cabbage pies appeared, garnished with onions and cucumbers. One girl even brought a hot frying pan of sizzling scrambled eggs. We ate, drank milk, and enjoyed the villagers' attention – and our own boldness at singing and dancing in sight of the enemy, from which we had snatched the cattle the previous night. Finally, at parting, Sergei said: 'Come and visit us, you know where we are. And bring up any weapons you can find: rifles, barrels and even spent cartridges.' The occupation had come to this place so quickly that many of the guys never had a chance to be drafted: now, by agreement with the local Communist Party, we were permitted to take them up to the forest: but only after faking their execution, so as not to leave their families vulnerable to German reprisals. Thus the Fritzes were running their mobilization and we ours.

We would have to make a circuit of 20 kilometres so as to enter the village from the other side. We came to Ushachi in the evening and stopped near an outlying shack. Sergei walked around it. Glancing into the windows he noticed nothing suspicious. Then he ordered: 'Ivanov, have a good look in the loft.' A ladder was leaned against the loft and Ivanov went up halfway, then suddenly declared he would go no further. 'Get down, you chicken!' said Zebik angrily. Ivanov quickly ran up the ladder and peered into the loft. Coming back down, he reported: 'Nobody up there, Comrade Commander.' And so we entered the shack. The hostess agreed to keep two of us for the night, so Sergei left me and Zebik. The rest had to split into groups and find places for themselves in the huts. All this was arranged to give the enemy the impression that lots of Partisans had been around. In the morning, our hostess produced a safety razor wrapped in a rag: 'Have a shave, it's my husband's. He's at the front.' Zebik and I thanked her and began shaving, soaping ourselves with the husband's shaving-brush.

As arranged with the local Communist officials, we now took the village men who were to join us as Partisans. But first we had to feign their executions. A little drama would be played out for the Germans' benefit, in which our recruits would be taken from their homes into the forest and 'shot'. Zebik and I made our way through the crowds of villagers to a shack where the first man was to be taken. Sergei was waiting for us and when all was ready, the show began. With sombre faces, we entered the man's home, several women and children following us, weeping and wailing. In a loud voice, for all to hear, the man's wife rebuked us, and tearfully addressing Sergei, said: 'Comrade Commander, what is it all for? It's not his fault, have mercy on the kids! Where are you taking him to?' Sergei replied sternly:

'We'll take him where he'll get what he deserves. He should have thought better beforehand!' Meanwhile, the man stood hanging his head. I was stricken by the realism of the scene and of everyone's acting. I didn't know what kind of thoughts and feelings the man was having. Was he thinking all this might be real? Was he thinking about his family, how they would get on without him? And more importantly, would they be able to deceive the Germans?

After the histrionics, we all went out in a body and walked towards the forest, not forgetting to take shovels, as if for digging a grave. Sergei stopped the locals: 'No one to follow us! Not a single man!' We needed to break away from the witnesses in order to feign the execution. We entered a pine forest, and when we were confident no one had followed us, quickly dug a 'grave' in a small clearing. We backfilled it as quickly as we had dug it, leaving this evidence to stand out as a hump of dark earth on yellow sand, just in case of a check. Serezha shot twice into the air. Then, on the advice of our recruit, we went deeper into the forest, where three others were to be taken. Down there we dug and backfilled another hole. When the others were brought up, three more dry shots resounded ...

As it happened, we received some extra volunteers – men who felt confident of quitting the village without putting their families at risk. The whole group then headed away from Ushachi. We walked through the forest, parallel to the road. Presently, a cart containing two milk churns appeared on the road, driven by a man in a black raincoat. Misha Chaikin stepped out onto the road and stopped the horse: he wanted to ask the driver if he had heard about our deeds in Ushachi. 'Cattle were snatched from the Germans,' the man said, 'people say: "The Partisans pinched a pillow from under the Germans' head." ' Mishka, pleased with that, asked: 'What are you carrying?' 'Milk to the butter works.' 'So, you're carrying milk for the Fritzes, are you? Get off the cart! Take the churns off!' He pierced the churns with a dagger. Then he noticed the driver's German-made trench coat: 'Where did you get this?' The man quickly threw off the coat and shoved it into Mishka's hands: 'Take it, take it! You need it in the forest and I'll get by without it.' Then he drove off, without waiting for thanks. Mishka came back, both pleased and embarrassed, and explained how it all happened. Then one of our new volunteers gasped: 'But he was a Polizei from Ushachi!' Everyone was appalled: due to our lack of experience, we had misunderstood the situation on the road and had let a Polizei escape ...

We crossed the road and Sergei called a halt: 'Nikolai, you'll lead the recruits to the camp. Zebik will go with you. We still have things to do here.' I remained with the group of volunteers, and was supposed to lead them across a countryside I knew nothing about. Zebik knew nothing about it either. My only hope was to act like a confident commander, who knew what he was doing. The sun was bright after the rain, but my boots, which had become soaked, were tight and rubbing my feet raw. Although it contradicted my notion of a commander's image, I had no choice but to take them off and walk barefoot.

After some time, we came to a river and I confidently led my men across a familiar ford. There were about twelve people in the group, averaging forty to fifty years of age. Only Zebik and I were armed. Everyone wanted to tell me what had been happening during the occupation, how much they'd been wanting to join the Partisans, and I felt like a real commander. But Zebik treated me strangely, showing respect in a patronizing kind of way. Eventually, we came to a village about 10 kilometres from Istopishe and decided to stay overnight. We knocked at the outermost house and were allowed in. It was warm inside, kindling was burning cosily, and there was the delicious scent of freshly baked bread. I explained to the host that we couldn't split into groups, and we were lodged in a big storeroom, each with a bundle of hay.

In the morning, I saw two of my men lying in a corner chewing bread, breaking off pieces from a big loaf. Knowing that yesterday we had eaten everything we had been given, I asked: 'Where did the bread come from?' One of them answered timidly: 'There's a trunk here, Comrade Commander, and inside there were three loaves. We commandeered two.' Now I faced a dilemma: whether to forgive this misdeed and walk away quietly, or whether to make the fighters understand that having joined the Partisans, stealing from the people was unacceptable, as it would stain our reputation. In the event, I called up the host and apologized for the stolen bread in front of all.

When we finally arrived at the camp, I informed Dubrovsky that the group of recruits from Ushachi had reported for duty with the brigade. At that time it was as if a dam had burst: people were coming to us from villages near and far, sometimes in ones and twos, sometimes in groups. The brigade was acquiring people on a daily basis.

At the end of September, the brass hats of Dubrovsky's and Nikitin's brigades decided to conduct a raid on the German garrison at Ushachi, and at the same time, to execute sentences on a whole number of traitors and Polizei. We formed a group in Istopishe, in a large, boggy forest not far from Ushachi. I prepared leaflets and placards, and found myself a rifle for temporary use: since I'd only just joined the brigade, I still had no weapon for myself and would have to get one in combat. We met with Nikitin's people on the edge of the Istopishe Forest, near a forestry warden's shack, and when the sun slid behind the clouds, we were ordered to set off.

Nikitin's people were unlike our disciplined brigade. Having marched hundreds of kilometres through the enemy's rear with heavy fighting, they seemed brutal to us. I closed my album, in which I'd been sketching the meeting of the two brigades, and shoved it into my bag of ammo. Having moved into the shade of the forest, we moved along the road that led into a ravine. After marching some 2 or 3 kilometres, it became completely dark. Strangely, I couldn't remember a darker night in my life. It engulfed and concealed everything. We could only get our bearings from the backs of those who walked ahead. Having covered 10 kilometres, we saw some lights on the horizon and the silhouette of a bell tower.

We approached Ushachi and set up our command post at a cemetery. It was decided to strike at the town from two sides. I was in the group charged with the task of capturing the Commandant's office and executing the Polizei traitors. We made our way to the centre along the backs of houses, via vegetable gardens. Suddenly, a green flare soared into the sky and a machinegun opened fire from the bell-tower, pinning us down. I lay on a bed of cabbages. Tracer bullets were falling nearby, disappearing into the ground – a few metres closer and a bullet would go through my head. I didn't want to die now: so much so, I began digging a hole for my head, not realizing the futility of the exercise, as the machinegun was firing from above! But I felt better when digging.

Soon it became a bit quieter: or to be more precise, the machinegun switched its fire sidewards. We stood up and rushed to the houses. I couldn't restrain myself and stuck a leaflet to the wall of a log cabin: next day, the occupants would see it and say: 'The Partisans have been here!' Running in a group of about eight, I hid behind a house and managed to stick up another leaflet. We began making our way to the centre, and how astounded we were when we saw my poster on the Commandant's office notice board: 'Death to the Fascists!' It meant that Karaban had already been here with his guys, smashed the glass, and posted this announcement. Mikhail had gained a lead over us: the Commandant's office had already been smashed up.

We split into groups, so as to raid Polizei houses. Suddenly, a figure in long johns appeared from behind a corner, armed with a rifle. One of my comrades grabbed the weapon: 'Your password?' The correct answer was 'Two', for we had agreed on a strict password system, so as not to compromise our safety in the dark. But the man replied: 'I'm one of ours!' I pointed my carbine at his stomach and pulled the trigger. A misfire! He dropped his rifle and took to his heels. I took a shot at his back but missed. Then I snatched his rifle and rejoiced. Glancing around, I saw that my guys were already far away ...

Rushing from one house to another, under the light of flares and to the incessant accompaniment of machineguns, we darted into the home of Burgomaster Vasilevsky: he had been sentenced to death for betraying a group of Partisans. He was shot with a submachinegun, although it would turn out later that he survived in the 'bracket' of two bursts. The fighting continued. Our group was moving from one Polizei's house to another. We had just rushed into one shack when a runner followed us: 'We're pulling out!' We read the traitor his sentence, shot him dead, and ran into the inner porch. Suddenly I saw – by the light of a comrade's torch – paints scattered all over the floor. They were oil colours in tubes! I fell upon them and found a whole crate of goodies – obviously stuff from a looted bookstore. At that moment the fighting ceased for me, such was my joy! My mate with the torch had already leaped out, but I was still groping about in the dark, picking up paints. I stuffed them into my pockets, down my blouse – everywhere. Then I rushed into the yard and headed to the command post, but I couldn't drop to the ground anymore between runs, for the paints were in the way, so I had to make do with running slightly bowed. Suddenly I saw a figure beside me: 'Who are you?' I asked. 'It's me, Kolya – Two!' That was Zebik! 'I was looking for you: everyone's pulling out – time to get away!' We ran together. By the barbed wire fence we saw something stirring in the bushes and aimed our rifles at it: 'Who's there?' 'Two!' came the answer. It turned out to be our Olen'ka, the Secretary of the Chashniky District *Komsomol* Committee. Her real name was Katya Zakhovaeva, which she guarded like a precious secret: but everyone laughed, for the Fritzes wouldn't bother about names if they caught her – she'd be hanged as a matter of course, with this name or that. Olen'ka had got her hair tangled in barbed wire and couldn't get free. Without hesitation, Zebik cut her hair with a knife ...

All three of us got back to the command post. I reported why I was late and it caused some bewilderment: what was the point of endangering myself on account of some paint? I was aware that after my captivity, they would be inclined to keep an eye on me: perhaps it was no accident that Zebik had been sent to look for me? And then there was the incident with the man in long johns. It turned out I had shot at a man from Nikitin's brigade – the long johns actually being white trousers. Regretfully, I handed over my rifle. I'd been so happy to get it, but in doing so, had nearly killed one of our men!

But the paints were mine and I was glad. Actually, at first, no one shared my happiness. My deed seemed strange to the Partisans, who took the paints for tubes of Vaseline. The guys laughed at me – what do you need 'Vaseline' for? But later, when the brigade moved camp, I painted a banner on a bed sheet with my paints: then everyone understood the significance of colours, even if a submachinegun is the main tool. Dubrovsky and Lobanok – the brigade Kommissar – immediately decided to use my art in the cause of the struggle against the Fascists, and an order was issued in the brigade: if anyone found paints they were to bring them to Headquarters and hand them over to the Artist! (Although Nikolai Goutiev and I were scouts from that day on, everyone would call us 'the Artists'.) Some days after this order, a big guy tumbled into our dugout, bringing over 100 tubes of lipstick! We would make a lot of use of that! We made many placards on paper and white canvas with the lipstick – the demand for posters was very high. Meanwhile, Zebik was in trouble after the operation. Olya was upset because of her hairdo and was angry at him: 'What have you done? What have you done to me?!' Zebik laughed it off: 'I couldn't see back then how to cut your hair, could I?!'

On this occasion we failed to dislodge the Fritzes from Ushachi, but next morning, after the raid, the Polizei left no stone unturned searching for the 'Bolshevik propaganda'. More raids on the garrison followed, and a month later the Germans had to leave Ushachi, for the security of the garrison was soaking up too many troops.

CHAPTER TWENTY-SEVEN

Savaging the Fascists with Images and Verses: October 1942

The Partisan camp was situated in the Istopishe Forest. But the place was becoming too small for our expanding brigade. It was also uncomfortably close to the German garrison, and we were under constant threat of encirclement. And so, in the middle of October 1942, the commanders decided to relocate from the Ushachi district to the Lepel district and the vast forests of the Berezinsky Reserve. The 3rd Detachment of our brigade, commanded by Dmitri Timofeevich Korolenko, had already been there a month, having cleared the Fritzes from the area. Now we had to establish a winter camp over there and set up food storage. A severe winter was due, and the Partisans would need billets, food, ammo and clothes. One evening, an order came for the brigade: we were to move, all gear was to be gathered, and at five o'clock we would march off. One detachment was to stay for cover.

Many parts of the forest around Antunovo were prone to floods in the spring, and in other parts there were bogs. For these reasons, a place on upland sandy islands, with ancient pines and spruces, was chosen for the camp. The forest had never been cleared there: trees fell, having lived out their years, and new ones grew in their place. The scenery of the forest camp seemed to me the most picturesque. The tapping of axes was heard everywhere, somewhere iron was being hammered, and the smell of smoke lingered among the trees. The first thing I saw was the hastily built log cabin of the smithy. Next to it, near the forge, the Partisans Tsar and Perednya were fixing up a machinegun mounting with wheels. Meanwhile, dugouts for the Kommissar, Chief of Staff and Kombrig were nearly completed. On the other side of this forest 'street', accommodation for the scout platoon was being dug. Kolya and I, along with Misha Chaikin and Vanya Chernov – aides-de-camp of the Kombrig and Kommissar – were digging an earthen shack for ourselves. Ladik, a signaller with a crippled leg, was digging one nearby, aided by his wife and others. Our earthen house was small but cosy, with a large window and two plank beds, each big enough for two men. Fedor Salnikov, a doctor, was also building a dugout for himself; the *osoby otdel* was building a big one, with much assistance. A large dugout for Olya and Galya – secretaries of the secret komsomol district committees – was built in front of us. Later, when I began working even harder on my pictures, the commanders would give us this dugout and transfer the girls to ours.

I began to draw pictures from my first days with the Partisans. Initially they were mostly leaflets, placards, slogans, and maps of localities for the commanders, which were used for combat operations. I made fake documents for the scouts as well. But after the action in Ushachi, when I managed to get paints, I began to paint in oils. The first things I did with a dry brush were two panels on bed sheets: on one I depicted the Bolshevik hero Chapaev on a horse, rushing into battle; on the other I depicted my comrades during the action near Borovka, when they wiped out a German convoy of eleven trucks and an armoured vehicle. This had been the first major operation of the brigade, which had been building up its strength. The inscription across both panels was: 'Long Live the 25th Anniversary of the Great October Revolution, 1917–1942'.

The dry, warm autumn of 1942 was on, people's mood was on the rise, and everyone had faith in victory, which replaced last year's gloom. Armoury workshops, a hospital, a bathhouse were all built; a dry-mess and forest bakery were already operating. Although this was done before my eyes, each new day surprised me with a fresh discovery. I began to experience a joyful conviction that everything the war had stripped us of could be returned – that we could do it!

The festivities for the Anniversary of the Revolution were coming, and our newly built camp was decorated. Footpaths between dugouts were sanded, spruce branches were stuck into the ground. An arch with a red banner across it was built in the middle of camp, and a huge tree stump became a dais or rostrum, displaying Stalin's portrait, framed with garlands of spruce branches. My pictures were fixed on both sides of the arch. The effect of all this decoration was astounding. People who had suffered so much under the Germans rejoiced to see Soviet power returning: many wept for joy.

We have to remember that apart from military warfare, the most critical psychological and ideological clash between the Germans and the Partisans was on. The Germans terrorized the civilian population with all possible propaganda, trying to convince them there were no Partisans as such, only forest bandits and murderers. We had to counteract this, to prove to people that we were fighting for our Motherland, for the liberation of our people. Partisans who took off for combat or sabotage missions adopted the custom of leaving a leaflet or a poster at the scene of action. They would leave posters for secret fighters in the district centres of Lepel, Chashniky and Ushachi, sticking them on walls, in German barracks, on Polizei houses. It made a great impression: it proved that the Partisans were everywhere and there was no peace for the enemy. When leaving for an operation, Partisans begged for at least one poster, but as Kolya and I took part in operations too, we had to make leaflets during breaks between combat tasks and sleep. In fact, the trickiest thing about producing posters and placards was thinking up memorable slogans. It wasn't hard to find a theme for a drawing, but when it came to composing the accompanying text, our suffering would begin. We would walk about mumbling words and looking for rhymes, but to our dismay, only swear words ever seemed to fit! But when a rhyme came out well we received our reward, for not only the Partisans and civilians remembered it, but also the Polizei: wherever we went, everyone knew and recited our verses! The lights in the Lepel movie theatre would flare up, and on the walls our posters would be in place, savaging the Fascists with images and verses. People would learn our rhymes by heart before they were torn down, passing them from one to another.

A portrait of Hitler hung on a wall of the Commandant's office in Lepel. Kolya Goutiev and I drew a similar one, but comprised of hanged men and corpses, and one night our scouts replaced the German portrait with ours. This picture stayed up for three days in a row with a guardsman below it! But gradually, people began lining up to see it. At last the Germans discovered the substitution. How indignant they were! And our people were gaining more faith in us: look, the Partisans even managed to replace Hitler, and that was in the centre of town – and the Fritzes didn't even notice! Later on, I would do posters only occasionally, for I would be busy with pictures, so Nikolai Goutiev occupied himself with placards, leaflets and a newspaper design. He would make placards on linoleum, then do large print-runs on paper. Many people came to our earthen house, from private fighters to the Kombrig and Kommissar: everyone was eager to see what 'the Artists' were up to.

CHAPTER TWENTY-EIGHT

Evil Times and Difficult Choices: November 1942

In autumn I took part in a big raid near the old frontier of West Belorussia. For the first time the brigade was armed with a 45 mm cannon, and we planned to use it in the coming attack. We'd been on the march for two days when, about one o'clock in the morning, we came to the village of Ugly. Mitya Frolov, head of the brigade osoby otdel, Misha Chaikin and I knocked for some time at a dwelling. There was no answer for a while, but eventually the door opened and a young woman let us in. Her husband lay on a plank bed above the stove, and a teenage girl occupied a wide bench beside it. We were received reluctantly. I asked the host: 'Why did you send your wife away from the fireplace and not come to the door yourself?' The woman laughed: 'He is afraid of getting it in the neck and hoped I'd draw it off!' We rested till dawn, then headed towards the railroad.

Yarmosh, an ex-artillery captain, set up the cannon among pine trees near the track, while we hid on a nearby hillock. Soon, a long train appeared, snaking up the track, bellowing steam. Yarmosh aimed the cannon and shot at the engine point-blank. The engine disappeared in a cloud of white smoke: the shell had scored a direct hit on the boiler! The train skidded to a halt amid a sickening, metallic screech. A second later there was another explosion: this was the work of miners, detonating TNT under the tail of the train. Five minutes later a flare soared up and everyone dashed towards the wreckage. No people were found in the train, but several mangled wagons were loaded with grain. I was at the head of the train when a heavy machinegun opened fire from one of its flanks. Another flare – a white one this time – went up, telling us to pull out. Vanya Kititsa handed me a red torch from the train and we rushed back to the woods, German machinegun fire stuttering along the railway line.

We were glad to be pulling out, everyone talking of his impressions and deeds. I was proud of my red torch: we would make good use of it in photography.

We returned to the same shack. This time our hosts did not shun us, but entertained us with boiled potatoes. The husband turned out to be the Starosta of the village. His wife was Polish – humorous, cute and deft. Her name was Jada, short for Jadwiga. The former frostiness of our hosts evaporated in the warmth of jokes and laughter. Mitya Frolov made an arrangement with the Starosta: as soon as we quit the village, he would run to the district Polizei barracks and report all that had happened. But as the Starosta would have to walk some 15 kilometres, we estimated that by the time he made his report, we would already be far away – and naturally, he could not be blamed for the delay.

Some time after, when we were again on our way to the frontier and stopped at the Starosta's place, Jada discovered I was an artist. She asked me to draw her portrait, so I seated her by the window and began sketching. As I was working, a Partisan came into the shack wearing a field cap with a red star. Jada snatched the cap, set it on her head at a jaunty angle, and pointing at the star said: 'I want you to show this as well!' When I asked why, she replied: 'When the war's over I'll say that I used to be a Partisan too!' And so I portrayed her as a fighter, with a red star on her cap. The portrait came out well.

Three more weeks went by and during this time, three more sabotage operations were carried out on the railroad near the village of Ugly. Each time, the Starosta properly reported events to the Polizei. But when I returned to Ugly, the Starosta was no longer among the living: he had been executed by the Germans after a search of his home revealed Jada's portrait with the Partisan's cap. She was shot dead too. Her death made a strong impression on me and I still feel guilty. The war was full of nasty surprises like this ...

When it got dark, Dubrovsky called me up and charged me with a task: 'You'll go with Boulba to accompany the 1st Detachment: the excavator near the railroad siding is to be blown up.' Boulba was the nickname of Stepan Nikolaevich Shenka, who worked for the Fritzes on the railroad. Shenka was a short, stumpy, fair-haired man, who spoke with a West Belorussian accent. He was on duty every third day, and was thus able to pass information to the brigade and return to work on time.

The detachment dodged through the forest for a long while. Boulba and I sat in the Commander's sleigh. Stepan Nikolaevich was telling about every feature of the terrain: where it was best to hide or find cover if the Germans were shooting from the station. It was dark and chilly: a blizzard began blowing in our faces. At last we approached the station and lay on the ground, in a line on the edge of a forest. Miners advanced into the dark to place detonation charges in the excavator, which was used for railroad construction. The minutes sloped by agonizingly slowly. Suddenly, the demolition men came back: it turned out there was not enough TNT – they would have to get more and put the charges in again. A young Partisan was lying next to me. He asked me in a whisper: 'Guvnor, where should I aim?' I explained that after the blast, when the Germans moved on us, we would have to aim at them. More minutes ticked by. It was remarkable how these young guys were thrown across my path: either in camp or combat, there had always been such a thirteen- or fourteen-year-old around me.

A buzz of alarm went up at the railway station and the Germans poured out. There were plenty of them, for a special train full of Fritzes was right there in the station. They began strafing the edge of the forest with submachineguns: perhaps they'd noticed our demolition guys. More time passed, but there was no explosion: it meant they would have to crawl out and put the charges in yet again! But as soon as the scouts moved towards the railroad, everything lit up and the ground shook – an explosion had struck! The German machineguns opened fire, and we returned it. My young Partisan pressed himself against me, but was shooting properly. And yet, something very unlikely happened to me: the breechblock of my rifle came unscrewed and fell into the snow. Knowing I shouldn't give away my nervousness, I began reassembling it thoroughly. At last I did it, but I'd been so engrossed by this business, I didn't notice that everyone had gone: my teenage mate and I were alone. We made our way out through the bushes, explosive bullets blowing up around us, and it seemed that shots were coming from all over the place. Eventually, we found our way back to the detachment, which was retreating through the forest. The operation had been a success: there were many dead among the Germans, yet we'd lost none. At three in the morning we were already home in Ugly, sharing our impressions with the guys of the 3rd Detachment.

We spent the day in the village, returning to the railroad again at night. I was in Mitya Korolenko's detachment. Boulba led us to the railroad embankment near a bridge. He told how many guards were there and where they were positioned. Then he gave information on the railway timetable: at one in the morning, a special train from Germany was to pass through and ten minutes later, a westbound train would cross the bridge.

At 12.50 am we wiped out the guards, put charges on the bridge and in front of it, and stretched out fuses. We decided to blow the bridge as soon as the first train tried to cross. We didn't have to wait long. A mighty explosion deafened us, billowing clouds of black smoke rose into the air, spitting fire and flying debris. The bridge was rent asunder and the train, unable to stop, plunged into the gap. Our machineguns opened up, perforating the carriages. Rifle shots were drowned in a frenzy of automatic fire. A heavy machinegun began strafing us from the station and we had to change position. But then a loud 'hourrah!' rang out, and the Partisans rushed into an all-out attack on the train. The Germans, slowly coming to their senses, returned fire, but our onslaught forced them back amid a storm of gunfire and grenade explosions.

Now the westbound train was approaching. The engine stopped several metres from the wrecked bridge. It was strafed by machineguns but returned not a single shot. Korolenko sent demolition men to blow up the engine, then sent Petro to join them with a 50 kilo bomb. Petro stumbled towards the embankment, sinking in the snow, cradling the big bomb in his arms. The demolition men ran to meet him, but Petro spotted Fritzes in the dark, deploying into an extended line, an officer quietly giving orders: 'Schnell, schnell, Partisan kleine Gruppe!' ['Faster, faster, there's a small group of Partisans!' – Trans.] Petro ditched his bomb and dashed towards the bushes bounding the railway line. He was a gigantic man and had to thrust his whole weight upon the small spruces to break through: but the rifle slung over his shoulder got caught and the thick wall of spruces thrust him back towards the Germans. Petro was captured but broke away and dived among the trees. The Fritzes failed to snatch him, and they couldn't shoot without giving away their position.

Korolenko was furious. His men had failed to blow up the engine and had even left the explosives behind! Two demolition guys stood in front of him and he told them in a whisper: 'The TNT must be detonated or brought back here. We ain't gonna leave it for the Fritzes! Bring the TNT back and report.' The two demolition men turned back. Only their quick wits helped them execute the task. The Germans had scattered in a file along the length of the train, but the men sneaked through. They reached the rear of the train and crawled forward under the carriages. They picked up the TNT blocks around the engine, right under the Germans' noses, and exited the scene the way they had come. Wounded men were moaning inside the carriages, medical orderlies were running about. The demolition men fetched the TNT back to Dmitri Timofeevich, but one of them returned with grey hair! That order had been brutal, but the fighters knew there was no other choice. The 3rd Detachment, led by Dmitri Timofeevich Korolenko, was the most reliable and the most disciplined in the brigade.

Fritzes were leaping out of carriages and closing on our flanks. Korolenko ordered us to pull out and we retreated into the forest. The task was only half completed, for we had failed to blow up the second train. It turned out to be full of troops: we hadn't expected this and pulled out under threat of encirclement. Three days later we discovered that several hundred Germans had been killed or wounded in the action. It was our first major raid on the railroad. The practice showed we had to look for new solutions. To derail or blow up an engine or train wasn't enough. A special tactic was needed to destroy every carriage, down to the last one.

By dawn, the brigade was on its way back to the camp. Nikolai Goutiev and I were on flank cover – a column always had a reconnaissance group ahead of it and about 150 metres on both sides – the flank cover. We were supposed to scout everything around us to prevent an ambush or sudden strike. Two days, two marches, and we were home. Kolya and Tass, my dog, were so happy to see me! A new bathhouse had been built and it was constantly stoked. Naked guys kept leaping out to roll in the snow or scoop cool water from the well, before jumping back in again. It was a great joy to have a bath after combat, to put on clean underwear and get back to your dugout, where your work and your mates were waiting for you.

Two days later, some Polizei came to the brigade, asking to join the Partisans. One of them said: 'When you were coming back from Ugly, where you blew up the train, there was an ambush in your way. We were concealed in the snow under a fir wood. Then two of your guys came up, squatted straight in front of us, did a dump and moved on. We thought about shooting them, but how could we?! We expected a small group to march past and we'd have a chance to strafe it, instead we saw a whole brigade!' And it had been me and Nikolai on flank cover! There were about thirty Polizei in that ambush and almost a third of them came to join us. As that Polizei had said, they'd been so impressed by our 'diversion', they had realized their defeat. But Nikolai and I had stuffed up big time – we hadn't noticed the ambush concealed in the snow! You never know when you are next to your death, or what is going to turn it away from you.

Pavel Vasilievich Khot'ko and I were sent to contact the Vlassovites [Followers of Andrei Vlassov, a former Red Army general who, having defected to the Germans, raised rebel battalions from POWs, for service against the Soviet State – Trans.]. It all began the following way: one night I was summoned to the dugout of the osoby otdel to see Mitya Frolov. Khot'ko was already there. Mitya asked me if, when at the Borovukha camp, I'd known a POW named Sakharov. I recalled someone of that name, a man around thirty-five years old, who wore gumboots and a green, wool-lined jacket. He had been an engineer and seemed like a good guy. His first name was Sasha. 'So,' said Mitya, 'this Sakharov is now in charge of a Vlassovite battalion. The battalion is based in Borovka. Sakharov says he wants to join us with his battalion. He wants Khot'ko to meet with him – but in Borovka!' Other information had been obtained. Learning from the locals that Khot'ko had been Chairman of the Lepel Soviet [the district counsel – Trans.] before the war, and later, one of the organizers of the Partisan movement, Sakharov had promised the German Commandant of the Lepel garrison to capture Khot'ko dead or alive. As I was to discover later, this information had been conveyed by one of our agents, who worked as a typist in the Commandant's office in Lepel.

We discussed what to do: should we send Khot'ko or not? Did Sakharov really want to join us, or was he playing a double game? The meeting had been scheduled to take place at the house of a friend of Khot'ko's in

Borovka. I suggested that I should enter the house first: after all, Sakharov and I had known each other. He would be faced with a surprise, we'd win a minute or two, and maybe learn something. So it was decided. It was impossible to guess what Sakharov was up to – it could only be discovered by a face-to-face encounter, and we were not in a position to pass up a chance to bag a whole battalion.

Next day, Misha Chaikin gave me his *polushubok* [a short sheepskin overcoat – Trans.] and Nagan pistol. I put my album and pencils into my map-case – that was the extent of my preparation. Before departing, we were counselled by Markevich, the Kombrig's deputy on reconnaissance, Frolov, chief of the osoby otdel, and Dubrovsky. We were going to the district centre for a week. We would have to contact agents among the locals, charge them with new tasks, and receive information gathered by them on German positions and intentions. But the main object of the trip was to contact Sakharov. 'The condition of his joining us is strict,' Dubrovsky concluded, 'only with his battalion! He has offended the Soviet authorities too much.' 'And no agitation!' Frolov added, 'your task is to convey the conditions!' We made our farewells. Dubrovsky took me aside and warned: 'Remember, Nikolai, Pavel likes a booze-up, that's why you mustn't let him go too far. You're responsible for the success of the mission.'

The end of November was cold and the frost was keen. Pavel's grey horse was harnessed to a light sleigh. Soon, snow was creaking under the runners. But inwardly, I was uneasy. The first thing we had to do was call at a village near Antunovo, to execute a woman who, according to her fellow-villagers, was seeing a Polizei in Lepel. The woman wasn't one of the locals, but an evacuee. I didn't like the thought of this task: after all, who wants to shoot a woman? But an order is an order, and the fear of the people she lived among could not be dismissed lightly. By visiting her Polizei sweetheart in Lepel, the woman was spreading alarm among those in the village with Partisan connections. People were in fear for their lives. And so, seen in this way, our brutal orders became understandable: to protect those fighting the invaders. Markevich began repeating what they'd been saying at our brigade staff meeting: 'Will Nikolai be able to shoot? Will the Artist be able to kill?' I had obviously created an impression of being a soft man: but the struggle was cruel and confidence in each fighter was necessary ...

We approached the village at night. No light was seen in any window, the huts stood as dark silhouettes, a forest loomed behind. Khot'ko stopped the sleigh near the shack we were after: 'Here we are. Nikolai, go and carry out the order. You'll see shortly what kind of a Polizei she is!' He was trying to embitter me, harden me, knowing it would be difficult to do the deed. Seeking support, I asked him to come inside with me.

An old man opened the door. Walking ahead of us, he led us into the shack and lowered the light in a kerosene lamp hanging on the wall. The light was weak but seemed bright because of the darkness. It lit up a plank partition covered by pink wallpaper. Through an aperture without a door, we saw an ageing woman lying on two chairs pushed together. I asked the old man: 'Who are you lot?' He replied that he and his wife were evacuees from Leningrad. He stood looking at us helplessly, wearing a woman's knitted jersey, his neck wrapped in a rag. 'And where is the other tenant here?' I was speaking loudly, trying to sound stern in an effort to arouse indignation against the traitor-woman: but it felt strange, awkward, and annoyed me even more. 'Nadezhda? She's here ...' said the old man, pointing at another aperture screened by a curtain. 'She's an evacuee from Leningrad too.' I moved the curtain aside and saw a young woman lying on an iron bed with two kids: a boy and a girl. The girl was probably about three, the boy looked older. A whirlwind of emotions rushed through my soul! I had to carry out the order!

Nadezhda stood up silently. She was wearing a man's white shirt, her face was pale and puffy. I began telling her that she had been sentenced for her behaviour, for her connection with a Polizei: 'The people accepted you as an evacuee! And you paid them back in such a way that the whole village fears you. Now they're afraid to help the Partisans in case you rat on them!' She stood as if petrified, head lowered, arms hanging. I was shouting the most offensive words, all the time thinking: yes, I will take her outside and shoot her dead, then I will come back to the room, for I will have to do something with the kids. The elders won't take care of them – they are barely alive themselves, and after all this, no one from the village will look after them. Where will I put them? Was it possible I would have to leave them on their own in the cold room?

I turned to Khot'ko: 'Pavel, what should I do with this scum?' Pavel was upset too. He replied frostily: 'You've got your order – so you carry it out.' I saw that none of my harsh words had made an impression on the woman. She stood frozen, shocked, as most people would on hearing a death sentence. I started again: 'How could you not think about your children? How could you flirt with the enemy? You fled from Leningrad because of the Fascists and now you go to Lepel to see your enemy!' But I could see the uselessness of my words. I made up my mind: I had to walk her outside, make her feel the fear of death, and then talk to her. 'Get dressed,' I hissed, 'we're gonna go outside.' She sat down automatically, obediently shoving her feet into big army boots, threw a wool-lined jacket over her shoulders, and followed me. 'Take a shovel,' I said, 'you'll be digging a hole for yourself. I'm not gonna make anyone from the village do that.'

We came out onto the inner porch. I could hear through the chinks how the wind was blowing snowflakes about the yard. And again the same thought struck me: what will I do with the kids? The woman came out and walked across the kitchen garden, the shovel in her hands, shuffling along in her huge boots. 'Well,' I said darkly, 'dig down here!' She tried to stick the shovel into the frozen soil, then suddenly began to twitch and whimper. At last I'd broken through: now I had to get her back into the shack and talk to her again, to try to find a way out. Once I knew why she had been going to Lepel, it would be clear what to do with her.

We entered the shack. Pavel was sitting at the table, the old people were huddling on their chairs, the kids were asleep. The lamp was still casting its pathetic light. And again I felt dismay deep inside. 'Nikolai, you have to make a decision,' said Khot'ko, 'you are taking too much trouble with her.' We sat at the table and she began crying. I asked: 'Tell us when you were in Lepel and what for.' She sobbed, her face buried in her hands, her shoulders were trembling: 'I went to the bazaar ... my dress ... the blue crêpe de Chine one ... I wanted to sell it ... to feed the kids. He came up and said, "Come with me, I'll buy your dress." I did ... he said, "I'll give you a bucket of rye, I like you." We came inside and he dragged me to the bed ... He gave me grain. I went home. They were hungry at home, after all ...' She was shivering with fear and the memory of her disgrace. She wept, but couldn't do it aloud for fear of waking the kids.

I felt chilled to the bone; and I felt sorry for her: I saw that she was telling the truth, shaken with the horrible nature of her reality. I had to execute a death sentence on a woman broken on the wheel of misfortune. Suddenly it dawned on me: she wasn't guilty! The circumstances were against her, so it wasn't her fault! Forgetting I would have to bear the responsibility for disobeying an order, I reached into my map-case and pulled out the album. Khot'ko looked at me with astonishment – what I was going to do? 'Well, Nadezhda!' I said, 'today you understood how your life could have swung! You could have left your kids orphaned. Don't even think about going to the Polizei again! Or even to Lepel at all! For the time being, I'll give you a note for the brigade storekeeper. You'll go to Antunovo and get half a sack of rye. You may ask for some kind of job – there are workshops over there, they sew camouflage cloaks for us ...' 'Nikolai, are you mad?!' Khot'ko couldn't contain himself. But I felt easier now. Nadezhda took the note, her hands shaking, and I stood up from the table. Khot'ko stood up too, and the old people from Leningrad came up to us. I told them: 'Keep your eyes on her, stop her from doing anything silly. Otherwise there won't be any place for the kids.'

It was time to go. We retired into the howling wind and icy sleet of the bitter night. The horse, which was frozen through, quickly pulled the sleigh and we slid over the snowy ground. Khot'ko said: 'Bloody Germans. Perhaps you're right – after all, there is no place to put the kids. Maybe everything will sort itself out. We'll just have to call in on the way back, to tell the villagers not to touch her.'

Only recently, in November, a Polizei from Ushachi came to Antunovo, saying he wanted to join the Partisans. But Headquarters reckoned he was a traitor, charged with the task of sneaking into our camp. And so one day, when Markevich and I were about to accompany this Polizei from

Putilkovichy to Antunovo, Sergei told me: 'Dubrovsky ordered us to shoot him and you'll have to do it. I'll be walking by your side and you'll shoot.' I shot and he fell down. The incident shook me. It was just after this that I was ordered to execute the woman from Leningrad. Of course, the way I handled the situation with Nadezhda was risky: should she return to Lepel and be spotted by someone who chose to report it, my fate would be decided the same way as that of the Polizei I killed. But I couldn't trample over the lives of the kids.

Yes, those were evil times and difficult choices had to be made. That's why, when the life of the Partisans is depicted as some kind of picnic in the forest, it's a gross mistake. Every moment was coupled with risk, every step a struggle to stand up for oneself and keep a clear conscience. Any compromise could lie upon one's whole life, like a grave sin: a millstone hanging round one's neck.

I behaved with some bravado after killing that Polizei, but I couldn't close my eyes to sleep, for I dreamed of blood. Such was the autumn of 1942 for me, when I joined the Partisans. I am sure other Partisans experienced blood and killing the same way, and not everyone could keep his emotions under control. Partisans often displayed a craving for pre-war things, mundane things – anything that reminded them of a time unburdened by war – and many of their deeds, which may seem naive and funny, become understandable when we remember this. For example, when I photographed the female Partisans of our women's platoon, they would wear their carefully preserved blouses and skirts, instead of a fighter's uniform with firearms.

Strange to say, after the episode with the woman from Leningrad, Dubrovsky – who was angry with me at first – began treating me with more respect. In fact, he placed so much confidence in me that soon after the incident, when we were pulling out of an action, he entrusted me with his submachinegun, asking me to give him covering fire.

We rode past Putilkovichy and stayed overnight with an acquaintance of Pavel's – he had friends in every village. In the morning, we took Ivan – a young submachinegunner from the 4th Detachment – as our driver and headed for Voron. It was our outermost garrison: beyond that, the Germans held sway.

We left Voron by night, in a raging blizzard. We would have to cross the main road between Lepel and Borovka under the Germans' noses, but Pavel knew every path and pothole, and we made our way without difficulty. Soon we came to the embankment of the Lepel–Orsha railroad, which would soon cease to exist, thanks to Misha Didenko's detachment. We reached Borovka, left the horse with Ivan, and made our way through backyards to our rendezvous with Sakharov. At last Pavel pointed at a house. I pulled a grenade from my belt and advanced across a kitchen garden. The shack was dark and the stillness absolute. I tapped on a window. A grey blotch of a face flashed behind the glass and the door opened. Pavel came up. The host immediately relayed a message from Sakharov: he wasn't able to make the meeting and suggested we return next day. Was he simply checking how we went about our business? Meanwhile, there was nothing to do but hand over letters for the Vlassovite soldiers, appealing for their support: the host agreed to circulate them and we parted.

We lay behind some logs, bellies on the snow, until a patrol passed, then leaped across the street and found our submachinegunner with the horse. The snow was beginning to lay – we had to get on the road so as not to leave footprints. But suddenly a thought came to Pavel's mind: 'Kolya, let's enter Borovka from the other side and have a look round the Vlassovites' barracks – three of our 76 mm guns were left over there. Also, a mate of mine lives nearby and knows where soldiers buried hand grenades in 1941.'

We skidded through a young pine forest, and in an hour we were on the spot. Pavel and I crawled towards the barbed wire surrounding the barracks. Brick buildings loomed in the dark, guards stood about 100 metres apart, a sentry patrolling between them. We scrabbled around for a while, sinking into the snow by the fence, and at last found the gun barrels buried beneath the snow. One gun was lying just inside the fence: provided we timed it right, this prize could be snatched away. And so we silently observed the sentry's movements, counting the minutes it took him to complete his patrol. It turned out the gun was out of his sight for almost two minutes. This meant that if everything ran smoothly, the gun could be stolen away without the Vlassovites knowing. We crept away, then stood up and stumbled into the night, unable to move quickly because our feet were numb with cold. Our horse cheerfully took off when we tumbled into the sleigh – she was chilled through too.

But still we were not finished for the night – we had to find out where the hand grenades had been hidden. Again, I was holding a grenade in my hand, and we were making our way through kitchen gardens along palings and bushes. Pavel's dark silhouette was ahead of me. Then he turned to a shack. We tapped lightly on a window and Pavel whispered into the very glass: 'Maxim, it's me, Pavel Khot'ko, open the door.' The door opened noiselessly and we slipped inside. Immediately, a child cried in the dark. We heard his mother speak softly, soothing him to sleep. We conversed with Maxim in whispers. We learned there were plenty of hand grenades – ninety-seven of them. Maxim said he would unearth them himself and hide them till we came to pick them up. Pavel couldn't keep his own promise and said to the host: 'You, my dear comrade, should help warm up our artist from Moscow – know what I mean?' Maxim nodded and whispered something to the hostess. She handed the kid over to her husband, then produced a bottle of *samogon* and a lump of pig fat [samogon is illicitly distilled vodka, while the pig fat would have been roasted, somewhat like 'crackling' in Britain – Trans.], apologizing for the meagreness of the snack, and for keeping us in the dark. I drank half a glass. A moment later we thanked them, said goodbye, and emerged into the stiff night air.

Ivan, our driver, was chilled to the bone. Suddenly, Khot'ko pulled a bottle from his overcoat: 'Have a gulp, warm up!' Then he turned to me: 'You, Nikolai, don't go thinking I stole this bottle. Maxim gave it to me himself, and it would be unethical not to polish it off!' Pavel Vasilievich was almost illiterate but enjoyed the respect and fondness of others for his fairness. Many times I went out with him on reconnaissance: he knew all the people and places of the district and I saw that, even during those difficult times, he was always warmly accepted; everyone trusted him, and would do anything to help him, even at the risk of their own lives. Because we usually moved about under cover of darkness, we often arrived at people's houses at midnight or after, yet we were welcomed like esteemed guests, arriving for an appointment just in time. We would go out on reconnaissance for a week or two, and I was supposed to keep an eye on Pavel, who liked a drink. Indeed, I was responsible for reconnaissance. Yet without Pavel I would have been both blind and deaf. The people we met were his old acquaintances, people he used to work with when he was the chairman of the local Soviet.

By now, the cock had crowed twice: it was time to leave Borovka. Again we were riding through the forest, dodging from one track to another. By dawn the snowfall ended and we had to follow the trail. 'Here we are in Sosnyagy,' said Pavel suddenly, 'we are riding over the place of our first dugout, which we built in 1941 with Lobanok and Kostya Yasko.' I remembered the story told by Volodya Lobanok – the brigade Kommissar – about the way they'd built this first dugout in the dense Sosnyagy Forest. He'd been charged with the task of remaining behind to organize clandestine activities in the Lepel district, where he had been appointed Secretary of the District Party Committee shortly before the war.

It was daylight when we arrived at our resting-place, an island in a bog, overgrown with small gnarled pine trees and brown reeds. It was here, at this spot, that the brigade had been created in the winter of 1942. Korolenko came here to join Lobanok with a group of those who had found themselves surrounded, and in March they began to operate in small groups. Lobanok's detachment of about ten or twelve people, isolated from the rest of the world, spent the winter in the disguised dugout. This was placed so skilfully that when the Fritzes were combing the forest in search of Partisans, they walked on the roof of the dugout – right over the heads of the guys – and noticed nothing! The dugout had lasted well, but the disguised bathhouse, built for steaming out lice (that horrendous scourge of the war) was in even better shape. We decided to spend the day in it. We unharnessed the horse, gave her hay, and lay down to sleep, having buried ourselves in straw. Only occasionally did we quit our sanctuary, to have a look at what was happening in the outside world.

When it grew dark we harnessed our horse and headed towards Borovka again. We managed to get there without trouble. Again, Khot'ko and I made our way to the shack where Sakharov was supposed to be waiting. At the approach, I took a hand grenade from my belt and unbent the wires holding the ferrule, so as to release it quickly if need be. We didn't know what was waiting for us. Perhaps Sakharov had prepared a trap and an ambush was awaiting us; or perhaps he would feel out the chances of penetrating the brigade: in this case, we would ease his caution with promises and hopefully secure our safe return. We knocked on the window. The host opened the door immediately: 'He's waiting – on his own.' We entered the inner porch and I stepped into the room, Pavel stayed behind.

Sakharov was sitting by the stove at a small table. He was dressed in an Oberleutnant's uniform. A kerosene lamp was burning. Originally, we had counted on an element of surprise: Sakharov was expecting Khot'ko but instead I would walk in. Yet in the event, he didn't even look around or raise his eyes. I walked up to the stove and sat on a bench, for I considered it humiliating to stand in front of him. I tried to look into his eyes but he sat with head lowered. He could see my hand, still clutching the grenade, which was ready to explode: 'Sasha Sakharov, we used to be in the same camp of Borovukha and were in the same working corps. I drew Germans in the Commandant's office, Major Menz, and you were a sewerage and water supply engineer. Maybe you remember me?' The room was in semi-darkness, and perhaps it was due to this that he didn't acknowledge his recognition of me, but merely beckoned. I began again: 'Sasha, I'm gonna talk to you. But if something goes wrong I'll pull the pin. You answer my questions. You called up Khot'ko. You conveyed via the host that you wanted to see Khot'ko. The osoby otdel of the brigade decided to send me instead of Khot'ko, since you and me know each other. You can give me your answer in a letter to the Kombrig – I will pass it on to him. I've been entrusted to tell you: the brigade commanders agreed on accepting you with your battalion.' Again, no answer.

At this moment, Khot'ko stepped over the threshold, shutting the door behind him. He walked over silently and sat on a stool near the window, on Sakharov's right. Pavel's right hand was in a pocket of his overcoat, holding a pistol. I turned to Pavel: 'I guess no one minds if you get the torch ready, in case the lamp goes out.' Pavel wiggled, pulled out the torch, and turned it on with his left hand. 'Well, Sasha, be quick, we're short of time. Do you agree to join us with your battalion?'

Suddenly, Sakharov began babbling incoherently that the Germans were watching him; that he feared he would be given away, even though he had trustworthy people. This talk was inconsistent. Then he looked up: 'You know, I'm ready to cross the line myself! And I'll bring in more people, reliable ones I vouch for.' Again he was wriggling and dodging: it meant that the aim of the meeting was to fulfil his promise to the Fritzes to capture

Khot'ko. Surely an ambush was waiting for us? We had to play our trump card: 'We can't return to Dubrovsky without a firm answer. You should write that you're ready to do it. Write it to the Kombrig.' He produced a sheet of paper and began scribbling. The atmosphere was tense. I clearly understood that the negotiations had fallen through, that Sakharov was being evasive: the defection of his battalion was out of question. Sakharov certainly wasn't speaking like a man who had realized his sin against the Motherland and was ready for action. I asked him to read out what he'd written, and this was his reply: 'I want to redeem my sin against the Soviet State and ask to be accepted, with my comrades, in your brigade.' I felt a spasm in my throat of tension, strain, disappointment. I didn't believe what he'd written: he just wanted to drag out the negotiations. But what for? Maybe the answer was waiting for us in the inner porch, or behind the walls of the shack? 'We should go,' I said quietly, 'I guess the Kombrig will give his consent . . .' 'We'll convey the answer in a week,' Khot'ko added, 'we'll fix a place for the meeting ourselves.'

We stood up, but I asked Sakharov to remain seated till the host returned. We walked out backwards, keeping Sakharov in the beam of the torch. We stepped over the threshold into the inner porch and shut the door. The exit door was already open, the figure of the host looming in the gap – he was showing us with his hand that the way out was free. We rushed out and bolted around the corner, running across kitchen gardens to the sleigh, stopping every so often to pull our legs out of the deep snow. We heard the voice of Ivan, our comrade: 'Come here, here I am!' We relaxed – there was no ambush!

A minute later, Ivan lashed the horse with his whip and she dragged us out of Borovka and into the dark. There was neither pursuit nor shooting behind us, but we knew for sure that Sakharov was up to something: perhaps planning a long-term operation to penetrate the brigade. Khot'ko burst into a long speech: 'Look, Kolya, what a bastard he is! What a skunk! I was sitting and thinking, "I'll shoot him now, only move and I'll shoot!" And you, Kolya, did well. We are lucky we were together, one wouldn't have handled this snake. He's gonna come himself, eh? He wrecked so many of ours and now he's gonna come by himself? Alone? And what's on his mind – scouting or sabotage? For sure he wants to gain favour with the Fritzes and that's why he's gonna cross the lines – not with a battalion or a company – but with two or three of his buddies. The Fritzes won't let him take more! Let him wait for our answer. In the meantime, we have to snatch away the gun and take the hand grenades from Maxim.'

We went over the details of this meeting again and again – after all that had passed, it was hard not to. We had been ready to die, but now we were trotting home under a starry sky. But the cold shadow of death seemed to be pursuing us, digging into our backs as if with pincers, forewarning us that something unexpected was imminent. It was hard to believe our luck in holding on to life, such a precious gift. Later, there would be a lot of conjecture as to why Sakharov hadn't prepared an ambush, and why there had been no pursuit. Maybe he had hoped to capture Khot'ko himself? Maybe he had arrived at the meeting without telling anyone? But we were not to find out what lay at the bottom of his mind. Yet we understood he'd been driven by fear of the Germans. Nevertheless, our letters were handed over to Sakharov's battalion, proving that our mission had not been futile. The letters reached people whose hearts awakened with courage, and they began looking for a chance to meet us. In September 1943 a whole company of Sakharov's men – a third of his battalion – joined us with weapons in their hands. They joined us during hard times and fought well.

Once again, we holed up for the day in the Sosnyagy Forest. The horse peacefully chewed hay, and I slept or drew, awaiting the night. When it grew dark we headed towards Borovka again, where we had a meeting arranged. Besides, we decided to sneak back to the Vlassovite barracks to examine the gun, for we would have to report its condition precisely.

These night-time raids were very exhausting, and for this reason, returning to camp was a joy, and on this occasion it was no different. We reported all our information and handed over Sakharov's note. Dubrovsky read it and swore: 'He's a coward and a vermin!' But then, realizing there was a chance to steal a gun from under the very noses of the Vlassovites, he called up Korolenko, and we reported our plans to Dmitri Timofeevich, an ex-artillery man. Having listened to us, he said: 'We'll snatch the gun. I'll order the blacksmiths to prepare a reinforced axle – we'll make a limber for the gun.'

For me, this time of winter scouting merged into one night, as if there were no days. At sunrise I would sleep, waiting for dark, when we would head off again. My sense of hearing intensified, detecting any sound and the direction from which it came, even at long distances: for a sound might herald a threat. Indeed, an awareness of fate hung in the very air. How many times did danger pass us by – especially in enemy territory, with its outposts and patrols? Of course, to make our traverses in the daytime was out of the question. Thus my memories of this time evoke a life north of the Arctic Circle, under permanent night.

But when I returned to camp after these raids and reconnaissances, walking on crispy snow glittering in the sun, it felt like I was at some festivity. The firewood was crackling cheerfully in the oven, an electric globe was shining. We had our own power station – the pride of the brigade! Four men lived in our roomy earth house: Misha Chaikin – the Kombrig's aide-de-camp; Vanya Chernov – Lobanok's aide-de-camp; Nikolai Goutiev and me. We had a large window above the ground in front of the door. There was a table under the window with a 200-watt bulb above, a wardrobe left of the entrance, and a plank bed. The wardrobe was simply a column of shelves rising to the ceiling, containing all our gear: weapons, underwear, paints, paper, cameras. Near the door was a small iron oven with a flue. My dog Tass lived with us in the dugout.

Tass was a German shepherd with his own story. A former border guard dog who became a 'POW' during the first days of the war, he was claimed by the Commandant of the village of Kublichy. One night in September of 1942, Partisans snatched the Commandant from the garrison, which put up a desperate resistance. The Commandant was shot after interrogation, but the dog – following the footprints – found us next morning. I managed to tame him and the faithful Tass became my partner in many operations.

CHAPTER TWENTY-NINE

Granddad, We're Gonna Burn Your School Down: December 1942

Preparations to seize the gun from the Vlassovites got into gear. While the blacksmiths made the axle, and the grooms fixed up harnesses for the horses, I drew a leaflet and prepared canvases and stretchers for pictures. For the Revolution Days [celebrated on the 7–8 November – Trans.] I had made a portrait of Stalin for brigade Headquarters: now it was hanging on a wall in front of the door to Dubrovsky's dugout, attracting the attention of all incomers.

One day, Dubrovsky and Lobanok entered our dugout. I had decided long ago to draw a portrait of Dubrovsky and suggested: 'Fedor Fomich, pose for me, I'll make your portrait.' But he replied, 'Lobanok and I have come together, so draw us together, not one at a time.' And so I began to draw them: the Kombrig and the Kommissar sitting next to each other in identical green officers' blouses. I understood I had to make a portrait showing their friendship and unity. Their detachments had merged into a brigade only recently, receiving a new name, neither Dubrovsky's nor Lobanok's, but something derived from the surname of Dubrovsky: 'Dubov's Brigade.' Dubrovsky was Secretary of the Chashniky Clandestine Party Committee, and Lobanok – of the Lepel one. Even their fur coats were identical – white and long, both taken from the Fritzes after the destruction of a train.

I started chatting so the sitting would be less tiring for them. I asked Dubrovsky: 'Fedor Fomich, how did it all start, how did you master people?' I knew Dubrovsky had fought as far back as the Civil War in the 1920s, and was a political officer during the Finnish War of the 1930s. Now he told us how he began his Partisan life. It turned out his group had been sent behind the front line back in October 1941, to organize a Partisan movement in this district, where Dubrovsky used to be director of an MTS [abbreviation of Machine Tractor Station, a state-owned enterprise in the USSR working for collective farms – Trans.]. They crossed the front line at night, amid fighting, near Velikiye Louky and then moved downstream of the River Dvina in Belorussia: 'Not many of the group reached the final spot,' said Fedor Fomich, 'we stopped for a day or two in the village of Pligovka near Ushachi. We had a bath, spent two days there, clarified the situation. There were Germans in Ushachi – they were conducting a draft into the Polizeitruppe, promising people money. We decided to hide, to go underground and set up contacts, to look for our people. Our Headquarters was near the village of Zhary at the Vatslavo Farm. I met Koulakov: he used to be a teacher before the war and was now doing work among the teachers of the district. He maintained contact with me and would come to Vatslavo himself. In March 1942 I decided to gather all the people I'd been in touch with in the Istopishe Forest and switch to combat operations. Koulakov was captured by the Germans in Zhary on his way to this meeting. They broke both his arms and cut skin from his back to make a star – they prepared him for interrogation this way. They held him in a school basement. They tortured him but he said not a word. Then they put out his eyes and cut off his tongue. They made him dig his own grave with broken arms and buried him alive in it.

'We retired from underground work and moved to the forest for open struggle. The first thing we did was avenge Koulakov's death – we destroyed the garrison in Zhary. We had two submachineguns – mine and Kraban's – and one rifle. The German garrison of about fifty men was located in a school. There were seven men in our group. We closed in from the side of the cemetery and I began to yell as if leading a battalion: "Company One – keep left! Company Two – close in from the right! Attack! Hourrah!" The Fritzes didn't stand up to the psychological attack and fled, leaving a machinegun, three submachineguns, several rifles and ammo. After this success men and women began joining us. The group grew into a detachment: this was in April 1942. We conducted several operations. We made an ambush near the Kroulevshina Forest by the village of Voron, destroying two vehicles and wiping out seventy-two Germans. Back then, Nikolai Safonov led one group and Vasya Nikiforov another. The detachment already numbered about 100 people. In May, eighteen people joined me for one operation. During the action a bullet whipped my hat off, another struck my arm. There was no doctor in our detachment and I was treated in Melnikov's brigade. When I returned, about seventy people who had known me before the war came with me. The detachment was growing, people were coming from everywhere ...'

It was already past midnight. I felt I had to have a heart and let Dubrovsky and Lobanok go, otherwise they might not pose again. I photographed

Dubrovsky and Lobanok with my 'Fotokor' so as to work out their figures from photos, without posing, and the Kombrig and the Kommissar stood up. Tass sat by the door, as if he wanted to walk them out, but in reality he wouldn't have let anyone out before I called him back saying, 'Take your place!' I made an arrangement to continue drawing next day, for I knew I couldn't postpone my work, as some surprise might change the situation and no one would care about the picture.

The portrait of Dubrovsky and Lobanok greatly impressed the Partisans, for many of them had never seen any original artwork in their lives. Now Partisans began coming to our dugout: Kolya and I would make portraits of our comrades, and they would readily pose for them. The brigade brass hats, seeing this level of interest from the Partisans and their desire to be portrayed by artists, decided that only those who distinguished themselves in combat would be portrayed. We were provided with a large dugout for our work. We had a gramophone and marvellous records in our dugout. Lots of people would come to our place every evening, but Kolya and I kept working. We couldn't afford to be idle – we had to draw pictures, leaflets and documents. We also sketched various plans and locality maps. We did not have enough official maps, so we had to copy them from the district ones, previously owned by local councils.

Work on the axle for the gun we were going to steal was nearing completion. It was reinforced by a thick wooden beam and large cartwheels. Thus, a robust limber was constructed and the gun mountings would be secured to it by a cable. All would have to be assembled in a few short minutes, and for this reason we made meticulous preparations. We selected six strong horses, taking time to adjust their harnesses and the riders' saddles. Speed and secrecy were crucial to our mission: so we worked out how to muffle the sound of the horses' hoofs, using special 'shoes' that could easily be discarded should we have to break away from pursuit. We also decided to tie up the horses' snouts in such a way as to prevent them from snorting. Then, having packed all this gear, Mitya Korolenko, with a platoon of his detachment, headed off for the gun. Khot'ko and I followed as guides.

Once again, Pavel and I were riding in the sleigh, harnessed to our horse, Old Grey, which – since we had shared so many dangers – had become a friend to us. The day was cloudy, the frost had gone, but the rivers the horses would have to cross with the gun were packed with ice. Thus our party reached Ostrov, where we stopped for a day. Leaving the rest of the group behind, Khot'ko and I went on ahead to reconnoitre and contact our agents.

We approached Voron via an open field. A thought came: what if there is an ambush behind the outermost shack? We had to decide what to do if this were the case. I said Khot'ko: 'I'll be sitting at the very edge of the sleigh. If there's trouble I'll jump off and start shooting; you can turn the horse around, I'll catch up, and we'll bolt.' And so we advanced, ready for action, me with my right leg dangling over the edge of the sleigh, ready to jump off. We trotted into the village when suddenly a rock, hidden under the snow, struck my instep. The pain was terrible and I felt my foot go numb. Pavel tried to calm me down: 'We'll fix it up shortly, let's ride to see the medical attendant.' Fortunately the medic was at home. Already it was impossible to take off my boot, so Pavel cut the stitches on the back seam. Having finally got the boot off, we saw that my leg was blue and swollen. The medic said it was possibly a sprain, but might be a ruptured ligament. I had obviously taken a hard blow from that rock. But nothing could be done quickly, and there was only one cure – to lie down. Walking would do no good at all. It was horrible! After all our careful preparation I had let everyone down by my carelessness. And I was supposed to guide Korolenko and his men to the gun! What could I say to Mitya – that my foot was sore? Khot'ko shared my torment, for we would both come out of this badly. But he had never given up before and now suggested: 'Bear up, Kolen'ka, I know a man here, we'll go and see him. You'll have a glass and not only forget your bad leg, but the good one too!' So off we went.

The host opened the gate, recognizing Pavel, and walked us into the shack. Pavel addressed him formally (I didn't know why, but whenever it was a question of being entertained, he always switched to an austere tone): 'Look, Ivan Makarovich, what a misfortune has befallen us! There is an artist from Moscow with me, he's come to draw this countryside. If you fix him up he'll portray you as well.' Despite the pain, I couldn't help bursting into laughter. The host didn't wait for the end of Pavel's speech, eagerly interrupting with: 'Well, Pavel Vasilievich, we got it just yesterday. Top stuff – it burns!' He searched in a wooden dresser, produced a Red Army flask, and poured me a full glass. We asked him if there were Fritzes in Voron and whether the Polizei were preparing anything nasty? We were about to leave when the host suddenly suggested: 'Leave your jackboot here, I'll sew it up. Take my *valenki* [i.e. felt boots – Trans.], they'll feel softer and looser on your leg.'

Although my head was spinning, and everything around me was swaying from side to side, I still couldn't step on my foot. I barely managed to walk back to the sleigh, leaning heavily on Pavel. We got in and went to see Nadezhda Alexeevna, a woman Pavel had been getting information from. He jumped off near the porch: 'I'll be back in a moment!' And in fact, he came running out in a minute, and we headed towards Ostrov: 'Listen, Kolya, Nadechka [a diminutive of Nadezhda – Trans.] said that she wants us to return as soon as possible – she's got important information, but we couldn't talk because the hostess was around.'

I begged Khot'ko not to tell Korolenko about my accident. And when he tried to persuade me to remain in Ostrov till the platoon returned with the gun, I would not listen. Pavel's 'medication' was working so well, I was adamant I would not be left behind – unwilling even to consider that by coming along I might be a burden to the detachment. The thought 'I MUST!' stuck in my mind like a pole hammered deep into the ground. And so, Korolenko and I set out from Ostrov after 4 pm. Again we were ahead of the rest. Pavel was driving. I checked the grenade on my belt and decided that, should something untoward happen, I'd be able to make use of it ...

Dusk was quickly descending when we entered a forest. We rode carefully. I remember that we stopped once, to put the 'shoes' on the horses' hoofs and muffle our wheels. The night air was cold, chilling me to the bone, yet my leg was burning with a sickening pain. A thought came: if I fell out of the sleigh during the action I'd be helpless, unable to crawl to safety. But I lacked the stomach to admit to Korolenko that I was in such a condition. Pavel comforted me: maybe, there would be no action, and even if there was, he wouldn't leave me alone while he was alive.

At last, Pavel stopped the horse. He gave me the reins and told me to stay put, leading the detachment towards the barracks himself. I sat quietly, listening and waiting, although the pain was so bad I kept dipping into unconsciousness. After a time, a crunching of branches sounded and Pavel appeared before me. Scrambling into the sleigh, he took the reins: 'They've already hooked it up and turned it around. You and me can go now, it's been quiet so far.'

We rode through the forest. I searched my belt and to my horror realized the hand grenade was missing! How had it come off? Maybe I had fastened it the wrong way? Maybe it had dropped off when I was checking it before? Maybe the sleigh had tilted and the grenade had been torn off by a branch? Whatever the explanation, the fact remained: the grenade had gone! To me, this seemed the summit of my misfortunes. I kept cursing myself: how could I be such a loser, such an impractical soldier? To have struck my foot against a rock and nearly screwed up the whole operation! How could Mitya trust such a man? It depressed me so much, I never told anyone about this accident ...

The detachment carried out the operation successfully. All our precautions had been to our advantage and the guys had skilfully snatched the gun without a single shot. They led a team of six horses to the spot, a rider on each of them: thus, if a horse was wounded, its rider could cut the traces. About 100 metres from the barracks, the riders turned the relay around with the limber against the fence. The guys crawled up, dragging a long piece of rope behind, then cut the wire of the fence, brought together the mounting plates of the gun, tied them up with rope and jerked it, giving the riders the signal to go. The horses took off noiselessly in their 'shoes' and pulled the gun away, disappearing into the swirling white wisps of a welcoming mist. Soon, the whole column was obscured by fog and we pulled out of Borovka unseen.

Two days later, the gun was hauled into camp. Sergei Markin, the chief of our Partisan artillery, examined it. The gun appeared to be in order, even the bolt was in good condition. The only problem was the gun sight, but our armourers soon fixed it. The gun was cleaned up and soon after, in Antunovo, next to the artillery Headquarters, two 76 mm guns and Karaban's 45 mm gun stood side by side. Dubrovsky thanked us for the successful reconnaissance work, and Mitya Korolenko thanked us for the efficient operation. Lobanok unfastened his TT pistol from his belt and handed it over to me: 'Here is my gift to you, for the successful operation!' But my joy was tainted. It is not always possible to explain, even to yourself, that a misadventure could not be helped. Now I understood the importance of taking care, of constantly watching oneself, so as not to become a burden to comrades or compromise the success of a mission. It was a tough lesson, and I took it so hard: some of that bitterness still remains with me.

Meanwhile, I lay day after day on the plank bed, for I couldn't put my foot on the ground. I passed the time drawing sketches for a big picture featuring the brigade. One day, Lobanok and Dubrovsky came to our dugout to have a look at the sketches and drafts. Fedor Fomich examined everything closely and suddenly said: 'Everything is fine but the artist himself is not in the picture. Now, he could be put in the driver's seat on the gun relay.' Thus I got the right to draw myself into the picture. Sergei Markin had been depicted as the first driver and the second one would become my self-portrait ...

Khot'ko and I were on our way back to camp from a deep reconnaissance, but we would have to stop at Voron before going home. We had to see Nadezhda Alexeevna, for we needed to obtain precise information regarding the Germans' intention of occupying this place. Evening was drawing in, the air was frosty and the track icy. Pavel was counselling me on the way: 'Once we get to Nadezhda's place, I'll be courting her. Don't you get surprised, Kolya, even if I lie down with her – we'll need to do some talking in whispers. You take care of Lizka, take some liberties, kiss her, and say that you've been missing her. Tell her whatever you want ...' Lizka was a Polizei's sister. He had been Polizei Chief in Voron, but now served in Lepel. Nadezhda Alexeevna – the wife of a Red Army officer who had died in the first days of the war – lived at her place for safety. Exploiting this location, she'd been finding out about the Germans' preparations against the Partisans. Khot'ko pretended he was in love with Nadezhda, and I, for the sake of security, was supposed to convince Lizka of my feelings for her.

As usual, we left the horse one house short of our destination. We tapped on the window with the customary knock and walked to the door: 'Who's there?' a familiar female voice asked. Having made certain it was us, Nadezhda let us in and slid the door bar. We entered a dimly lit room. Some kind of bustle began in an adjacent chamber and a moment later, the curtains parted and we saw Lizka with a lamp in her hands. The golden light illuminated her fair hair, making it gleam. He face was round, sprinkled with freckles, and her lips were full: she was very attractive. Pavel immediately began clowning around, sitting next to Nadezhda, hugging her, and saying how much he'd been missing her. Then he had a go at me: 'Why are you standing in the middle of the room like a sentry! Go to Lizka, talk to the beauty.' I took the lamp from Lizka and we retired behind the curtain.

What should I tell her? I put the lamp on a table, laid my submachinegun next to it, and suddenly blurted out: 'If your brother pops home, what an encounter there'll be!' She laughed: 'I'll go lock the yard gate.' Nervous sparks rushed through me – Pavel and I were really clever, we were having fun with the gate open! What if she didn't slide the bar back but opened it up? I followed her with the lamp, as if wanting to give her some light, but at the same time had a look at the kitchen, inner porch and the door. We returned to the room. I seated Lizka on a bed and sat next to her. I began my courtship with the silliest questions: 'Do you frizzle your hair? It curls nicely ...' then, touching her hand, I asked: 'What do you wash your hands with, since your skin is so smooth?' I was waiting for a signal from Pavel: he couldn't stay with Nadezhda for too long for fear of arousing suspicion. There were special customs here: it was one thing to pay court to a woman in front of other people, but quite another if you were tête-à-tête with her for too long inside a house. I asked Lizka if her brother had been coming frequently. She laughed archly: 'Oh, how cunning you are! You want me to tell you about my brother. He told me not to tell anyone.' She was watching me while I stroked her hand and then suddenly blurted: 'My brother will live at home soon! And you won't be able to come around, nor Pavel to Nad'ka.' 'Hmm, has he been fired from the Polizei, has he made a slip? Let him join us, the Partisans!' 'No, not fired, simply quit. He'll serve here.' 'Where is he gonna serve here? In the church or at school as a teacher?' She shook her head: 'Not as a teacher but at school!' 'Well then, as a sentry?' She shook her head again. She liked to talk in riddles, but she wasn't pulling her hand away from mine, as if she had forgotten about it.

At last, Pavel glanced in the room: 'Nikolai, what's happening with you? Ah, you feel so warm with Lizan'ka, you've forgotten about time? You dare, maybe, to make a proposal? I guess her brother won't give her away!' I replied in tune with him: 'I'll steal her then, if she's in love with me! Liza, will you marry me?' I was glad this date was over, but I felt sorry for her. I picked up my submachinegun and kissed her on her cheek. She suddenly blushed and looked at me resentfully: 'Look, he's already covering me with kisses.'

We left the shack and Pavel said straightaway: 'Such a thing, Nikolai, the Fritzes will be around here any day now. They want to set up their garrison at the flax works and in the school. What are we gonna do?' Now I knew why Liza had told me that her brother would serve in Voron at the school!

Obviously, they had decided to place the Polizei in the school and to lodge their own garrison at the flax works. We couldn't let them settle so close by! Our garrison in Pyshno was not far away, but we had no time to ride back to the camp and report it. All this rushed through my mind with lightning speed, but there was no time to think it through, we jumped into the sleigh and rushed to the school: we would burn it down before they could occupy it . . .

We tied the horse to a column and entered a cold, echoing vestibule. Two people, an old man and woman, sat near a stove in a side room. Khot'ko addressed the old man: 'Granddad, we're gonna burn your school down, otherwise the Fritzes will occupy it tomorrow.' The old woman groaned: 'Oh, good gracious, how come?' 'Collect your gear,' said Pavel, 'and we'll get ready and set it on fire.' The granddad was rooted to the spot, he couldn't believe his ears. Meanwhile, the old woman cried as she piled up pillows on a blanket. I helped her tie up a bundle and dragged it outside. Then we carried out a table of crockery. The granddad took a study globe from the top of a locker and picked up some clothes from a hallstand. Then he took the clock from the wall, and not forgetting the school bell, carried them out to some willow trees on the riverbank. Meanwhile, I carried out buckets and cauldrons and gathered felt boots and footwear in a tablecloth.

A stack of notebooks lay on a desk. I picked them up, put some of them into my map-case, and took the rest for kindling. Khot'ko and the old man smashed chairs and desks with axes and began carrying the debris into the outermost classroom, piling them up as if for a bonfire. I crumpled up paper and stuffed it underneath the pile, then went for a kerosene lamp. I poured kerosene over everything and using the lamp, set the place on fire. Now it was time to open the windows. Cold air blew in, the paper blazed up brighter, and the flames began licking around the bonfire of planks and chairs, lighting up the classroom walls. The old man stood next to me watching. Suddenly I heard him sobbing. I escorted him out.

The old woman was wailing on the front steps, people were gathering around, having seen the fire in the school. Voices were heard: 'Was it possible not to burn it out?' 'Such a good school it was. They built it shortly before the war . . .' Pavel was explaining that it was impossible to leave it in one piece, for the Germans wanted to make their barracks out of it, and then there would be no chance of driving them away. For this reason we had to do it, to stop them consolidating their grip here. I declared: 'Carry out benches and chairs, stack them up on the bank. Maybe something will be left – it will be yours. For the time being, don't touch the fire, or the Polizei will decide it was you that started it.' The women wailed even louder, but scattered into the classrooms. Smoke was already filling the corridors and suddenly the flames grew stronger and began to drone. Pavel and I got into the sleigh and rushed towards the flax works.

The flax works were not far away, about 3 kilometres from Voron. An old friend of Khot'ko's, Nikita Petrovich, lived at the works' gatehouse and Pavel was looking forward to seeing him. We turned off the road before we reached the place, so as to approach from the rear, emerging from the side of a field, beyond which was a forest. We left the horse behind a shack and walked towards the works, which stood on a hill beyond a deep ravine. The trunk of a huge fir tree was thrown across the ravine: black water glinted below, in a pool on the ice. The trunk lay high above and was iced over. An occasional protruding branch offered some hope of holding on to the trunk should we slip, but the fear of falling was sickeningly real. Somehow, we managed to get across ...

The watchman's family was sitting in the gatehouse in a small room with a low ceiling. Nikita Petrovich met us, and we were greeted amiably by his wife and daughter – I liked this cute, hazel-eyed girl very much. Her name was Lena. We had come across people we hadn't contacted for a long time, reconnecting with a seemingly long forgotten atmosphere. Hot potato soup and thinly sliced pig fat appeared on the table. Rubbing his hands, Pavel excitedly explained to the host: 'It's become known now, dear Nikita Petrovich, that the Germans are going to lodge in the flax works and set up their garrison. They wanted to do the same in Voron, so we had to burn down the school. Now we'll have to do the same here.' According to Nikita Petrovich, Germans and Polizei had ridden past that morning in sleighs, from Lepel towards Pyshno, and three Fritzes had stayed for while to look at the works. Khot'ko and I exchanged glances. We couldn't delay: if the Germans came here they would control the whole road to Lepel, build fortifications, and it would be impossible to scratch them out. I spoke to Lena. It appeared she was a teacher of Russian from Leningrad, but when the war started she moved here to her parents. Nikita Petrovich poured some liquor but I suddenly got a sore stomach. It was so bad that I only managed to say: 'I'll be back shortly.' Closing the door behind me, I found myself outside.

The moon was high in the sky, snow lay like a grey shroud, shining here and there and highlighting our footprints. It was quiet. But in the distance I detected shuffling, thudding sounds drawing near. I strained my ears for a minute, stress rising. My stomach cramps disappeared, eclipsed by panic, as I realized the shuffling noise was the sound of sleighs sliding over the frozen ground, and the pounding thuds the clattering of many hoofs. The Germans were approaching the works! I leaped into the room and grabbed my submachinegun: 'Pavel, follow me! We have to burn it now or it'll be too late!' Pavel stared at me madly, then guessed what was up and managed to say: 'Thanks for everything! We'll finish our drinks when the chance comes!'

We rushed across the yard towards the huge wooden building of the works, then swung the gates open. Pavel began collecting wood for the fire, I searched the floor, piling up loose fibres. But the oakum didn't want to burn, being damp, and simply smoked up. Stumbling about in a fog of smoke, we piled a big bonfire against a wall and began fanning the flames. Everything was done in silence, the approach of danger lending urgency to our movements. We had just minutes to complete our task. At last the oakum blazed up. Flames flicked against the wall, fluffy with dust, as we tore planks from the floor to feed the blaze. The room filled with suffocating smoke and we ran outside.

Coughing and sneezing we ran down the hill. Here was the ravine. I glanced back. Bloody hell! The works stood dark – no fire gleamed in the glass of windows! 'It went out!' I wheezed, 'head back! The windows!' The fire had gone out because we'd forgotten to smash the windows! We climbed the hill towards the works. I fell over and cut my palm on the ice, but felt no pain in my fury. We were up on the hill now. The voices of sleigh drivers could be heard. We ran into the building and saw nothing but thick smoke. We began smashing windows with submachinegun butts. The panes were small squares and we had to smash one after another – and on both sides of the building, to open a way for a draught. I threw myself at the extinct fire, fell down next to the smoking debris, and began frantically blowing with all my might! Some dry wood and oakum caught fire. I jumped to my feet and yelled to Pavel: 'Come on! Finish up!'

When we ran outside the German convoy was pulling through the gates on the opposite side of the huge yard. Shouts! Curses! They realized the works was being set afire. Submachinegun bursts resounded, bullets chipped splinters from wooden walls, but they didn't know where to shoot, and we were rushing towards the ravine crossing. Again the same fear of balancing on the ice-covered log! I fell on the opposite slope, and bending down, ran towards a shack. Khot'ko was behind me. Faster, faster, up to the sleigh! Looking back I saw bright flames joyfully licking scorched timbers. Running Polizei were in pursuit, shooting bullets and curses. Now Old Grey was our only hope! We threw ourselves into the sleigh, the shooting growing stronger and more accurate, for now we could be seen on the white field! But at that moment a cloud screened the moon and in its shade we rushed across the field towards the forest, which stood as a dark wall. At last we were on the road. Old Grey began to wheeze easier and the sleigh flew lightly over the frozen ground.

Not until the approach to Pyshno did we pull ourselves together: 'Did you see that? I thought that was it!' But now my hand was burning badly. I glanced at it: the palm was black all over with clotted blood – I'd injured it when I fell on the hill.

That same day, in Pyshno, we found out the Fritzes had advanced on the local Partisan garrison. They wanted to destroy us, 'to make an end of Partisans in this district'. The action lasted all day and in the evening the Germans pulled back. But instead of the anticipated 'lesson to the Partisans', the tables were turned and it was the Germans who received some education, fleeing with seventy corpses and more than 200 wounded. Furious at the setback, the Fritzes quit Pyshno, hoping to find shelter in Voron. But there they found smoking firewood instead of the school they planned to occupy. And so they pushed on to the flax works, and straight into another misfortune, for it was set ablaze right in front of them! A chill seized me when I thought what they would have done to Khot'ko and me had they caught us during the arson. They would have cut us to pieces! But Fate did not want to give us away yet and we were spared ...

At the end of December I chanced to do some work on my picture of the brigade. I made a sketch and it was hotly discussed who would be depicted and on which spot. I took a sortie for an operation as the subject of the picture, so as to portray as many people as possible. Such a moment had always been very solemn. The brigade would pull out of the forest and head towards Antunovo, which was called 'Little Moscow'. The Headquarters of our Partisan artillery was based there: brass hats would come to the place, orders would be given to detachments, then all would go their own way. And the operations we conducted then were big – sometimes it was a raid on a railroad, sometimes an attack on large garrisons, such as the one in Chashniky or Lepel: up to 1,000 fighters took part in them.

CHAPTER THIRTY

One Who Survives the Gallows Cannot be Hanged Twice: January 1943

The January sun shone brightly, casting dark-blue shadows. Shaggy chestnut horses, harnessed to our big guns, ploughed through snow, snouts smothered in silvery hoar frost. I sat in a sleigh with Semen Borodavkin, the brigade Chief of Staff. Before the war he used to be a public prosecutor, then the Secretary of the District Party Committee in Ushachi. The brigade stretched out before me, over a series of snowy hillocks. Fighters marched, carts moved in convoy, machinegunners rode in sleighs – for they were a privileged caste amongst us.

So far we had been operating in the Lepel district, setting up ambushes and raiding the German garrison in Ushachi. Now we had achieved our goal of forcing the enemy out, we were marching on Chashniky. This would be a major operation, involving all five Partisan detachments, led by the Kombrig, Fedor Fomich Dubrovsky, and the brigade Kommissar, Vladimir Eliseevich Lobanok. The brigade was strung out over some 5 kilometres, its head entering a new village while its tail was still in the one before – or the one before that! Many Partisans wore short, white, sheepskin coats. The brigade had its own tanneries so the coats were home-made, though frost-proof and with furry collars. Against the white of their coats, weapons gleamed and glittered, reflecting sunbeams: 'As good as archangels!' The old *babushkas* [i.e. grandmothers or old village women – Trans.] told each other. Many eyes watched the brigade, both good and bad: let them report our movements to the Fascists; let them know such a force is marching!

When Dubrovsky entered a village, a mob of women, old people and children quickly gathered round. To tell the truth, Dubrovsky – a stout man seated on a Herculean dapple-grey horse – looked like a *bogatyr* [a noble knight – Trans.] from some old Russian epic. He wore a long trench coat, binoculars on his chest, a Mauser in a yellow holster on his side, and a submachinegun round his neck. It is hard to overestimate the effect the brigade's march had on the villagers: our very presence gave strength to the weak and hope to the disheartened.

We stopped for an overnight rest in one village and had a quick bite. Someone dragged a pile of cold smelly hay indoors, to which we added some straw, spreading it on the floor. Then we laid down in a row with firearms beside us or under our heads. Next day there was another march, and another overnight stop in the village of Medvedky. Next day we would be in Chashniky. Before I settled down for the night, a Partisan came around: 'The Kombrig is calling for you and all your drawings.' I picked up my map-case, containing my album, and quickly followed the messenger. There were many people in the shack, Dubrovsky sitting at a table in the centre. I reported my arrival. Fedor Fomich laughed: 'Look, Nikolai! Did you want to draw a bearded Partisan? Such beards are grown in Kirpich's brigade!' I laughed too, for I remembered Dubrovsky had recently reprimanded a commander for not shaving before an operation. He had even rebuked Boris Zvonov, one of his favourites, in the following manner: 'Are you a commander or an anarchist? Would you present yourself to the colonel of an army unit like that, eh?' In our brigade it would have been absurd to imagine someone had grown a beard – it was unheard-of! The bearded chap – a young fellow – was laughing too and Dubrovsky ordered: 'Hey, hostess, give us more light! Let the painter draw the whole of his beard!' He was a picturesque man and I set to work, drawing the bearded Partisan who had impressed the Kombrig so much. The hostess lit a new wooden taper and a bright light flashed, lighting up the colourful interior.

Among those entering the room was an old man with a small moustache, wearing a canvas raincoat and a Polish cap. This was Boulba – Stepan Nikolaevich Shenka – from the Western Zone. He was a short, stocky, fair-haired man with greenish eyes, who spoke with a West Belorussian accent. Knowing the brigade had approached Chashniky, he met us in Medvedky to warn us of German reinforcements. Then tall Misha Didenko arrived, bending down in the doorway, followed by Boris Zvonov. The Kombrig began giving out tasks: 'You, Mikhail, together with Boris, will occupy the Chashniky–Lepel road and wait. If vehicles with reinforcements move down from Lepel, strike! Now we need to set up one more roadblock, to stop the Fritzes getting out of Chashniky ...' New commanders were coming for orders all the time. I fell asleep near the fireplace and only awoke in the morning.

The final march to Chashniky was about to begin. I washed my face with snow and returned to the shack. A fire was burning and there was a big frying pan with *dracheniks* on the table. I had always been astounded how quickly the womenfolk could cook! It seemed our hostess had not slept late like the rest of us: the fireplace was stoked up, the dracheniks and scrambled eggs were served – and she was not in the least bit irritated!

Once again, the column stretched across a snowy landscape, the sleighs carving out a road. Tass, my dog, was with me. Semen said: 'We will approach Chashniky in a small group from one edge of the woods, the rest – from the other side. We must not reveal ourselves. We must sit quietly and wait for the operation to begin. We will detain anyone walking towards the centre, so as not to let anyone know about us prematurely. You are assigned to work out who is going to the town and what for.'

It was already evening, and a crimson sunset was dying behind a hilltop cemetery when we entered a hollow on the outskirts of Chashniky. What would we find? Where were the Germans? Where could the Polizei strike from? There were three huts in the hollow: one of them was enclosed by a solid fence and a dog suddenly began barking behind it. I went up to the shack and knocked at the door – no answer. I knocked harder. At last an old man's voice asked: 'Who are you?' I said sternly: 'Host, take your dog away so it won't bark.' The voice grumbled: 'What can I do about it?' I threatened to shoot the dog. The door bar slid open. Holding Tass back, I said to the elderly man, a priest: 'Take your dog away or I will unleash mine.' Noticing Tass, the old cleric got scared. We entered the yard together and I made him open a shack, put the dog in, and lock the door. He did everything reluctantly and I disliked his attitude more and more.

I was joined by more Partisans and we began looking around the old man's shack. From behind an icon we pulled out a bundle wrapped in a sock. Unpacking it carefully, we found batches of greenish papers with Swastikas – 2,500 German marks. The man was an enemy. The door swung open and a messenger came in: it turned out that Borodavkin, who was in one of the other huts nearby, had summoned me. I left the priest's place and followed the messenger.

The shack I entered was full of people, sitting and standing. When Borodavkin saw me, he announced: 'Here is a representative of the osoby otdel. He'll make a decision on the whole lot of you. Nikolai, I leave all the detainees with you. Sort out who was going where and what sort of people they are.' This was a tough task. Who among them would want to admit where he was going or what acts he might have committed against the Soviet authorities? I pulled out a child's notebook with double lines and began recording details: names, ages, occupations and so on. Then the questions began in earnest: 'Do you work for the Fascists?' 'How do you help to fight the occupiers?' 'Have you betrayed any Soviet people?'

A man of about forty, neatly dressed in a pre-war army jacket, stood before me. I began by asking him to empty his pockets. He pulled out a slide rule, playing cards and a silver Bure watch [a famous and exclusive brand – Trans.]. As I jotted down his personal details, I asked why he was not in the Red Army, for people his age had been drafted in 1941? He explained there had been some confusion in the military commissariat when the Germans had approached, and as a consequence, he never received his call-up papers. I pricked up my ears at this, while agreeing that his story might be true. Then I asked him to explain why he was walking about at such an early hour with a slide rule and a deck of cards? He admitted he was on his way to the German Commandant's office, where he worked as a land surveyor. I immediately observed: 'Apparently, you enjoy some respect there, and that's why the Fritzes haven't taken your watch?' He wavered but had to agree. Then I asked: 'In what way do you struggle against the Fascists? Do you assist the Partisans?' He hesitated, then launched into a series of apologies: 'You see ... I had no time ... I didn't know ...' But it was clear that, had he been a patriot, he would have gone east with thousands of others. He might even have gone to the forests to join the Partisans. I asked him about it. He replied: 'It never entered my mind ...' I was outraged: it hadn't entered his mind? Yet it had entered his mind to work at the Commandant's office! It had entered his mind to survey and allot kolkhoz land to the Fascists! I asked: 'What kind of land do you survey? Who is it given to?' The surveyor explained without embarrassment: 'You know, once an officer of theirs receives two Iron Crosses, he is entitled to 100 hectares of land on occupied territory ...' This man preferred a comfortable job with the Fritzes to risking his neck with the Partisans. He'd been playing cards at the Commandant's office, waiting for the defeat of the Red Army. Now he was talking as if we both understood everything as intelligent men – all the particularities and difficulties of his situation! I couldn't hold back and asked him directly: 'Did you betray your Motherland? Did you betray the Soviet State? Are you a deserter?' He hadn't expected these questions and began babbling: 'No, no, not like that ... no, how could I? I've done the same thing as others ... I was forced to work, otherwise they would have sent me to a prison camp ...' This guy couldn't see that it was better to be in prison than to collaborate with the Fascists. I had no doubts, writing in the margin next to his name: 'To shoot for deserting and collaboration with the Fascists.' I asked him to sign it. He refused. Of course, the sentence was not strictly right, but there was no time for a full inquiry: a battle might erupt any moment, letting him off the hook for his crime, then he would have won the battle for his life.

Some women came up. It was found that one of them was carrying milk to the Commandant's office, another one was a cleaner, and a third was going to the bazaar. The last two pointed with their eyes to a stocky man in a big overcoat, with an astrakhan collar and matching hat. I took him for interrogation. He turned out to be a doctor and produced a stethoscope. In the meantime, to my astonishment, a Partisan brought up a hunting rifle and cartridge pouch, found in the doctor's sleigh: 'You work in a hospital, right?' I began. He agreed. I continued questioning him, asking him to sign every affirmative answer: 'Why do you have your own equipment?' 'I am the chief doctor and I need to visit sick people.' 'Were you appointed by the Starosta or by the German commandant?' 'Commandant.' 'Why were you appointed out of all the other doctors?' He wavered – obviously this was not a pleasant question to answer, for it turned out all the other doctors had been shot. I asked him why his colleagues had been executed and he replied, 'As Communists and Jews.' Naturally, the question then arose as to who had betrayed them. The man shrugged: 'I don't know.' I pressed on: 'Why do you have a rifle and ammunition?' He replied that he needed a weapon for self-defence. 'Defence against who – Gestapo or Partisans?' He evaded the question: 'From various mobsters and bandits.' Then I remembered Shultz's words back in the prison camp: 'Nikolai will fight not against his own people, who swore a military oath, but against the bandit-Partisans.' I asked the doctor if he had been betraying our Soviet people. He answered in the negative. 'Who gave you permission to carry firearms?' 'The Commandant did.' 'By your request or as a reward?' Silence. What could he say? Everything was already clear. I asked him to sign the protocol. The interrogation was over. I wrote 'Execution' next to his name and again my conscience was clear.

Logic was my only weapon in prosecution. I had neither witnesses nor time – logic alone had to prove a man's guilt or innocence. Meanwhile, my ears were straining in anticipation of the battle-sounds that might bring judgement to my own fate.

The door swung open and Mitya Frolov, head of the brigade osoby otdel came in. Mitya glanced over my interrogation notes and whispered: 'What have you scribbled? There is no confession but you have written "Execution" – you may as well be shot for such protocols!' 'Mitya,' I replied, 'why would he admit to treachery and betrayal? I am confident that he is guilty of both.' Then Mitya saw the surnames of the surveyor and the doctor: 'Wait, Nikolai, what a scoop! We've been chasing these guys for a year! They betrayed Communists in Chashniky, and Jews and doctors of the town hospital were shot thanks to this surgeon.'

The detainees were led to a neighbouring shack and those who had drawn no suspicion were released. Mitya and I left the shack and stopped by a stack of firewood. Mitya was still talking about the traitors: 'These two were sentenced to death by the Chashniky raikom last year, but there was no chance to get them. As the sentence was passed in Chashniky, it's their business . . .' Suddenly, a machinegun burst smashed through the firewood stack behind us, bullets burrowing into the snow by the doorstep of the shack we had just left. Our machinegun struck back. The battle was getting closer. It was time to make a decision about the traitors: 'Get them out here,' Mitya ordered. I dashed to the detainees' shack, told the surveyor and the doctor to come out, and returned to Mitya. A field spread behind the shack, and beyond it rose a hill topped by a church and cemetery. The two traitors turned into the field and began walking away from us, in the direction of the enemy: a few more paces and they would get away. 'Alright,' said Mitya, 'you take the one on the right!' We shot and the two figures fell.

I rushed forward, past the bodies of the betrayers, and up to the church on the hill. Entering, I climbed up to the third level of the bell tower and began shooting at the running figures of Polizei on the street below. A bullet whizzed past me, chipping an ornamental baluster. Then came another one, a little higher, which hit a wooden handrail. Hell, they've zeroed in pretty good! I decided to change position, then saw our main forces withdrawing back to the village. It meant we had to join the brigade. I crawled back to the hatch and climbed down to the second level: one more stairway and I was on the ground. It was not as uncomfortable here as upstairs, where I had been vulnerable from all sides. But Dubrovsky didn't throw the brigade into battle. Didenko's detachment was covering the main road to Chashniky, so as to hinder the arrival of enemy reinforcements. Having gathered other detachments, Dubrovsky decided to leave the village for a while and withdraw to another place, so as to strike from the other side. It was typical of Dubrovsky's tactics. There were only three artillery pieces in the brigade with scant ammunition: our main asset was our people. That's why Dubrovsky chose to harass the German garrisons without major assaults on fortified positions, for this would have cost many lives.

The brigade was moving in a circle, bypassing Chashniky from the other side. Dark clouds crawled across the sky. We reached the village of Vaskovshina, where we were going to stay till nightfall. I was immediately summoned by the Commander. Three maps of the village were required for detachment leaders and I would have to prepare them. The time and location of each detachment's combat engagement would have to be plotted on these maps, so my task was urgent. I returned to my shack and began work. Mitya Bourko, Frolov's deputy, arrived and passed on an order for me to report as soon as I'd finished the job. Bourko added: 'You will ride into the forest on my horse and shoot a traitor-woman.' I took my maps to Dubrovsky and went straight to Bourko. The woman was standing in his room. 'This viper had been warned already,' said Bourko, 'and now she's given away a Partisan's family. She reported to the Commandant's office that Partisans had been visiting a neighbour's shack. She brought the punitive squad herself! They locked the women and kids in the shack and set it alight.' The woman kept quiet the whole time, and this silence was menacing, unnerving. Bourko read out the sentence: 'For the betrayal of the Motherland and the Soviet people – execution.' Then he led her out of the house and I followed. Bourko turned to me and gave the following order: 'You'll be accompanied by my brother, Semen. Shoot her dead in the forest and come straight back.' Senya [a diminutive of Semen – Trans.] was a young Partisan, only sixteen years old, and it crossed my mind that by sending him along, Mitya wanted to accustom him to the sight of death. But then again, maybe Mitya suspected I would disobey an order again, and Senya would be his witness – a thought that did not please me.

A black stallion was waiting in the yard, harnessed to a small sleigh. We seated the woman between us, and I drove towards the forest, which loomed darkly behind the village. The road descended into a ravine, then followed a hollow up a hill. A thaw was setting in and the wet, sombre trees stood like black posts on the white snow. We entered the forest. I stopped the horse after a turn: 'Seems to me that's it, we are on site.' We stood up and stepped down from the sleigh, including the woman, who remained silent. I asked her how she could betray people she'd known as her neighbours, understanding they would be killed as a result? She answered simply: 'I didn't do enough of them ... That's why I have to die myself.' I said: 'Walk on ahead, I'll shoot you.' I raised the rifle and shot. The woman fell down. The report from my rifle made a dull sound in the wet forest. Having checked the woman was dead, we returned to the sleigh, turned the horse around, and rode back to the village. It had served this viper right: but the lives she'd snuffed out could not be restored; and the pain and torment of grieving families could not be removed. Yes, it had served her right – but still I felt uneasy. We reported to Bourko: 'In the forest, around a turn in the road.' Mitya said: 'Alright, I'll send them to bury her now.'

What's the duty of a scout? Not just to look out for something hiding behind a bush. We had to act, to unite people around us, to instil faith in our victory. We had to punish traitors so others would not follow their example. The whole purpose of executions was to show the enemy and their informers that the Soviet authorities were close and would call treachery to account. We also had to protect the people who were helping us. Deep inside the occupied territory, we were representatives of the Soviet State and executors of its laws. All possible means were used by the Fascists to convince people of the strength of their New Order: radios clamoured, newspapers bawled, placards wailed, trying to make every traitor believe it was safe to collaborate. Informers and turncoats in a garrisoned village or town did not foresee the possibility of finding themselves before a Soviet court of justice. Meanwhile, as a result of their treachery, people were tortured and hanged, their eyes were put out, stars were carved into their backs. And yes, people were burned and buried alive. But when night fell, a scout would come and do justice for the villainies committed. The collaborators saw that retribution would come unexpectedly; and this was a weak point in Fascist propaganda: no assurances of German omnipotence could stop Soviet law being exercised.

We spent the night at Vaskovshina, and by eleven or twelve o'clock, having waited till dark, our detachments approached the town of Chashniky again: this time from the side guarded by the flax works, where the Polizei garrison was located. The windows of the works' building were plugged with sandbags, but loopholes had been left in-between. There was no chance of dislodging the Polizei from such a fortress without artillery, so we set up a gun and the shelling commenced. One explosion followed another in the works' inner yard, but then a shell struck the main building – crash! The jingling of broken glass! Tongues of fire blazed and fighters of the 2nd Detachment ran past us. I was at the command post with Chief of Staff Vasili Nikiforov, and he dashed forward yelling: 'A-a-h, Yaponsky bog!' [literally, 'Japanese god!' – a consonant substitution for a much ruder Russian oath – Trans.] And I followed.

The Polizei kept pouring machine- and submachinegun fire on us and didn't spare the ammunition. Suddenly I saw Vasili's submachinegun fall into the snow. I ran up to him. He was swearing with gusto, spitting out a stream of obscenities. He had been wounded in his right hand. I grabbed his submachinegun and we rolled down into the ravine where Dubrovsky and Lobanok were. Dubrovsky asked: 'Where is Vasili wounded?' 'In the right hand,' I replied. 'Take him away now and put a dressing on.' 'Maybe you will have to stay with him,' Lobanok added.

Vasili and I rode to a neighbouring village on his horse, stopping at the very first shack. The host, having discovered I'd brought the wounded Nikiforov, opened the gates – it turned out they knew each other. 'Leave the horse harnessed and give it hay,' Vasili told me. I led him into the shack and pulled out a first aid pack from my bag. I diluted permanganate powder in warm water and washed the edge of the wound with a lump of wool. Thankfully, the bones were intact, although the palm had been shot through and the thumb was paralyzed. The wound was not dangerous but the bleeding was heavy. I applied a bandage and the bleeding subsided. I dabbed the edges of the wound with iodine and dressed it. With the aid of the hostess, I tore a towel into long strips and tightly bound the hand. Then we lay the wounded man above the stove, where it was warm. I asked Vasili if he felt well enough to be left on his own: 'You go,' he said, 'leave me the horse and the submachinegun – I'll catch up with the brigade if need be.' The host, turning to me said: 'I'll give you my horse.' We walked out into the yard, harnessed up a shaggy steed, and I rode back to the battle.

When I reached the forest, our gun was already withdrawing. I came across Frolov and he waved his hand: 'Bad luck. Reinforcements broke through to them and Dubrovsky withdrew.' It turned out we were retreating to the village I'd left Vasili in. I turned my horse around and rode back. The host rejoiced when he saw I had brought his horse back! Meanwhile, my patient was sleeping and that was a good sign. I waited till morning, sleeping fully clothed on a bench. My heart was easy, for Vasili was nearby, and I was cheered that I had returned to combat and had not taken advantage of being an attendant.

In the morning I caught up with Salnikov. Fedya Salnikov, our surgeon, having examined the wound, said the dressing had been applied well. A phalange of the thumb was smashed and time was needed to let it knit. The hand was dressed again and immobilized. A bullet, having pierced Vasili's hand, hit his submachinegun, leaving a dent in its breechblock. He was lucky!

The Partisans had no opportunity to conduct trench war against fortified garrisons. Since the time of Denis Davydov [a Hussar officer who operated with Partisans on French lines of communication during Napoleon's invasion of 1812 – Trans.], a sudden strike on the enemy's convoys had been typical tactics for a guerrilla war. This method brought excellent results for us too. Partisan ambushes constantly operated on the roads around garrisons. Stockpiles of bread, cattle and other foodstuffs for the German Army, which were stored in garrisons for transportation to the front by rail, failed to reach their destination. They were intercepted on the way by Partisans, who knew – thanks to local informers – when, and by what route, a German convoy would go. The whole reason for a garrison's existence was to hold territory and supplies. But because of the Partisans, these garrisons had to be protected by additional forces. Thus, a garrison could become a nuisance instead of an asset to the invaders, drawing off troops from the front. Using these tactics, and avoiding a major clash, the Partisans forced the enemy to leave occupied areas. It happened this way in Ushachi: later, the same tactic was used to liberate the Chashniky district.

The prolongation of the Siege of Chashniky in January 1943 was caused by a specific situation, which I only discovered later. It turned out that the raid on Chashniky had been undertaken by order of the Vitebsk Clandestine Party Committee, in order to draw off the enemy's forces: since at the same time, the Germans were conducting a major punitive operation in our district and several neighbouring brigades were in trouble. For nearly a week our brigade was in combat with the enemy. Only when the Germans had begun to muster large forces around Chashniky, augmented by tanks and artillery, were we ordered to retreat. Manoeuvring at night, our detachments quit the outskirts of the town. Later, we found out the Fritzes in Chashniky had already loaded their archives on trucks: so one more strike and they would have left the garrison!

The brigade was on the road again and I sat in Borodavkin's sleigh. The wind had changed to the westerly during the day, it got warmer, and as darkness closed in, it began to snow. The wind was whipping up snowdrifts as we approached a big village. I came up to Partisans standing behind a shack, sheltering from the wind. I'd just lighted a smoke when a messenger ran up: 'Quick, Korolenko is calling you to the detachment!' Everybody ran, and although I was from reconnaissance and the order didn't apply to me, it seemed improper to stay, so I ran along with the rest.

The detachment was gathering on the edge of the village. Mitya lined up the fighters and I joined the file too. We stood on the edge of a hollow, a village looming on the opposite side. Korolenko gave orders quietly, in a hoarse voice: 'The Fritzes secured the village for themselves. We have to lure them into the hollow and make them reveal their positions. Ten people will go in a line. First section – two steps forward.' Korolenko strode along the file, glancing into the eyes of each fighter. Having reached me – I had joined at the end of the row – he asked in amazement: 'Why are you here? Step out of the line!' 'Let me stay, Comrade Commander.' Korolenko waved his hand in agreement and commanded: 'Carry out the order. The interval is twenty steps.' We stepped down from the hillock into the darkness and began our descent into the hollow, stretching out in order to cover as much space as possible.

Soon, the line broke up, each of us becoming a little island, knowing that any moment the enemy could strike. My heart shrank in suspense. It was fearsome to wait for the moment when a shot burst out and you'd get your 'nine grams'. But behind us was our brigade, and here, in this hollow, a trap was being prepared for it. This was our duty to our comrades.

Maria was to the left of me, Afonka to the right. Like me, Afonka was from the staff scouts: most likely it was he who had warned Korolenko about the Germans' ambush. The ground was frozen. As we approached the village outskirts, remains of hurriedly dug foxholes could be seen. Not yet buried beneath the snow, these foxholes had been abandoned only recently. We came across a second row of slit trenches. Fine snow was falling: our black silhouettes would be clearly seen against this white background. Suddenly a machinegun rattled into the night from our line, immediately answered by another situated in the village. A command was heard: 'Drop down!' We immediately fell to earth. Silence. Someone ran along the line to the source of the firing. It turned out our machinegunner had been shot dead. Walking with a light machinegun, he had spotted an enemy, but managed to shoot only one burst before he was hit by submachinegun fire. Again an order: 'Move forward – but with caution.'

The suspense was agonizing. Everyone expected to be the next to fall. Suddenly a flare soared above us, spilling a wave of blood-red light all over us. At the next instant, machine- and submachineguns began their work. Sparks of tracer bullets came straight at us, scoring green and pink dashes in the dark, lighting up our snowy hollow with a bright glare. An order to withdraw swept across the line. We turned and ran. But the hollow was already flooded by a solid rain of fire, and the snow was boiling with fountains of bullets, any one of which could take your life away.

Afonka, Maria and I ran, but quickly lost our strength. I saw that Maria was no longer running but struggling to pull her feet from the snow. I myself could not run for much longer. I took the rifle from her and we switched to walking, but it was impossible to get through this hail of fire. Still, we pushed on over the boiling snow, and it seemed strange that we were still intact. Maria walked ahead and disappeared out of sight – she had probably reached compacted snow, enabling her to make better progress. Meanwhile, my feet felt like lead weights and my rifle became insufferably heavy. My will-power, like my energy, was sapping away and a thought came: 'They'll kill me anyway, a step further or a step closer ...' Having come to myself, I noticed that I wasn't walking anymore but dragging myself along, staggering. Afonka was hobbling next to me. We climbed the hill where the village was located, and from where we had started. A heavy machinegun began tapping out a jerky staccato. A little more effort and we breasted the hill. Four hours later we caught up with our guys.

In the morning, Mitya Korolenko's detachment returned to the brigade – the guys were chilled through. It was at this point that I discovered we had been under fire from a whole battalion! Dubrovsky, advised by his scouts that the Germans had set up an ambush on his line of march, had switched the brigade to another road, ordering Korolenko's detachment to cover the brigade. Mitya had decided to lure the Fritzes into the hollow, to strike and destroy them: in other words, to turn the tables and ambush the ambushers. In the dark of the night – just as Korolenko had counted on – the Germans had taken us for the vanguard of the brigade and engaged in combat: but facing no fire in return, they realized their plan of a sudden strike had failed. Mitya had expected the Germans to pursue the brigade and had kept his detachment in ambush for the whole night. In the morning, his scouts reported that the Germans had withdrawn to their garrison. Victory was ours! The brigade had been moving through occupied territory while the Fritzes had been mustering forces to destroy it. But having found us, they lacked the guts to attack, and had crept back to their garrison under cover of night.

One day, in Medvedky, me and another Partisan were called to the Kombrig: 'You, Obryn'ba and Kazachonok, are ordered to execute traitors of the Motherland.' We answered: 'Yes, Comrade Kombrig.'

Markevich specified the order. The man I was sent to execute didn't work for the Germans, but he was a brother of the Polizei Chief, and often spent time in the company of Polizei. People feared him, and the demand to get rid of him came from his fellow-villagers. Meanwhile, Afonka would have to shoot another man from the same village, accused of being a German informer. We would have to cross a frozen lake, some 3 or 4 kilometres wide, leave our horse on the bank, and walk to the village. Sergei explained everything in detail. The first man's shack was near the Polizei barracks. I would have to pass the sentence, shoot him, run back to the horse, and wait for Afonka. It was a dangerous mission, for the Polizei might easily spot us as we recrossed the lake, the surface of which was smooth and white, with no place to hide. Sergei advised: 'The main thing is not to make too much noise. Do your job and return immediately.'

Winter days were short, so we wasted no time in harnessing a sleigh and taking off. It was cold on the move, thanks to a strong headwind. Afonka and I didn't talk on the way, both wrapped up in our thoughts. I felt uneasy: the assignment was difficult, and I would be the last to see the eyes of that man . . .

An hour later and we rode up a steep, icy bank. I tied the horse to a willow and Afonka said: 'Don't dawdle over it, Nikolai, do your job and get straight back here. I'll do the same – bang and done! I will wait for you in the sleigh.' With these words we parted. I walked straight to the shack as directed. It was not late and the door wasn't locked. I opened the latch in the hallway and entered a spacious dining room with a whitewashed floor of wide planks. In the middle of the room stood a woman in a long white chemise. She held a baby in her arms. In a corner, next to a small table with icons, sat an old woman. An icon lamp burned. I asked: 'Where is the master?' The woman with the child shouted: 'Ivan!' A man of medium height, about thirty-five years of age, came out from behind a partition holding a *valenok* [a winter boot made of felt, the plural form is valenki – Trans.]. For some reason, he spoke in a guilty tone: 'The valenki are worn out, I'm mending them.' In my mind an inner voice spoke: 'You won't wear them, you don't understand that your fate is up.' But I had to speak out loud and was bracing myself. It was difficult to deliver a death sentence straight into someone's eyes. The guilty man's eyes were one thing, but the eyes of his mother and wife, full of fear, were another. At last I found my voice: 'You're accused of connections with the Polizei. Of being with them all the time. You've been sentenced to death.' A shocked silence. I ordered: 'Let's go.'

I led him out, set him against a wall, raised my rifle, aimed it at his head, and pulled the trigger. But there was no shot – it was a misfire. I repeated the procedure and again there was silence after I pulled the trigger. I took out a cartridge. There was a dent in the primer but there'd been no shot. I fired a third time and again there was a misfire. My thoughts began to tap in my head like flies on a window. What to do? What to do? Three misfires! Should I shoot after all this? And what about the order? Should I smash his head with the rifle butt? I had to decide what to do! What if he yelled and they heard him at the Polizei barracks? I was looking for a way out – how to avoid another shot. And here a salutary thought came: I remembered that one who survives the gallows cannot be hanged twice – he must be pardoned. It meant I didn't have to overburden my conscience! If I killed the man now, after all this, it would be not an execution, it would be a murder. I would show Dubrovsky the cartridges with the striker dents. But how to explain it to these people? I spoke quietly: 'You see how frosty it is, I have to grease the breechblock. Do you have any kerosene? Let's go inside and grease it.'

The man seemed hypnotized by my composure and we stepped up to the porch. Now our roles had switched: he could grab an axe, any piece of iron, and hit me! He could run or yell for help, knowing that my rifle was disabled. Instead, we entered the room and he brought kerosene. The hostess lit a lamp. I disassembled the breechblock and rubbed it clean – fully disarmed in front of him. The breechblock worked alright. What was the problem? It must be the ammunition: that's what decided his fate. The woman said something, took a jug from the stove, and gave me a cup of hot milk. I had to say something. One thing was clear to me: I wouldn't shoot him. I began talking about his child: 'He has just been born! Your only one! How could you not think of your family? How could you hang about at the Polizei barracks? What on earth made you befriend them?' 'I've been going there to play cards,' he answered, 'so they wouldn't harass me. My brother is my brother, of course, but still they pester me, asking: "Why aren't you in the Polizei?"' His words sounded convincing. And three misfires in a row were too many to ignore. 'Use your brains!' I said, 'once your brother is in the Polizei, you have to be with the Partisans. You reckon you won't have to pay for this? Our folk will come back and you won't get away with: "I used to go to play cards . . ."'

I was looking at the old woman, crossing herself in front of an icon, and I couldn't get rid of the thought: how would I explain to her the reason I hadn't shot him? Suddenly, I asked the *staroushka*: 'Did you pray to the Blessed Virgin to have mercy on him?' 'I did, sonny, I did.' 'Then you write a note saying you won't pray for him anymore.' 'But I'm illiterate, I cannot write!' At the same moment, I heard a shot not far away. It meant that Afonka had carried out his order. Silently, I tore a sheet of paper from my album and wrote quickly: 'I, such a person, Ivan Lozhkov's mother, won't pray for his health before the Blessed Virgin should he do something against the Soviet State.' I put the note on the table in front of the staroushka: 'Put a cross on it. And you, Ivan, remember what has happened today. The Blessed Virgin saved your life for the sake of your child.' I was not going to talk about wet ammunition. His wife came up: 'Maybe, you need something? Maybe, you're hungry?' I hesitated on the threshold, but remembered about underwear, for we were short of it: 'Some underwear for the guys would be good . . .' She quickly opened a trunk and threw several rolls of underwear into a pillowcase. I ran down the bank, back to the sleigh. Afonka was there, huddling himself up and cursing: 'Why was there was no shot?' 'I'll explain later.' I put the bundle under my knees and pressed myself against the seat. The horse, being fairly chilled, ran quickly over the ice-covered lake. There were no shots and no yells. I felt completely confused, for I understood that I was bringing Dubrovsky a strange document instead of a report confirming his order. And this was the second time! How would he take it? Then I remembered: I was bringing the cartridges dented by the striker too . . .

We arrived in Medvedky late. In the shack where Dubrovsky was billeted a kerosene lamp was burning. I entered the shack, where Mitya Frolov and Markevich were sitting with Dubrovsky. I handed them the note. Markevich read it, then Frolov, then Dubrovsky, who hurled a long, unbroken burst of foul language at me: 'How many notes are you going to bring me? First you gave grain away! Then the Blessed Virgin stood in your way!' Frolov came to my rescue: 'Fedor Fomich, Nikolai showed his worth in combat. He found the traitors. True, the protocols were not formally correct, but in essence were very just.' Dubrovsky softened up: 'They said he couldn't kill a man and it's true. Well, tell us how it was.' I told everything, just as it happened, then pulled out the cartridges. 'Come on, Afonka,' said Dubrovsky, 'load your rifle.' Afonka loaded his rifle with my cartridge and a shot resounded. I said again: 'Well, that's fate ...'

Some time went by. In spring, the brigade marched back along that road and Ivan Lozhkov came to Dubrovsky to ask for his mother's note back. By that time he had begun working for us, but his mother – bound by the note – didn't dare pray to the Blessed Virgin for her son's salvation. Naturally, she took his escape for a miracle, and believed in the Virgin even more than before. And why wouldn't she believe? He'd been taken out to be executed, she had prayed, and fortune had turned death away from him three times!

After a ten-day raid to Chashniky, the brigade returned home to the camp. My heart was full of joy: I was alive, at home again, and not back there, in the hollow, where cold fountains of bullets were ploughing up the snow ...

The Fritzes, finding the main force of the brigade had gone to Chashniky, had tried to advance on a Partisan garrison in Pyshno, but had been beaten off. In revenge, they organized a punitive expedition to the villages of Pounishe and Slobodka nearby. They'd surrounded the villages, set the huts ablaze, and massacred the residents. In the evening of the same day Lobanok called me up: 'Tomorrow you'll ride to Slobodka with Goutiev. You'll both draw and photograph what you can. There is an order from the other side of the front to record Fascist atrocities. They want to issue leaflets based on these facts and to distribute them as soon as possible. Take off in the morning. Take guards in Pyshno.' I quickly collected albums, pencils, and a 'Kontaks' camera – a trophy taken from the Fritzes during an operation on the railroad.

In the morning, we harnessed my horse to a light sleigh and headed to the garrison. At about twelve o'clock we were already in Pyshno, drinking tea with the hospitable hostess of the house where Nikolai Safonov, commander of the 1st Detachment, was billeted. We organized a convoy of ten people, with a heavy machinegun on a big sleigh, to which a strong black stallion was harnessed. After Pyshno, we rode through a forest to Slobodka, halting in a hollow before the edge of the forest. Our scouts advanced to check if there was an ambush. In front of us stood a hill covered in blue snow. Columns of black smoke could be seen here and there, spread against the pale backdrop of the winter sky. But the smoke was not coming from chimneys: those were the burning homes of Slobodka.

We took off slowly, passing a dead horse on the road. And further on, when we entered the village, scenes of horror met our eyes, becoming gradually worse as we made our way to the centre of the settlement. In the middle of the road there was a woman lying with a child on her chest: both stabbed with a bayonet. Nearby, an old person and a boy with faces buried in the snow, both badly charred – apparently they had run out of a burning shack. The Germans had locked the locals in their huts and set them alight: those who managed to run out were shot dead. We walked a bit further and saw beheaded corpses of old people, their heads nearby on the ground. They made old people bend down, and chopped their heads on a birch stump, like firewood. Further away, near a burnt-out fence, was the naked corpse of a young guy, blue-black from scorching. The smell of ashes, the mournful flakes of soot flying in the air and settling on the snow, amplified the horror.

Emerging from my stupor, shaken by the view, I hurriedly began drawing sketches. My comrades set out guards, and with reason: the Germans were only some 600 metres away. Their outposts could clearly be seen, next to the outermost bathhouse of a neighbouring village. But strange to say, having noticed us, they refrained from shooting, and Nikolai Goutiev and I kept drawing. My album was quickly filled with sketches. The time was passing rapidly. It was very cold and already dusky – the winter day was going down fast. At sunset, the sky grew crimson, the frost strengthened, and the guards began urging us to return before dark. But as there was still a lot to do, I decided to let the Partisans go, reckoning that in case of danger, Kolya and I would be able to get away on our horse, which stood nearby.

As soon as our convoy, led by the sleigh harnessed to the black horse, managed to get down to the forest, a machinegun struck from trees nearby: an ambush! I hid behind the stove of a ruined house and began to shoot. But another machinegun opened fire at my back. I had to withdraw! The black horse pulling our machinegun rode past us. Kolya managed to catch up with it and jumped into the sleigh. The youngest of us, a fourteen-year-old Partisan, pressed himself up to me. He had got his rifle the day before yesterday and was in combat for the first time. Also nearby was Afonka, an experienced and quick-witted scout. My horse, scared by the shooting, rushed towards the forest and stiffened on the hill. Tracers were zooming at the prancing black stallion, pulling the guys away. If only we could get over the hill and then into the forest! I lay down to shoot while Afonka and the young Partisan ran; then they lay and opened fire while I caught up. I found the boy completely bewildered. He was crying, having thrown his rifle on the ground: 'Oh, uncles, don't leave me behind . . .' I had to shout at him to bring him to his senses. Making short runs, we pressed on. Then all three of us ran, and at last reached the hill near the road and began shooting back.

Dusk was descending and there was no threat of pursuit. I asked the boy: 'So, what's your name?' 'Volod'ka,' he replied. 'Why did you take off your camouflage cloak?' 'It was hard to run, uncle.' 'Why weren't you shooting?' 'Forgot about it, uncle.' Volod'ka was badly shaken. And it wasn't hard to sense the hand of death after all we'd seen in Slobodka! But the darkness came to our rescue and now we were plodding towards Pyshno across deep snow.

That night was pitch-dark. A blizzard arose, and after some time we began doubting if we were on the right road. Then the outline of an edifice showed black in the distance. We didn't know where we were. If this was Pyshno then all was well, but what if we'd walked directly to the Germans in Studenka or Zastenok? What to do? We decided that the guys would hide in the snow and I would reach a street and try to find out where we were.

I was standing behind a shack. In front of me was a fence, and beyond it a street with people walking by: 'Which village is this?' I asked. Someone stopped and a breechblock clicked: 'Which one d'ye need?' This time I didn't know what to say. If I said 'Pyshno' and these guys were Polizei, they'd start shooting straight away. Likewise, if I said 'Zastenok' and the men were Partisans, again the bullets would fly. 'I need to spend the night here,' I replied, 'don't you know where to stop, for I've lost my way?' Suddenly I heard: 'Kol'ka, is it you? You're a hell of a chump! We were ready to shoot!' I ran back to call my comrades. Afonka was waiting for me on the spot but Volod'ka had bolted. We looked for him until midnight but failed to find him. Obviously our hero had been really scared!

In the morning, our artillery – a 76 mm piece – arrived in Pyshno and we saw Volod'ka near the grooms. Safonov, our commander, asked him: 'From which detachment are you, young fellow?' 'I, uncle, serve at the field gun.' 'What do you mean, "I serve at the field gun"? You're in my rifle platoon, aren't you?' 'No, I can only be near the field gun!' The thing was, Volod'ka had lost faith in his rifle, and it seemed safer to remain near the big field gun.

Back in the night, Kolya and I worked on drawings for the leaflets. By morning, sketches had been done and during the day we prepared 100 leaflets entitled: 'Take vengeance on the Fascists!' In the night, our scouts took off to spread the leaflets throughout the neighbouring villages and the German garrisons. Some were even dropped over Lepel from a kite!

The idea to make a kite, in order to drop leaflets from the air, was Misha Chaikin's. Not long ago, he had attended an aircraft modelling group in Dom Pionerov [i.e. 'Pioneers' House' – youth clubs with numerous hobby groups, which existed in the USSR until the late 1980s – Trans.]: now he was a dashing aide-de-camp, riding a horse like a true Cossack. Misha knew how to build huge kites, which could be raised up to a significant height. The wind would drive a small sail on wooden rollers up along the rope to the flying kite, which had a number of leaflets attached to it. The 'postman' – the name we gave to the sail – would strike the kite, opening the hook to which the leaflets were pinned. The wind would pick up the leaflets and carry them high above the ground, sowing legends about a Partisan aircraft. Since the leaflets' contents reflected the most recent events, people thought the Partisans had excellent communications with the mainland and maybe had their own aircraft.

That very day the leaflets were dropped from a kite for the first time. The impression was huge! An event had just happened and already there was a plane with leaflets from behind the front line! People could recognize the place on the drawing and that was especially convincing. Both the civilian population and the Fritzes reckoned we had an aircraft bridge with the mainland. They couldn't imagine how we had managed to produce a large number of leaflets referring to yesterday's events. They didn't guess that we had our own printing press in the forest.

CHAPTER THIRTY-ONE

Spitting Out Blue, Yellow and Green: February 1943

When someone set out on an operation or reconnaissance, everybody tried to supply him with the best stuff – weapons, clothes, and so on. Misha Chaikin promised me his overcoat, Vanya Chernov gave me two hand grenades, Kolya offered his gloves. Meanwhile, I had my own pistol and rifle. The album was ready and pencils were in order: I put everything in my shabby old map-case. Only Nikolai Goutiev remained to look after the household, and I entrusted Tass to him, as we'd been banned from taking our dog on a 'railroad operation'.

Everyone was preparing for tomorrow's departure, cleaning weapons, adjusting clothes. Dubrovsky and Lobanok took along three detachments, as the operation was to be a big one. Yesterday, Boulba – that is to say, Stepan Nikolaevich Shenka – had come a long way over snow to convey important information: which trains would pass through the Prozoroka station and at what times.

As usual, everyone felt nervous before an outing. We couldn't fall asleep for a long while, and kept talking in the darkness. Some recent events were discussed: Vasya Nikiforov, wounded in the hand near Chashniky, had become intimate with Alla Charikova, a Partisan from the 3rd Detachment – a beautiful girl with hazel eyes and slightly Mongolian face. They were a good couple: Allochka [a diminutive of Alla – Trans.] was a temperamental person, fervent and resolute; and Vasili was a man of handsome presence, one of the first-rank commanders in the brigade. In short, a wedding was required, but there was a law in the camp: no one was permitted to drink or to be in love. The times were harsh and these ascetic regulations were dictated by the life itself – husbands were leaving their wives and kids to fight the enemy, not to have a nice time. For breaching this rule, Vasili Nikiforov, Chief of Staff of a detachment, was demoted and Alla was to cross the front line. Kononov, a former accountant, replaced Vasili as Chief of Staff. He had recently arrived from behind the front line, sent by the Central Headquarters of the Partisan Movement. He failed to win recognition as a commander . . .

We woke up before dawn and jumped outside to wash our faces. The snow lay like a blue shroud, laughter and quick orders were heard all around. The horses were already harnessed up, muffled machineguns were brought and set on sleighs. We walked to the dry-mess, where aromatic soup was waiting in a big pot. The cook generously poured it into everyone's bowl. After this we were ready, and when the day began to break, the detachments lined up. They were inspected by the commanders and the brigade's senior officers. The scouts took off first, then Korolenko's detachment. Dubrovsky and Lobanok – both in identical sheepskin overcoats – rode each in his own sleigh. The column of Partisans stretched out: there were no less than thirty heavy and light machineguns on sleighs. Artillery pieces made by Partisan craftsmen were in convoy too – they were our pride.

I sat with Dubrovsky in a sleigh harnessed to his huge grey stallion. Dubrovsky told me how Mitya Bourko from the osoby otdel, who used to be a *Zootechnik* [a skilled livestock attendant on Soviet collective farms – Trans.] before the war and knew how to handle horses, had broken a kicking stallion. Dubrovsky was a good storyteller, it was interesting to listen to him, and I didn't notice we had reached a village. Here we had to wait for the moment to attack the special train.

By nightfall the brigade stretched out in column again and moved towards the railroad embankment. We approached quietly, left the horses and carts behind a hillock in a hollow, took up an arc-shaped position on a knoll parallel to the embankment, and set up machinegun positions and a 45 mm gun. Beside each man was a bundle of thatch with straps attached, so we would have our hands free when the time came to storm the train. We would have to set each car alight and destroy everything inside, but we had no petrol, and that's why we had bundles of thatch as fuel.

We heard the sound of a train coming: closer, closer, closer . . . We waited. We were ready. At last the steam-engine panted past, followed by the wagons. And then the gun struck. We shot point-blank at the engine. An explosion, a screeching of steel, a clanging of iron! The engine was enveloped in steam and the train stopped. 'Fire!' Dubrovsky shouted. Snarling machineguns began to shoot, a pillar of fire soared into the black skies. 'Forward!' The Partisans grabbed the bundles of thatch, hurled them on their backs and ran towards the train to set each car ablaze. Hand-to-hand fighting had already broken out in the sleeping cars, bags of grain and frozen meat carcasses were being thrown out of the goods wagons. Suddenly, crates appeared from under the carcasses, and in them were shells for tank guns! The train was moving to the front and the Fritzes had disguised the ammunition so as to protect themselves from the Partisans' action with so-called 'peaceful freight'.

The train was ablaze. The cars were turning into bonfires with tongues of fire breaking away from windows and doors. Dozens of peasants' carts were coming up to be loaded and driven towards the forest; Partisans in white camouflage cloaks were rushing about, driving the carts away; and a whole convoy of carts was already making its way into the forest. But then a heavy machinegun opened fire from the station. Dubrovsky turned to me: 'Check the horses – is everything alright?' I ran down into the hollow.

Tracers were dashing over me, slamming into the hillside, but the frightened horses bunched together and the grooms could barely hold their reins. One of the horses broke loose and ran away. Others followed in a headlong flow and the grooms failed to stop them. I managed to catch Dubrovsky's stallion by the reins but he leaped aside. I had no time to jump into the sleigh and was dragged across the bushes after him. Somehow I managed to pull myself up by the reins, shift myself into the sleigh, and gain control of the horse in time to block the path of the other horses. One of them fell, the rest struggled on top of it, and the grooms began jumping off, throwing the reins. 'Stop!' I yelled, 'unharness!' The horses leaped up. Dubrovsky's horse was snorting, but the first bout of fear had gone. Meanwhile, the grooms busied themselves with the fallen horse, rousing it and quelling the panic. And not a moment too soon, for a messenger from the Kombrig ran up: 'Bring up the horses! Faster! Withdrawal! Tanks are around!'

Crewed tanks had been on platforms near the steam-engine. They were already moving along the embankment – we had to withdraw. I heard a shout and turned back. Frolov's figure was seen on the hillock against the glow of flame: 'Nikolai, get the sleigh ready for Dubrovsky!' I rode up to Dubrovsky. He sat in the sleigh but I decided to hang around, for I wanted to draw the scene of destruction. I had just started sketching when Vanya Chernov rode up, yelling something at me, but I couldn't hear him. He lashed me with his whip: 'Watch out!' I turned around and saw a file of Germans approaching from the tail of the train! I ran after Ivan, grasping at his stirrup, and we managed to get away. When we caught up with the brigade, Vanya apologized for striking me.

We returned to the village rejoicing. Everyone was excited and exchanging impressions. I was told that some guys from the Didenko's detachment had found paint, so straightaway I ran to find them. How frustrated I was when I found them spitting out blue, yellow and green from paint-smeared mouths. It turned out the guys had mistaken the little bars of watercolours for candies and had eaten them up!

In the morning, again at first light, the brigade was withdrawing and the Germans were mustering for a chase. We gave out a lot of captured bread in the village and took the rest back to camp. The operation was exceptionally successful, due to intelligence gained by Boulba. But within two weeks, the life of Stepan Nikolaevich Shenka would end tragically. The Fascists found out he was a Partisan agent and hanged him. His wife and son were shot.

Our camp was expanding and becoming more and more habitable. Construction was so rapid that it was still late autumn when we took the bold decision to snatch a steam engine from a German garrison and set up electric power in the camp. We lifted it at night, having mounted it on runners harnessed to a pair of bullocks, for there was already a covering of snow on the ground. We built a huge shack, installed an iron chimney, and our camp reverberated with the puffing of the engine. Thus electric power came to our camp. Dubrovsky and Lobanok ordered the first lamp to be installed at our place, so I could work at nights and print photographs – this was necessary for our agents' documents.

Volodya Lobanok conceived the idea to organize a printing-works in the camp for our hand-drawn and handwritten leaflets. They brought remnants of a typeface from Ushachi and began sorting it out. We had the former editor-in-chief of the district newspaper in our camp, and he was entrusted to do it. We built premises for it, brought two female typesetters from Lepel, and began publishing district papers and a brigade paper. News reports were printed daily. Nikolai Goutiev was charged with publishing leaflets and posters. He cut them on linoleum and then text was printed at the works. Apart from that, we also made a large number of leaflets with carbon-copies, then tinted them up a bit with watercolours. Texts were written by hand or printed at the works.

The base of our brigade was located in a school building at Antunovo. The camp was 5 kilometres away and no strangers were allowed in there. There, next to the school, our guns were located, and artillery crews lived in the building. And in the forest, on some sandy island surrounded by a swamp, there was a bakery for those who lived in the camp, and for detachments and groups secretly departing for operations. Farmers brought foodstuffs to Antunovo, and from there Partisans would bring it to the camp, where stocks were made. Meat and sausages were smoked in the forest and bakers made bread – bricks of it, just like before the war.

On Sundays, those who wanted to join the Partisans would come to Antunovo to be examined. People would also come to sort out various issues. It was a centre of Soviet power in the Partisan area. By the spring of 1943 a pavilion was built here, and Partisans and youths from neighbouring villages would come to dance and stay with the Partisans. Partisan actors performed at this pavilion. They sang songs and *chastushki* [simple verses on topical subjects – Trans.], staged small plays, and recited poetry. A portrait of Stalin was always fixed on the Antunovo school. They also used to post up placards and news reports; and during holidays, the school was decorated with garlands of spruce branches and slogans on red fabric.

Many workshops were set up in Antunovo. Camouflage cloaks and clothes for Partisans were made in sewing workshops. And when aircraft began dropping bags of ammo and medical supplies for us, blouses and pants were made from the bags. Parachutes were also recycled – underwear was made from them. Meanwhile, warm winter boots were made from sheep's wool, galoshes were made from rubber tyres, and tanneries produced coats and hats of leather and astrakhan. Before the *rasputitsa* [the season of slushy roads in autumn and spring – Trans.] the Partisans needed to be shod with good boots. Horse hide was best for jackboots, so slaughtered horses were brought to Antunovo. The camp was situated in the Berezinsky Forest Reserve, that's why neither Partisans nor peasants were allowed to shoot wildlife without a permit, and it was watched vigilantly. But sometimes, when there was a shortage of food, two or three elks would be shot by order of Dubrovsky, and the skins handed to the tanneries. It was a huge undertaking to organize a tannery! They had to get tannins and find leather-dressers who knew the trade. Private currying had been banned before the war, that's why it was hard to find craftsmen who knew the whole technology. But already, in February–March, I drew pictures of Partisans fully clothed in outfits made on site.

An idea to mechanize our armoury workshop was conceived. Theft of a lathe in Lepel was arranged and it was brought to the camp. Having installed the lathe, the armourers could fashion many parts needed for maintenance. Home-made artillery pieces were produced, new rifles – more than 1,000 of them – were made from old, fouled ones. And tens of thousands of shells, retrieved from the bottom of the Dvina or brought from abandoned fortified districts [at the early stage of the war – Trans.] were cleaned up with brick-powder by our womenfolk. And such mortars were made! And submachineguns converted from semi-automatic SVT rifles! Trinitrotoluene or 'TNT' was smelted from artillery shells in special workshops, and landmines for diversions on railroads were made. I remembered a superb blacksmith called Ruba. He was sick with tuberculosis and was doomed, but joined our brigade saying: 'I want to be useful before I die.' He had enough time to make a mount for a 45 mm gun.

Plenty of machineguns had been taken from downed aircraft – both German and our own – but it was difficult to use them, as their rate of fire was too high. A blacksmith called Perednya from Putilkovichy invented a tripod mount on which a machinegun could be easily rotated. The very same Perednya invented a mortar from a pipe. It was designed for mortar shells of the 'regimental' calibre. This pipe did not shoot far but was impressive. The pipe would bang and a flying shell would scream wildly – a deafening sound, making a terrible impression on the enemy. Then a mine would explode with a huge pillar of smoke and a broad area of splinter strike.

The ingenuity of our people and the range of work they did were astounding. Some 300 kilometres of communications were laid and a powerful signal centre linking all Partisan garrisons was established. But before that we had to take those 300 kilometres of cable from the Fritzes! There was a kind of furious competition and each step, each breakthrough, each invention, was accepted by all with gratitude and goodwill. I remember this period as the happiest time of our common struggle – the sensation of unity was probably at its height. When I look back and try to imagine how many hours and days I spent on the hundreds of paintings I did back then, each of them requiring sketches and drafts! And paintbrushes, stretchers, primer coating – I had to make them myself. My best brushes were made with rifle bullets. I used to smelt the lead bullets, chop both ends, and insert a bunch of polecat hair, which Vasili Kosy, our scout, had caught for me.

And so it was a time of creation, even though fierce fighting went on nearby. In one place or another the Germans would massacre Partisans and locals. But there was no sensation of doom: everyone was suffused with optimism, joy and satisfaction at the struggle against the enemy. We believed in our immortality ...

CHAPTER THIRTY-TWO

Words of Pain and Love: March–April 1943

I was working on a picture entitled, 'The Echelons on Fire', but Dubrovsky said: 'Tomorrow, Nikolai, drop into Headquarters, there is a job for you. The guys from the landing party will have to go to Königsberg, you must think how to arrange passports for them.'

It was the most difficult thing, to make German Ausweis identity passes. If you made a mistake – even if you put a dot in the wrong place – then the agent was dead and it was you who sentenced him. This knowledge was an unbearable burden.

I couldn't forget the story of Natasha, our scout, who I had met when driving livestock from Istopishe to Antunovo. I had made documents for her many times, but then she was detained and sent to the Gestapo. I began looking for my mistake, riding around the district with Khot'ko, checking documents, disguised as Polizei. The Germans used a new stamp every month – 'Checked' – and I simply copied it. So why the exposure? What was different in Natasha's Ausweis? During a careful examination it turned out the Fritzes were using a code, carefully marking people's identity cards according to their village. For example, one village was indicated by a blue dot in the right-hand corner of the card; another by a small plus sign at the top; another by a green bar on the reverse; and so on. At first glance everything looked accidental, but in reality a strict method was in place. Thus, if you added a mark incorrectly, the bearer of the Ausweis was detained. All this played on my mind and I couldn't be cold-blooded about it. Whenever I finished a document and an agent went off on a mission, I lived in a kind of limbo, waiting for news. Now Dubrovsky wanted me to prepare documents for people heading to the very den of the enemy. Would I have enough wit and experience to foresee everything?

In the morning I walked to Headquarters, tense and concentrated. Dubrovsky called me up and a resplendent and shining girl emerged from a neighbouring room – God, what a beauty she was! I mustn't let her down! Lobanok, Mitya Frolov, and a tall, blond, Aryan type followed. Volodya introduced us: 'Nikolai, meet Anna and Anton.' These guys would head off, believing in my craftsmanship. Indeed they had to believe in it, for their very lives depended on my skill. I could not dent their confidence by expressing doubts or admitting the difficulties I faced. They must believe everything would be alright, that I was confident in my trade.

Mitya and I walked to the dugout of the osoby otdel. He showed me a German passport from Königsberg. But that was an out-of-date type and we had to get a new one. Apart from that, we needed blank passport forms. In fact, everything had to be German – photographic paper, film, developer and fixing agent – in order to look as authentic as possible. I knew that Mitya would call up our agents and order them to contact underground comrades in Lepel, to whom money requisitioned from the Polizei would be given, to allow them to buy or barter everything I needed from the Germans. But Mitya and I didn't talk about it: I simply listed all that was required.

While waiting for the materials, I had time to draw a picture entitled, 'The Brigade Goes for an Operation'. My work on this picture moved along slowly, as I rarely had time for it. Apart from that, I was also drawing, 'The Tread of Fascism', depicting events in Slobodka, based on sketches made back there. And then there was a picture called, 'In an Occupied Town', based on a photograph captured from the Fritzes. During our operation to destroy the special train, the Chief of the Western Railroad was killed and we took the film from his camera. There was a woman on one photo, plodding along with her head bowed. There was so much grief and pain in her figure! There were Fascists cackling behind her back, next to a post, from which a Partisan's body was hanging. After the war it was revealed that this picture was taken in 1943 in the Surozhsky market in Minsk. This photograph shook me with its cynicism and I decided to draw such a picture: people had to know what was happening in occupied towns. The picture made a strong impression on everyone.

Mitya Bourko rode to the Headquarters and dropped in to see us. He used to be Deputy Chief of the osoby otdel, but now he was the commander of a detachment, half-manned with former Polizei who had deserted to our side. Mitya asked: 'Look, Nikolai, give me Tass, I'll feel safer that way. And so as not to leave you missing him, I'll give you Essa, my sheepdog. She is a good companion, but untrained.' Of course I agreed, but warned him he would not be able to handle my dog, since Tass could be vicious. Mitya just grinned. I led Tass out of the dugout, Mitya whistled to him, and to my great astonishment, the dog obediently ran after him. Thus Tass and I parted. He was killed in combat like a soldier ...

The day when I could start work on the passports approached. Nikolai Goutiev and I kept arguing over how best to forge the stamp on a passport: should it be drawn directly on the document or carved on rubber first, then literally stamped on? I favoured the former method, Nikolai the latter. And yet, despite this argument, the fact remained that we needed to produce many forgeries: it would be impossible to draw a stamp so many times. Nevertheless, I took Frolov's passport and tried to draw a stamp. It came out perfect. Back then I had sharp eyes and a pretty faultless hand – I could reproduce a stamp, including all its distortions, with great precision. Meanwhile, examples of documents arrived at last. Our agents in Königsberg had managed to obtain – at great expense – not two but four blank forms, plus several completed passports as examples. And our agents in Lepel had bought photographic paper and developer from the burgomaster. Film was found in the 'Fotokor' camera, which Dubrovsky had presented me with.

Now, Anna and Anton were coming to our dugout all the time. This association brought us close together, and they soon became our kinsfolk. I began taking photos of them: I had to guess the exposure, for I didn't know the speed of the film. At last, Kolya and I managed to produce 'German' photos, just like in a Königsberg studio. We were assisted by Fimka the machinegunner. Fimka was from western Belorussia. The Germans had shot dead his kinsfolk and he joined the Partisans with his father. He knew German and was invaluable when working on documents. I drew stamps, scrupulously putting in dot after dot – every minor touch. Finally, we compared everything with a magnifying glass, and brought our work to Dubrovsky and Lobanok. Everything was checked again with a magnifier and we decided everything was accurate.

The day of parting came and we said our farewells. Anna, the beauty, kissed me; Anton hugged me tight and kissed me too. Everybody was laughing and joking when they left, but I was worried! Suddenly, I seemed to remember leaving a tiny puncture in a round stamp, thanks to the sharp point in a pair of compasses. It began to worry me and I told Nikolai: 'No, not at all! You worked with it on a backing sheet.' He calmed me down a bit, but still I was worried ...

In 1965 or 1966 I went back to the Berezinsky Reserve for drawing exercises and recognized a scientific worker as Anna. She told me that Anton was alive as well: both of them had returned from their mission, but to another brigade. At that time the blockade of the Partisan area, which had disrupted the positions of all our brigades, had already begun. In this way I discovered my documents had withstood the test.

Before May Day, Poznyakov, the Second Secretary of the Vitebsky *obkom* [i.e. provincial committee – Trans.] of the Party, arrived to examine the brigade and hold a festive rally. Dubrovsky and Lobanok proudly showed him the camp. They also showed him the pictures and leaflets made by the brigade artists, and told the story of our appearance: how we had run from Borovka, where the German Administrative Headquarters of the Occupied Territories of Belorussia had been based. But having seen our combat maps and discovered that we'd been producing documents for our agents, Poznyakov was horrified: 'What? Ex-POWs in the heart of your brigade?!' And he instantly demanded we be removed as far as possible from the Headquarters, to some remote garrison. Dubrovsky told me about his conversation with Poznyakov, concluding with this advice: 'You, Nikolai, don't pay attention, but don't say too much to him.'

Several days went by. Then Poznyakov came to our dugout to get acquainted, and to have a look at what we were doing. I showed him some leaflets and my picture, 'The Echelons on Fire', which I had taken from Headquarters for a while, as I needed to work on it a bit more. Poznyakov leafed over the sketches and albums, and I could see from his expression the distrust that the very word 'POW' was arousing among those in the rear. Meanwhile, for those of us who'd been through captivity, such people did not ignite pleasant feelings, but rather a desire to ask: 'How come hundreds of thousands of fighters found themselves surrounded?'

I was sitting on a plank bed, waiting for his words, and so as not to snap, began reloading the drum of my submachinegun. Externally I was calm, but inside I was boiling like a kettle. At last he asked: 'Were you a prisoner?' I didn't hesitate: 'What about you?!' 'No!' he replied, in such a way as to reject even the very idea. 'Then I cannot trust you!' I retorted, 'you're still an untried man to me! Because I saw there a lot of people, of various positions and ranks in the army, and they were as good at treachery as ordinary Polizei!' My hand clutched the submachinegun and I waited for his reaction. But he replied quietly: 'I've given an order not to engage you in staff work.' I answered that I wasn't chasing high rank, and had been 'engaged' by the commanders to do what was necessary to hurt the enemy.

He stood up and left without saying goodbye. I thought: he feared to shake my hand in case it desecrated his 'clean' one. I burned with bitterness and contempt. Most of the Partisans and commanding officers of the brigade inspected by him were *okruzhenets* from previously surrounded units, and former POWs who had escaped from captivity to fight the Fascists, but it didn't make him think it over. And he couldn't be unaware that I, as a staff scout, knew many things: so his order made no sense at all . . .

During these last days before the festivity, I was charged to draw a slogan on the red silky cloth of our banner: it was the face of our brigade. I thought long and hard what should be written on the banner. Eventually I decided on, 'For the Motherland!' And in the middle, above it, 'Workers of the World, Unite!' On the other side of the banner (it was a two-ply cloth) I wrote, 'Dubov's Partisan Brigade'. By the evening I had finished decorating the banner, and in the morning it was already embroidered. The embroidery was done by our girls: Lena Sharaeva, political leader of the 2nd Detachment, and interpreter Vera Ladik, wife of our two-way operator. The fate of Vera Ladik and her husband would be tragic. During the blockade of the Partisans' forest, when the Germans were combing the woods, Ladik hid in some moss with his wife and brother. The punitive squad approached, and Ladik knew he and his companions would soon be found. He pulled out his revolver and shot his wife, his brother, and himself, to prevent them from being tortured and giving away his comrades ...

Many of our people were dying, but every death was a strike for freedom. And our girls did their best to attire a fallen man for his funeral, making flowers and bows of paper. Everyone would come to say a final farewell to a fallen man. Then the coffin would be borne to the cemetery and the fighter would be buried amid speeches. These speeches were important for those who survived.

The cemetery was an old one, situated about 5 kilometres from the camp, near the village of Putilkovichy. It was considered a Partisans' cemetery – our cemetery. The fighters looked after the graves, planting flowers. The graves were nice and the living didn't worry that they would be abandoned. Many people worried a lot that their bodies would be abandoned and put at the mercy of the forest beasts. And everyone's will was: 'Bury me with my comrades.' Each of us knew that should he die in combat, the words of pain and love would be said about him too, and a salute would be awarded him. It strengthened people's spirit. It comforted them to believe in memory, and in the fact that a man sacrificed his life for the salvation of the Motherland.

So far, I'd thought that life and death were the main issues. But it turned out that people were tormented by what would happen to them after death – where they would be laid to rest. And how strongly all of us wished to lie next to his comrades – in our cemetery!

CHAPTER THIRTY-THREE

No White Spots of Tranquillity: May–June 1943

Brought in on the night of 1 May, killed in action, were Mikhail Zhukov and his Chief of Staff, Vasili Nikiforov. Their bodies were laid out on tables at Headquarters, decorated with tree branches and posted with a guard of honour. Zhukov's wife, Zhenya Lyabikova, cried next to his coffin. Zhukov died a hero, as he had promised, leading his detachment.

Nikiforov had been the first to break through to a Vlassovites' gun, scattering the crew and yelling his famous, 'Yaponsky bog!' The gun crew scarpered and Vasili captured the gun solo. Partisans running to join him saw Vasili seize the mounting, and yelling, 'Swing it around!' try to turn it about and strike the enemy with their own gun. At that moment, some of the retreating Vlassovites turned round and shot him in the back. Vasili had been reinstated as Zhukov's Chief of Staff, after falling from grace for loving Alla Charikova, but the injustice of that demotion still hurt him. He wanted to prove something, looked for an exploit, and died as a result.

I worked on Vasili's portrait all night and by morning it was finished. But I had no chance to rest. On the morning of 1 May, a new German advance began on Voron, where Vasili and Zhukov had died, and a detachment of Partisans, led by Dubrovsky and Lobanok, rode out to rescue their comrades. The fighting near Voron lasted a whole day, and we returned to camp late at night. And so the May Day festival, and the opening of the exhibition of my paintings, occurred without me.

In the middle of May, the front line was approaching Belorussia. The Germans started a simultaneous advance on all key Partisan positions, trying to mop up the rear of their army. The enemy engaged in fierce fighting around Staisk, but Safonov's detachment put up a tenacious defence. They'd run out of ammo for a 76 mm gun and there was no opportunity to take it to Antunovo, so it was decided to bury it. For two days we dug a huge pit, in which to hide the gun from the enemy. The artillery battery was commanded by Sergei Markin and the gun's crew commander was Ivan Artemenko – the same guy I had escaped from Borovka with.

At the end of May, Lobanok and I headed off to Misha Chaikin's cavalry squadron. From there I got back to camp and Lobanok went to Staisk. Soon after that he was called up to Moscow and we wouldn't see each other for a long time.

In the middle of May 1943 the blockade of the Polotsk–Lepel Partisan area began. A new period full of strain commenced. Not only did we have to fight, we also had to construct an airstrip to receive supply planes.

In May I had been far away from camp, and when I returned, it had already been abandoned. Essa, the sheepdog, threw herself at me in greeting. Nikolai Goutiev was waiting for me in our dugout and told me all the news. The Germans were pushing into Pyshno. The capture of Pyshno would open a gateway into the area and give them an opportunity to break up the Partisans, annihilating each brigade, one by one. At the moment, Korolenko's detachment was in Pyshno, holding the advance of two German battalions – the fighting there went on day and night. The situation was difficult, the Fritzes were expecting support units with artillery, tanks and aircraft, in order – as they wrote in their papers – 'to wipe out the bandits' stronghold'. Nikolai explained: 'Dubrovsky has shifted the Headquarters close to Starinka, and he has ordered your pictures taken off the stretchers and sent across the front line.'

Nikolai had remained behind to wait for me under Dubrovsky's orders, for we would have to take all our art materials and make our way to Starinka. A camera-operator, Masha Sukhova, who had arrived from Moscow, would go with us: she had already filmed our camp, and we were ordered to accompany her to Dubrovsky's place.

We took off in the morning. About 5 kilometres from the camp we heard aircraft howling, as the Germans began dropping thermite bombs, setting the forest afire. I hid between the roots of uptorn trees, and in the gaping holes where they once stood. Essa followed, trying hard to crawl beneath me, whining pitifully. Time and again there was the howling of passing aircraft, explosions and creeping fire. Suffocating smoke was already covering the forest floor and dry trees were blazing like bonfires. We made our way by crawling over undergrowth, then quickly running across open spaces, covering our faces with field caps. The heat was scorching our faces unbearably. We rolled down into a river bed. It was shallow, barely half-covering us, but the water made the heat seem less intense. At last, the howling aircraft flew off: we had to get out before they returned.

We arrived at Starinka by night. The brigade was camped in the forest not far from the village. I reported to Dubrovsky's Headquarters and was immediately charged with organizing an airstrip to receive supply planes:

'Aircraft should be here at night,' Fedor Fomich Dubrovsky explained, 'they'll drop bags of arms. Light up three bonfires 50 metres apart. A plane will shoot out a green flare, you must reply with a green one too. Then they'll start dropping. Watch where the parachutes go while they are still in the air, otherwise you won't find any. Then take ten of our people with carts. You'll find the bags and bring them to Headquarters.' I stood up to go but Dubrovsky stopped me: 'Wait, Nikolai, sit down. Do you have any idea about airfields?' I answered that I had. During the first week of the war I had spent a day working at an airfield in Moscow, helping to camouflage it: thus I had seen how they were laid out. 'That's good,' said Dubrovsky, 'you'll be constructing an airfield. We will have to receive planes carrying ammo, and send them out with our wounded. You've got the job. Wait for the planes till twelve, and be in Starinka by three. You'll instruct local people, who we have mobilized. You'll be constructing the airfield over here. The strip should be 1,000 metres square. Do you know a hillock beyond Starinka on the way to Ushachi?' I knew exactly where he meant: 'But there is a swamp over there!' 'There is a hillock too,' Dubrovsky replied, 'so you'll dig the hillock out and fill up the swamp. There's no other place, it's already been checked out. Take a horse from Mishka's squadron. No deadline, but do it as fast as possible. See what's going on in Pyshno. If the Fritzes take it, they'll steamroll straight through to Tartak – then no airstrip will be needed ...'

And so I was charged to construct the airstrip. Borodavkin would have to provide a system of fortifications around it, to build earth and timber emplacements.

The work was backbreaking. First, we tried using lumps of earth from the hillock to fill the swamp. But the soil soaked up the water, which soon seeped out again. Then we began laying logs on the swamp. We lay fascines as a foundation on the bottom of the bog, then bundles of brushwood, and only then did we throw earth on top. I sent everyone with a cart to adjacent villages, to pull down sheds and abandoned huts for logs. The rest collected brushwood. In the meantime, I began surveying the airstrip with a rope, hammering in stakes. It turned out that it was impossible to make an airstrip 1,000 metres square. The only solution was to abandon the idea of paving the whole square, and simply make a diagonal runway. Even so, the runway was not flat, but sloped somewhat. But after hearing of an incident in Melnikov's brigade, when a cargo plane landed but failed to take off after bogging down, I decided the slope might not be such a problem. For instance, on landing, a plane would slow down when taxiing up the slope; while on take-off, a plane heading down the slope would gain extra momentum. Nevertheless, taking such a decision was nerve-racking: not only for me, but also for the Kombrig, who I told about it. The order to build an airfield 1,000 metres square had come from Ryzhikov, the First Secretary of the Vitebsk District Party Committee. And our readiness to receive aircraft would have to be confirmed by Poznyakov. Had the real situation been disclosed, I would have been shot for sabotage. But we had no choice: 'For us, ammo is the same as life,' Dubrovsky said, 'and we've got plenty of wounded too ...'

The workload was huge. Two-thirds of the strip covered what had been the swamp, one-third covered what had been the hillock, and which was now a hump. About 2,000 peasants worked on the construction. They would come to the strip before dawn, about 4 am, when no German aircraft were around. I agreed with the peasants that as soon as people reached their daily work quota, I would let them go: and so everyone worked fast, achieving high output. At eleven, I would let those who remained go, and the second shift arrived to begin work. It was early June and all the peasants had plenty of work to do at home.

Constructing the airstrip was wearing me out. I was swayed in the saddle from fatigue and lack of sleep. By the end of the day I wanted to collapse and rest, but when night came, I would wait for our planes to arrive, loaded with arms. I was accompanied by Borodavkin, his wife, and Dubrovsky's wife. It was just we four, so as not to disclose the drop and signalling points. We would light small bonfires, spreading bundles of thatch around them, so as to throw them on when we heard a plane. Then we would lay on the hay sheaves: this was my only rest, which unfortunately lasted but a short time – perhaps three or four hours. By one o'clock our hopes of getting a plane would melt away: Borodavkin would go back to Headquarters; the women would go back to Starinka; and I would go to meet the morning workers, for the nights were short and already it would be dawning.

Two weeks passed and the construction came to an end. Finally, we dug holes for the bonfires on one side of the airstrip, with a communication trench running alongside for riflemen. I suggested making lids for these holes, held open by struts. A person in the communication trench could then tug on a rope tied to the struts, the lids would fall, and the fires would be extinguished immediately.

After a flight of gliders, which had brought weapons, one of the pilots remained in our area. I was looking forward to meeting him, to find out if the airstrip had proved useful. At last the pilot arrived – a real one, in a peaked cap with blue hatband and a moustache. I told him that there was no airfield as such, just an airstrip, but that it had been built on a serious scale, taking into account heavy planes as well as gliders. Having walked along the whole strip, he said that its slope was ideal for takeoff and landing, and a whole airfield was not needed. My heart rejoiced: I had not let Dubrovsky down! The triumph was complete when he repeated this in front of Dubrovsky and Poznyakov. That same day, a radiogram was sent: 'Ready to receive a plane!' I was appointed by Dubrovsky to oversee the proceedings.

We had already organized night watches at the airstrip. On the third night, we heard an engine running. I fired a green flare and lit the bonfires. The plane was losing height and it seemed to me that it was about to land.

Then it lashed the field with machinegun fire! I was lucky to throw myself to the bottom of a trench and pull the rope that made the lids fall down and extinguish the fires. Thus the first reception of a plane ended unsuccessfully. In my joy, after a long anticipation and full of impatience, I hadn't noticed that the plane did not fire a green flare. But next night, our first plane closed in for landing ...

The beginning of the blockade came suddenly for us. On 17 May the Germans struck simultaneously in several directions: four divisions were thrown into the battle, and we were outnumbered by ten-to-one.

Pyshno was the key to our zone, and from the very beginning, the fighting for it was fierce. The Germans kept throwing one battalion after another into the battle. Their aircraft bombed the village and their artillery rained down a hellish fire. Soon, Pyshno was wiped from the face of the earth. But Korolenko's detachment held out tenaciously. In June it was replaced by Misunov's detachment.

After three weeks of attempting to capture Pyshno, the Fritzes reinforced their attacks with armour and threw in an infantry regiment. They broke through on the flanks and Misunov ordered a retreat. A machinegun platoon under Alexei Karabitsky remained to cover the withdrawal. Alexei was hit in the leg, the wound was dressed by a medical orderly, Nina Fligovskaya, and he was left with two machineguns. The first crew consisted of Semen Klopov, Nadia Kostyuchenko, and Vasili Buinitsky. The second machinegun was manned by Alexei Maksimovich Bourak and his seventeen-year-old son, Nikolai. The detachment managed to withdraw, but those who remained to give cover were killed.

Two more weeks of unequal fighting passed and the Germans withdrew. Preparations for the Battle of Kursk were in hand, and these echoed in our Belorussian forests too. The Germans had to take their troops away and transfer them to the Kursk salient. The territory of Pyshno became a no man's land. The German garrisons were on one side, and on the other – behind a forest – were the Partisans.

By order of Lobanok, who had returned from Moscow in one of the planes, I quit the airstrip and headed to Pyshno with my comrade, Petro. I packed my album and some food. Then we harnessed up the grey, shaggy horse and rode off. Misha from the osoby otdel came up and asked me to give him my submachinegun: 'Give me yours, because today I'm leaving for a dangerous area. Take mine instead: it's alright, but I'm short of ammo for it – only got two drums.' He had a German submachinegun and a cartridge-chamber for our ammo (which was a different calibre) was inserted into it. He was insistent that we should swap weapons and eventually I agreed. I tried shooting from his submachinegun and it worked. I thought: 'Well, at least I've got a horse and will be able to get away if need be.'

We rode along and soon Pyshno appeared in the grey haze of the morning mist. In front of us there were lime trees, and nearby stood the church and cemetery. Petro was the first to notice two cyclists near the graves: 'Ours or theirs?' 'Must be ours,' I said. It was too late to turn away. I decided we should dash in at a trot, and if necessary, I would mow them down with the submachinegun. And so I yelled: 'Ride!'

As soon as we got closer, the cyclists shouldered their rifles and shot. My horse fell, but I leaped to my feet, and as the distance to our enemies was short, I thought I would cut them down. I fired but only one bullet flew out. My submachinegun had jammed! The German cyclists returned fire and my field cap flew away, as if from a violent push. I tried to pull the trigger of my submachinegun but to no avail. Finally, I kicked it into place and again there was only a single shot! More Fritzes were running up from afar – obviously they had prepared an ambush for us. In the meantime, Petro threw a hand grenade. An explosion! The Germans hit the deck and I dashed sideways, hiding behind a fence near an elder bush. I rapidly began reloading the submachinegun. I took off the ammo drum and then understood that the drum was not the problem: it was the cartridge-chamber, which was jamming and not throwing out empty shells. It was impossible to fix it, and I realized there would be no shooting in bursts.

I was lying quietly, listening to my heart beating. Fritzes were yelling nearby. About ten of them had gathered, and they were looking for me. They seemed confident I'd bolted towards the woods and were searching thoroughly, combing the village and moving further from the square, towards some vegetable gardens. One of them even climbed a lime tree and peered through his binoculars. I lay close to them and saw everything, but they were not looking towards the bush. It hadn't occurred to them that I had not run away! But the situation could change any moment.

I managed to drive one cartridge into the chamber. Then I carefully removed my camera, and having unscrewed the object-glass, wrapped it in a handkerchief and buried it in the ground – the Germans would not get it! Recalling that I had a cut-throat razor in my pocket, I pulled it out, wound a twig around the handle, so as to keep it open, wrapped it in a rag, and clutched it in my hand. I was lying on my left elbow, holding the submachinegun: it would shoot once. I was doing everything quietly, having meticulously thought it through. If they found me, I would shoot the first one who appeared, then I would run: if wounded, I would cut my own throat. This would be better than being caught, tortured, and hanged by the jaws from a telegraph post for two or three days before dying.

It was difficult to lie still, for nettles were stinging me. Also, my body was going numb from immobility, and I was in intolerable pain. But I was kept quiet, listening to their steps. I couldn't feel my hands anymore, so I moved my fingers to keep some life in them. Meanwhile, the Fritzes couldn't figure out where I'd got to. They couldn't guess that I was almost under their feet. Time passed slowly. At last, the sound of German voices began to fade ...

I waited a while longer before crawling along a gully to a field, then through a ditch towards the woods. I was making my way through the trees when I suddenly heard a shout: 'Stop! Hands up or I'll shoot!' I dropped behind a stump and clicked the breechblock. Well, I thought, now it's the Polizei! I replied: 'Our side!' 'Who's "Ours"?' I played for time: 'Don't you hear – *our side!*' Suddenly I heard: 'Is it you, Nikolai? We'll save you!' It was our detachment, on a mission to find me! It turned out that Petro had run to Ostrov and told Misha Malkin what had happened. Misha contacted Headquarters and Lobanok ordered: 'Send the detachment to the spot and snatch him away – dead or alive!' A group of Partisans took off to save me: Andrei Korolevich, the detachment's Chief of Staff, Nastya Boulakh, our wonderful nurse, and others: a total of about thirty people. The operation was commanded by Vera Margevich, a platoon politruk. Vera was a former schoolteacher: a modest but resolute girl. She was only twenty-two years old and it was astonishing that she was a politruk. It was a huge honour and could only be earned by special spiritual qualities – yet she was not deficient in courage, for I once saw her walking into an attack standing upright.

Vera deployed her platoon in a file and we set off to dislodge the Germans – but they had already gone. I dug out my object-glass and joyfully photographed the whole detachment to record my salvation. But Vera didn't rest on her laurels and decided to pay the Polizei a visit. Meanwhile, she sent me, Andrei Korolevich, and a section of Partisans to Ostrov, to check out a road across a swamp. We had to survey the approaches to the village in the event of a German advance.

Despite the fact that this swamp was marked as impassable on the map, we managed to cross it by jumping from one hump to another, occasionally sinking up to our knees. Indeed, over my whole time with the Partisans, I never encountered an impassable swamp. We finally reached Ostrov after 2 am and fell on the floor of a shack where Partisans were sleeping: we were exhausted!

At dawn, Vera returned with the detachment and a herd of cattle: they'd slaughtered the Polizei inside their own garrison and snatched away their livestock.

It is impossible to predetermine one's fate; impossible to foretell the day you will die. One has only to believe in survival to stop thinking about death – but death was always around. There were no white spots of tranquillity in a Partisan's life, but constant anticipation.

Here we were, thirty men hiding in a shack and a bombing raid was on. Yurka Smolyakov was cracking jokes: 'How do I know, maybe one of you is a sinner and a bomb *should* hit him? I'd rather run under that lime tree and find out for sure: if I'm hit, then it's my destiny!' He made several leaps, found himself on the road, and a bomb hit him squarely. Later, when we looked for him, all we found was a bomb crater – a big hole in the ground – and the remains of his rifle.

Then there was Vasya Nikiforov. Unfairly demoted, he dashed alone onto a gun during combat and snatched it away. Vasili's death, as well as the fate of Alla Charikova, was on the Kommissar's conscience: for it had been unfair to punish them for being in love. Alla stopped taking care of herself after Vasili's death. In action, she walked towards the enemy's pillboxes standing upright – the girls from her platoon told me about it. Nikiforov was a strong man, brave and conscientious. I remembered one example of this. A Polizei named Vasilevsky had promised to co-operate with us, but turned out to be a traitor, directing a group of Partisans into a German ambush. Vasili and I were charged with annihilating Vasilevsky's family. Nikiforov leaped into their shack, saw me standing perplexed, and opened fire himself. When we returned to the brigade he didn't say a word ...

Vera Margevich met her end after a battle. She was in a group that had just liberated Lepel. Suddenly, she fell without a sound – not even a shot was heard. She was killed by a sniper sitting on a water tower. Nadia Kostyuchenko blew herself up with a hand grenade. And Nina Fligovskaya was killed trying to save Karabitsky, dragging him from a battlefield.

None of these fighters were awarded a Hero Star [the highest award in the USSR – Trans.], but I rank them with the heroes of this prestigious Order without hesitation.

CHAPTER THIRTY-FOUR

An Hour of Work, Ten Minutes of Rest: July 1943

I had to report to the Kombrig about my return from Pyshno and the burial of our comrades. Dubrovsky's Headquarters stood in front of an airstrip near Starinka. Goutiev and I were greeted by Sergei Markevich. Dubrovsky came out of a shack where he'd been a resting, kissed me, and asked in detail how it happened that the submachinegun had misfired. Having searched his cart, he pulled out a *limonka* [a hand grenade shaped something like a lemon – Trans.] and presented me with it: 'Always have it on you, just in case!'

In the morning, Kolya and I awoke with a terrible headache – the night before we had overdone it a bit with home-brew! A new day began for us, and for Fritz, who flew over at nine o'clock to drop 'lighters' [i.e. incendiary bombs – Trans.] on Starinka. They hit a shack and it went up in flames: but intense fire from our machineguns and anti-tank rifles broke out, so the Germans didn't dare make another pass and flew away. Finally, I came to my senses after the previous night's binge.

In Starinka, I drew several pictures and sketches dedicated to the Battle of Pyshno. The Partisans, both men and women, took it as an honour to pose for the portraits of fallen comrades. But daily air raids by German cadet flyers impeded my drawing – they flew regularly from nine to twelve. At first I worked in a shack, but then, so as not to jeopardize my work, paintings were taken outdoors and I drew in the shade. A trench was dug near the shack and Nikolai Goutiev and I hid in it during air raids. We tied a rope to our paintings, so as to drag them away in case a 'lighter' hit the shack.

The life of Partisans went on as usual. I went for reconnaissances, took part in operations, and at night I guarded the airstrip. Whenever I could grab the time, I worked on my canvases and watercolour painting. Meanwhile, Nikolai Goutiev made propaganda posters and leaflets. Partisans who visited

Headquarters always came to our shack. They came to see our drawings and pick up leaflets, which they disseminated during reconnaissances and operations.

In front of Headquarters, across the road, Lobanok was busying himself with TNT sachets, binding them with wire and selecting a proper length of Bickford's fuse. Two German POWs were sitting on a bench nearby and Partisans, being at rest, gathered around them. Both POWs were thirty-five to forty years old, from the second wave of drafts, and not on the active service list. One of them was tall, skinny and gloomy. The other was cheerful and kept joking with his sullen comrade.

A job was found for the POWs: to turn the dynamo machine, in order to recharge the batteries of a radio receiver, used to get communiqués. To our surprise, they refused. We were outraged! We fed them well (which was more than their camps did for our POWs) and they didn't want to work! We soon cleared up the reason for the refusal. The cheerful German said: 'My mate is an illiterate peasant. I will work and he will remain idle. I don't want to work for him. Give us a clock.' We brought an alarm clock and watched what they would do. They put the clock on a solitary, standing post, and set up the dynamo machine. The cheerful German said: 'It's gonna be alright now. An hour of work, ten minutes of rest.' We brought a blanket, so as to let them lie when at rest, and the Fritzes began working properly. But the jovial one again found an excuse to annoy his mate: he was poking his finger at the eagle on his chest and laughing. Our interpreter Fimka said that he was mocking his comrade: 'You're an ignorant hick! You eat the Partisans' bread but wear the Fascist eagle!' He himself had got rid of his eagle, having explained that he worked for the Partisans and no longer considered it his duty to wear Fascist insignia.

The tall chap sat sullen, keeping silent, but when his mate gave him scissors brought by our guys, he poked at the eagle on his chest with such a frenzy that he cut through his uniform jacket. This caused laughter among the Partisans. But at that moment an explosion resounded! All had been so absorbed by the prisoners' antics, no one noticed that Lobanok had lit up the Bickford's fuse, testing his system. The explosion had occurred so close that the tall German threw himself flat on the ground in surprise. To his misfortune, a puddle happened to be there, and he got up on all fours straightaway. His mate was running around, holding his belly and roaring with laughter: 'He ripped off his eagle and decided to drown himself!' Suddenly, the alarm clock began to ring and both Germans rushed to the dynamo machine, so as to keep working: that was how punctual they were!

These two Fritzes had fallen into our hands in a funny way. Our guys made an arrangement with two Polizei who had decided to change sides. The Polizei agreed that when on watch with two German guards on a bridge, they would neutralize them and snatch their weapons. This was a condition of their passage. One of the Polizei, when going to the bridge, had taken along several big carrots in his bag. During his watch, he took out a carrot and began eating it, repeating: 'Gut! M-m-m, gut!' The tall German watched for a while and then closed in, saying: 'Give it to me!' The Polizei readily gave him a carrot, and when the German had stuffed his mouth, the second Polizei threw his weight at the small German. The Polizei tied up the two hungry Fritzes and left them near the bridge with carrot gags in their mouths. Then they snatched the Germans' weapons and ran towards the woods, where our guys were waiting.

The Partisans were joyfully walking back to camp, carrying a captured machinegun, two submachineguns, two rifles, and leading the two Polizei. Suddenly, yelling and the crackling of dry branches resounded behind them: 'Comrade! Comrade!' Having got rid of the carrots and untied each other, the German guards were running behind the detachment, afraid of lagging behind and getting lost in the woods. They explained that for them there was no point returning to their unit. The cheerful German – a working-class man – was the instigator of it all. I guess he had saved himself and his mate by his humour and optimism. These sentiments were always comprehensible to a Russian soldier, and we could understand the jolly German with no tongue at all! The two POWs worked surprisingly well, but we were astounded that, most of all, they were dismayed by lack of order. They couldn't reconcile the possibility that one of them might work harder than the other! And the fact they were in captivity, working for the Partisans, seemed not to matter. On this, these two very different people were of one mind.

Of course, all this made them both ridiculous, and at the same time, close to us. They stopped being enemies. It had worked out strangely that they regarded us Partisans – who were 'bandits' and 'beasts' according to their propaganda – with less fear than their own officers, to whom they hadn't dared return without weapons. The Partisans would get so used to these two POWs that Lobanok ordered them sent to the mainland when there was space on a plane. The guys accepted this decision with joy, for there was no more malice towards them. On the contrary, all rejoiced that they would stay alive.

Later, we got another German, a cadre officer who helped us interrogate POWs. He hadn't been captured but crossed the lines as a conscientious anti-Fascist. He interrogated POWs very thoroughly, knowing the mentality of his countrymen, and their rights in the German Army hierarchy. This officer remained with the brigade till the end, taking part in the breakthrough of the blockade in 1944. I don't know if he survived the war.

Another funny story involved the Partisans of Sadchikov's brigade, neighbouring ours, who captured a tank in combat. The tank was in operating condition but needed petrol. This was obtained from the Germans themselves, at a price. Both petrol and salt were sold to us by one of their NCOs, who was a storekeeper ...

CHAPTER THIRTY-FIVE

Tobacco and Hot Bodies: August 1943

In July, our overgrown brigade was divided into two for greater manoeuvrability and flexibility. The Lepel brigade – called the 'Stalin Brigade' at Moscow's request – was separated from Dubov's Brigade, commanded by Fedor Fomich Dubrovsky (which kept its old name). Lobanok was appointed commander of the Stalin Brigade, but as he was recalled to Moscow, his deputy, Korolenko, was in put charge.

The light of a burning splinter was flickering over a large cauldron, shadows of people were flitting across the walls, girls and Partisans were sitting on benches, and a concertina was playing. The concertina player wore a *kubanka* [a type of a cylindrical Cossack hat – Trans.]. On its top was a white cross over a red background: that's why the Fritzes nicknamed the Partisans of our brigade 'Crosses'. We didn't wear a red band on the front of our kubanka hats but stars cut from anything we could find – tin cans, buttons from officers' trench coats, copper samovars. A pin was soldered to these makeshift stars so they could be attached to a hat, peaked cap, field cap, kubanka, and so on. Everyone wanted to be like the soldiers of the regular Red Army! The musician was playing a waltz, bowing his head as if listening to his concertina, and the Partisans, with their sub-machineguns behind their backs, were whirling the girls in a tight embrace. The air smelled of tobacco and hot bodies.

But then a guy dressed completely in black entered the circle. He had a revolver on his hip and two limonkas hanging from his shoulder-belt. His pants were tucked into the tops of tight-fitting jackboots, shining with orange on the top flaps – something considered the height of fashion. Everyone stepped aside, understanding that, at the very least, the guy was an anti-tank rifleman or a machinegunner – no less than that. They could be recognized by features that didn't require any insignia – neither 'cubes' nor 'sleepers' [officers' and NCOs' rank insignia in the Red Army, which remained valid up to 1943, but were later replaced by shoulder badges – Trans.]. This image of a Partisan machinegunner or anti-tank rifleman had firmly established itself in our culture. No one ever issued the Partisans with uniforms: our mode of dress evolved on its own, but became surprisingly stable. The guy stood in the middle of the shack and the concertina player changed the melody of the waltz to the rhythm of a chastushki. The guy tapped his foot in time and sang out with his hoarse voice. The chastushki songs were about Hitler. They had many words but only one sense – mockery and hatred. But his hatred wasn't of a weeping kind: it was the hatred of a strong man who'd seen the death of his enemies. One stanza followed another, and the fighter danced in between them, deftly slapping his hand on his boots, and holding back the dangling hand grenades to prevent them from falling from his belt. Suddenly, he began to sing about other stuff:

> These are the last days we go merry,
> These are the last days of our freedom.
> These are the last days of our guerrilla life,
> There'll be no more of our camaraderie.
> The life will scatter us far and wide,
> Will any of us remember old mates?

'And suddenly there was a call: Do remember! There've been tears, but there've been joys as well!'

His words overwhelmed me, and at first seemed paradoxical. We were waiting for the end of the war as for a rescue from suffering and anguish: how could one yearn for these harrowing days? And suddenly a thought broke into me: this life of ours is our happiness! Comradeship and camaraderie had been born in this purgatory ...

People were leaving the shack. They were sitting down, smoking, hugging the girls. But the new feeling that had just been born was probably nagging everyone's souls. Everyone was looking at his comrades as if bidding farewell. And again, I was astounded by our Partisan life – not a simple thing at all for people's hearts and minds.

The sun was falling beyond the horizon as I strode towards Ostrov. That was the place I had arrived at a year ago, having escaped captivity. The last turn of the familiar road, and the lights of the village showed up on the hillside. Now I'll see Maria, Korolevich and Vera – my saviours, our girls. Valya Matyush, Zhenya Rutman and others had been taken to Misha Malkin's detachment after the division of the brigade. A whole platoon of girls had been formed, commanded by Nikolai Nepomnyashy. But first I went to a shack where the commander lived, so as to report my arrival: 'That's great!' Mikhail rejoiced, 'come and join us – we've just got a guest from Moscow!'

There was food and a bottle of home-brew on the table. Andrei Korolevich and I hugged each other. I reached out my hand and was introduced to a young Sergeant. 'He's a paratrooper from Moscow,' Mikhail explained, 'he was dropped into our zone. There were two of them, but the second one with a machinegun was apparently swept away. We'll wait a bit longer and I'll send people to search for him.' My heart began to ache, for I thought about Galochka – maybe I'll have a chance to find out what it was like in Moscow? But the Sergeant said he couldn't tell me anything about Moscow, for his unit had been located outside, and they hadn't been allowed into the city. Meanwhile, I was greatly impressed that he was in the Red Army uniform and was armed with a PPSh [a Soviet-made submachinegun brand – Trans.]. I knew it was a submachinegun of a new model: we didn't have any of them yet. I began examining the submachinegun, inserting and removing ammo drums. The drums were odd – one was for a PPSh and another one for a PPD [a Soviet-made light machinegun – Trans.]. I commented on this, and the Sergeant told me that he'd had two drums for PPSh and one for PPD, but one drum fell off during the parachute jump.

Andrei brought another bottle and storytelling about our Partisan life began – everyone wanted to astonish our guest with a good story. The Sergeant listened with interest, but didn't say anything himself. We didn't pry, for it was forbidden to ask visitors from the mainland too much. And so the visitor remained silent, although he had already made a full report to Mikhail, proving his identity with all the necessary documents.

The talk continued and we drank to victory over Germany. I noticed that my tobacco pouch was empty but the guest from Moscow, seeing my distress, did not offer me his tobacco. I was displeased with his selfishness or slow-wittedness and said: 'Why don't you offer me a smoke? Do they provide you with Makhorka?' 'Well, I'm not a smoker,' he replied with some embarrassment, 'but I do have some tobacco.' He searched in his rucksack and handed me a sealed pack of Makhorka in a brown wrapper. It was already dark in the room, and I wanted to read some Russian words, which I hadn't seen for so long, so I moved to a bench by the window and began examining the wrapper in the dim light of sunset. Yes, we used to be supplied with tobacco like this when I had been in the Opolchenie. But then I saw something and could not believe my eyes – over and over again I kept reading some words printed in small type: 'Printing works . . . Vitebsk, 1943'.

My intoxication rapidly passed. I returned to the table wondering what I should do: the guest was obviously not from Moscow but from Lepel or Vitebsk. They had overlooked something in the sabotage school when kitting out this spy: there would be dozens of imprints on a sheet from a printing works, but they would rarely be found on a tobacco wrapper; it was accidental that this pack had come into his hands; that I had begun to examine it; and that I'd found this mark in the dark! But how to let Mikhail know about it? All this was rushing through my head.

I fell on a chair, swaying and pretending to be drunk. I made it clear that I had to leave the room as soon as possible. Mikhail was not surprised and helped me from the table. I held onto his arm and he led me out of the shack. When we reached the doorstep I told the commander: 'The Sergeant is not a Muscovite. On the Makhorka pack there is an imprint: "Vitebsk, 1943". We'll arrest him. I'll sit to the right of him and you'll point your pistol at him. We just need to warn Andrei.'

We returned to the room, Mikhail supporting me as I staggered like a drunk. Then, Mikhail called Korolevich out 'for a minute'. I sat down next to the guest and began apologizing. Next thing, the door opened. Mikhail came right up close, then drew his pistol. The trigger clicked: 'Don't move!' I grabbed the spy and held his arms. He didn't resist. Andrei tied the impostor's hands with his belt and searched him, placing the contents of his pockets on the table. Malkin invited the 'Sergeant' to get undressed: we had to search his clothes meticulously, as documents or poison could have been sewn into them. Andrei brought pants and a shirt from the housemistress and the spy changed his clothes, then his hands were tied again, but this time with a rope.

The interrogation began. The 'guest from Moscow' didn't resist, and we found out that at dawn the same day, a German colonel had driven him and his mate to Voron in an Opel: from there they'd come on foot. The second 'paratrooper' was supposed to come to Ostrov too. Then the 'Sergeant' announced that he was a double agent working for our intelligence; that he had been sent to penetrate the sabotage school in Lepel and was now returning to Moscow. We were not in a hurry to believe him. During that spring about 150 spies had been caught just in our zone, all of them sent on sabotage or murder missions. There'd been others like this one, calling themselves double agents, so as to play for time. Mikhail ordered the 'guest' locked up in the *banya* [a wooden sauna shack – Trans.]. A guard was posted and our sentries in the village strengthened, in case the 'mate' arrived.

Next morning came misty with a pale sunrise, but it was warm and cosy in the shack. We were drinking hot milk straight from the stove and discussing the spy's story. I was happy to be alive and up to the mark, having apprehended a man who had come for our lives. Who knew what plans the spy had had for that night?

Malkin rang brigade Headquarters at Starinka. At that moment Korolenko was acting kombrig in place of Lobanok, who had flown to Moscow. Misha reported that a spy from Lepel had been arrested, that he was claiming to be a double agent and was requesting a passage to Moscow.

Mitya swore: 'Alright, send him over, we'll sort it out.' We carefully wrapped the still sealed Makhorka pack – it was an exhibit now – and put it in the impostor's rucksack, with his uniform. The sun was already coming up when the 'guest' headed off to Starinka under a strong guard. Korolenko rang up two hours later: 'We got your 'parcel'. The guy's definitely from the sabotage school. His ammo drum turned out to be one of mine – with my sign!'

I remembered a story of Mitya's, how his men had once found themselves surrounded. They had stayed overnight in a banya and suddenly the Germans turned up out of the blue. He jumped out of a window, and when he was squeezing through, an ammo drum with his initials – 'DK' – [Dmitri Korolenko – Trans.] came off. Apparently, the drum had been found by the Germans and now, two years later, it found its way into a spy's kit. Thus a PPD drum, issued before the war even started, was returned to Korolenko, its rightful owner, courtesy of the Fritzes!

Later, I found out that the 'Centre' [Partisan jargon for the Moscow authorities – Trans.] had not confirmed the spy's story about being a double agent. Consequently, he was sent to Moscow for more detailed questioning. Seemingly, his mission had been meticulously prepared: but two insignificant trifles had betrayed him, sealing his fate.

Those were sunny August days and I was still in Starinka with Nikolai Goutiev and our irreplaceable helper Vanechka [a diminutive of 'Ivan' – Trans.]. When the brigade had been divided, the 'artists' had been divided too, but although I was listed in the ranks of Dubrovsky's brigade, I was actually still in Lobanok's brigade. There was a lot of work to do and I was working on a leaflet entitled, 'Strictly According to Plan', which was about Moscow, Stalingrad and Ushachi. Everyone liked the leaflet and the fact that I was drawing Ushachi along with Moscow and Stalingrad, causing some smiles as well as pride ...

CHAPTER THIRTY-SIX

Life Turned Upside Down: September–October 1943

It was September, two months had already gone by after the segregation of the brigade and I was still dragging things out, delaying my departure. Once, Zhurko and Vasili Kosy came to the shack where Nikolai and I were working. They came to Starinka for ammo, and at the same time passed me Dubrovsky's order: to report to brigade Headquarters at Lyakhovichy, on the Valovaya Gora. Vasili passed on Dubrovsky's words: 'If he doesn't come willingly, tie him up and bring him by force.' I had bitter feelings about parting with Nikolai, for we had come a long away together. Also, I didn't want to leave Korolenko and the airstrip behind. I did not want to go to brigade Headquarters, but I had to.

On the way, we stopped at Petro Litvin's detachment. Petro was a former tanker, an okruzhenets [nickname given to soldiers from an encircled unit – Trans.], and had become a commander of a Komsomol unit and a devoted friend of mine. We were happy to see each other and Petya [a diminutive of Piotr – Trans.] asked me to photograph him and the girl he was in love with. Next day, before the film was developed, Petro would be killed leading his detachment in an attack ...

At the new place I was lodged in, the shack was owned by the mother of Fedor Gaidukov, a young boy who had recently joined the brigade. The hostess already had lodgers: a woman from another village who had fled from the Germans, an old woodman, and our Partisan girl Shopoulya, who lived in the attic. I became the fourth tenant. I was given a young Partisan with artistic abilities, named Nikolai, as an assistant. At night I took part in ambushes. During the day I slept and worked, collecting material for a picture about our horsemen – the legendary squadron commanded by Mikhail Chaikin.

It was the autumn of 1943 and the Germans, Polizei and Vlassovites were retreating through our area, after their defeat near Kursk and Belgorod. They moved towards Chashniky, breaking their way through the Partisans' sector. Fighting raged several kilometres from Lyakhovichy. Zvonov's and Didenko's detachments were blocking the roads, engaging passing units, annihilating the enemy's manpower and snatching convoys. The retreating troops moved in large groups, often with horse-drawn wagons or motor vehicles stuffed with loot. The fighting was desperate and deadly. The Germans were joined by local traitors and Polizei, who were trying to lead their families away under cover of the soldiers' protection. And so the front line was approaching, and two wireless-operators were sent over from the mainland. As a result, not only could we receive communiqués from the Central Headquarters of the Partisan Movement, we could also coordinate our actions with other Partisan detachments, and later with the advancing Red Army.

The morning I was accepted into the Communist Party began as usual: three German cadet pilots flew over, machinegunning us, and I began to work. Nikolai, my assistant, was making copies of leaflets using carbon paper, and our hostess, Fedor Gaidukov's mother, began mending my pants. My dark-blue riding-breeches were completely worn through, and she proposed patching them up with broad bands of yellow sacking. Our supplies were dropped from aircraft in such sacks.

At dinner time, as we sat down at table, someone spotted a rama reconnaissance plane hovering over the village: a bombing raid was imminent. Nevertheless, we began our meal. But we didn't even manage a mouthful of bread before an engine roared and 'lighters' began to fall. One fell near the shack window. I grabbed a bread shovel [a common thing in Russian country households, where bread is baked at home – Trans.] and jumped through the window in my underpants. Seeing the blue-white flame, I immediately threw the bomb away. But when I turned back, the shack was already ablaze, for a second incendiary had struck the roof. I leaped back into the house but found no one inside – everyone had already run out. The place was filled with thick smoke, and I couldn't find my paints or submachinegun. At last, I fingered my painter's case and threw it out of the window. Then I rushed out through the porch, which was already burning. I saw a tethered cow under an awning, its eyes wild with terror. I rushed to save it, but the knot, made from thick rope, would not yield. The frightened cow was quivering in a corner, pulling away and tightening the knot. I thought: 'While I'm messing about here, my paints will burn!' I tried untying the knot with my teeth. Then the hostess ran up, clutching her sewing machine – with my pants still sticking out of it – and my submachinegun. When she saw me with the cow, smudged and naked, she began to cry, and handed me my small album of sketches. I imagined her rushing about the blazing shack, saving my things while her own stuff burned. But she had understood the importance of salvaging my pictures: images that told the truth about people's fates. Her conduct shook me, for it was a revelation, showing people's attitude to the work I did. Grabbing the submachinegun and the pants, I rushed back, hoping to salvage the paints. But I was too late: I saw the burning painter's case and little lumps of fire on the road – these were scattered paint tubes, melting and catching fire. A minute more and nothing was left but smoking bits of black ash.

The planes were climbing higher, preparing for another raid, while people ran along the street, rushing to a bomb shelter. A woman with a child in her hands, and a girl about twelve years old, leaped out of a neighbouring house. I picked the kid up and we hurried down the road. The roar of engines was growing. We threw ourselves into a ditch, avoiding a big puddle at the bottom. While they were bombing, I opened my album and began drawing the mother and child. The kid was crying and the woman was shoving her breast to him, to stop him from yelling. The girl was lying on the ground, pressing herself into the soil. Here was my landlady's son – a boy about six years old, hugging a kitten. He had run away from his mum and returned through the burning village to save his little friend. I just managed to scrawl this group when the roaring began again, turning into the deafening growl of a dive-bomber. I chanced to look up and saw black bombs falling, shining in the sun. I pressed my face into the grass and waited. An explosion came, shaking the earth.

When I regained consciousness I was completely wet, the bomb-blast having thrown me into the water at the bottom of the ditch. One of my arms – the one holding the album – was stretched up in the air, the pictures remaining dry in my hand. The roar of the planes was dying away. When silence returned we stood up and walked to the bomb-shelter.

In a cellar there were lots of women, children and old people. A dog was lying at a woman's feet, pressing close to its owner. I made myself comfortable on the steps and began drawing again. My mind rushed headlong into thoughts of blazing buildings. I couldn't stop myself from drawing one burning shack after another. The living village was becoming a scorched desert with burning huts and black hearths, and inside there was only one thought throbbing: why hadn't I salvaged my paints? I was shivering from my wet clothes, gripping my pencil as if bewildered. In delirium, it already seemed to me that it was I who had thrown the paints into the fire with my own hands. With this thought, with this image, my life turned upside down. Before that moment I'd been driven by one passion: a passion for the arts. At that instant I stopped being an artist. I couldn't draw anymore.

My doubts had surfaced earlier – after the cruel fates of the doomed lovers, Vasili Nikiforov and Alla Charikova – but I had been driving them away. Then, after the segregation of the brigade, I came to the Valovaya Gora and saw that Dubrovsky, my ideal of a commander, was becoming spoiled. Things were different here than at the Antunovsky camp. Now, drinking bouts began to be arranged, and in general, Dubrovsky was becoming less approachable. He had become vain. In the past I had drawn pictures in good faith, sketching and painting Dubrovsky and my comrades with joy: but when I began to detect a tendency to use me, to exploit me, I understood that I didn't need rats anymore.

The last thing I did was an album of photographs of our brigade. On the lid of the box that contained the album, I depicted Dubrovsky mounted on a horse. The old man who lived in the house of our hostess had made the box from black wood. This was the last thing I did for Dubrovsky. All my other pictures were made for ordinary people, as mementoes.

The darker it became, the brighter was the crimson gleam of the fire. I came up to a shack that had miraculously survived amid total destruction – the raikom would convene in it. A lamp was burning on a low table in the shack, a wounded Olya Zakhovaeva was on a bed in the corner. Chepik was busying himself with paperwork: many applications to join the Communist Party were to be discussed that day. Gradually, many people crowded into the house. Dubrovsky came in: as Secretary of the Chashniky Clandestine District Party Committee, he would preside at the meeting. Everything seemed to be so simple. I applied and was given recommendations by Dubrovsky and Borodavkin themselves. And now it was the moment of acceptance. Everybody felt tense. My comrades, who had been my friends just a minute before, now became my judges: they had to decide if my life had been lived with dignity. Markevich came in and reported the close proximity of the Germans. Dubrovsky ordered the 2nd Detachment sent to block them, and the session continued.

When they began reading my application aloud, including the lines, 'I will give my life and creative work to the cause of building of communism,' these words were absolutely real for me. I was ready to make the ultimate sacrifice any day, any moment. When dying, I would try to fall forward, to protect at least a piece of my native land with my lifeless body! I didn't believe I would survive and it seemed better to die a Communist – in itself, this would be a blow against fascism. I kept answering my comrades' questions about my captivity, and about my creative work. No one was asking me about our struggle – all that was in front of everyone's eyes. Then they were congratulating me, shaking my hand.

I left the shack, stood for a while, then walked down the road. My soul was full of joy. Without meaning to, I came across the shack of the female wireless operators. I entered, for I wanted to talk to someone. The girls were waiting for transmissions from Moscow, and as Anya was a Muscovite too, we began to reminisce. Then Anya began receiving a message. She suddenly looked at me with her big eyes. I felt she had learned something she wanted to share, to pass on, but daren't. We stared at each other, frozen in time, frozen in silence. At last she spoke: 'Not a word to anyone! Whoever is asking you – tell no one I told you. You are summoned! An order has been issued to Dubrovsky: to send the artists Obryn'ba and Goutiev to the Central Headquarters of the Partisan Movement!'

I'd never suspected that this message would stir such a thunderstorm of emotions in me. Everything was mixed up! Joy, fear (suppose something happened and things didn't work out?), hopes and doubts. Until now, no opportunity to leave, to see Galochka, had never been so concrete: but my desire to return was seemingly paralyzed. Before, I had accepted the impossibility of going home, and only occasionally would I see my wife in my dreams, and in the morning awake with yearning and some kind of pleasure. Now, suddenly, everything had changed!

In the morning, I went to Headquarters. The village was unrecognizable: only a stove remained of our old shack, blackened by the blaze, a pile of charred logs around it. I saw the hostess and her children in the vegetable garden: she was digging up potatoes, a calf was grazing nearby. Freshly unearthed potatoes were boiling in a bucket, hanging on a crossbar, the kids were warming themselves, extending their hands to the fire.

Dubrovsky's shack stood on the outskirts – that's why it had remained in one piece. Fedor Fomich greeted me warmly. I couldn't hold back and asked if there was any news from Moscow: 'No, nothing yet,' he replied calmly. Then he added: 'You're waiting for some, aren't you?' I was stuck. I couldn't say that I knew about the radio message, but was unable to think up another question. Dubrovsky laughed, and now I understood that he had guessed from the very first moment of our talk that I knew about the order. 'A wireless message has been received from the Central Headquarters,' Fedor Fomich said, 'you and Goutiev are called up to Moscow.' I went numb. It was one thing was to hear about the order and another to have it confirmed by the Kombrig. We hugged and kissed each other. Dubrovsky ordered Sharko (the brigade Chief of Staff) and Markevich to write a combat reference for me, and a recommendation for decoration with the Red Banner Order. He sent me to Borodavkin to get my personal file.

I went to the shack where the Chashniky Clandestine District Party Committee was lodged and where I had been accepted into the Party just the day before. Semen busied himself with the documents and I came up to wounded Olya – we'd always been good friends. Suddenly, the sound of tramping hoofs resounded outdoors and a rider shot past the windows: it was Katerina, Misha Chaikin's wife, riding her husband's horse, Orlik. I stood shaken. Another female story. For Katerina and Misha it had been the first love! And now we learned from her that Misha had been killed on this horse, which she could not bear to part with. The submachinegun hanging round Katerina's neck was Misha's. I said farewell and went to Headquarters to pick up my references.

Sergei and Pavel Sharko were still writing when I came around: 'Nikolai, draw a picture of us!' Sergei asked. I drew them a picture and we parted.

Then I went to say goodbye to the wireless-operators. Anya was fresh as usual, but Valya shed a few tears. It was sad to say farewell, for I had got used to them over that time. I was doing all that was necessary to prepare for departure, but the reality of my leaving had not struck me. I was still living a Partisan's life and didn't even try to think about a meeting with Galochka. I had become too accustomed to the thought that it would be impossible to return. The habit of being ready to die wasn't so easy to get rid of . . .

I needed to go to Starinka, to tell Nikolai Goutiev about the radio message. But I was riding in a cart heading for Ostrov. I wanted to say goodbye to the guys from Malkin's detachment. I didn't stay long in Ostrov. I saw Misha Malkin, Vera Margevich, Korolevich, Valya Matyush. Everyone was wishing me happiness, jealous that I would see Moscow. Vera would perish in a few days. When the war was over, Valya Matyush, her friend, told me that Vera had prophesied her own death. Just before her final combat she said: 'I'm gonna get killed today,' and named two other fighters. They, too, died in the same action. It was on that long-awaited day when Korolenko's brigade took Lepel at last. The fighting was ferocious, for it was the most heavily fortified garrison of the Germans and Polizei, with fire emplacements, minefields and barbed wire entanglements. The Germans were armed with tanks and armoured vehicles, guns, regimental mortars and machineguns. Nevertheless, the Partisans broke through and took Lepel. Everyone was cheerful, walking round the streets. A group of Partisans stopped in the square, talking about the fight, and suddenly Vera fell down. No one even heard a shot. It turned out that they'd shot from a water tower. A sniper was sitting up there. They rushed to find him. He was a Polizei. They began shaking him, asking why the hell he'd shot after the fighting was over. He said with malice: 'I wanted just one more and chose her – in a skirt but with a rifle!' He was sentenced straightaway and shot dead.

In Starinka I dropped into Korolenko's Headquarters (he was acting kombrig) and learned that an R-5 aircraft had arrived the previous night. It was supposed to pick up the wounded and a Partisan named Betta and her child. I found Nikolai Goutiev in the editor's office and we hugged each other. It was clear that both of us couldn't fly away at once, so we decided that I would head off first and he'd take the next flight. Nikolai led me to a shack where the pilot was lodged – he was a young Muscovite named Kouznetsov. At first he upset us by saying that he had to evacuate the wounded and there was no room for anyone else. But then, feeling compassion for me as a fellow Muscovite, he suggested: 'I have one seat, actually, not a great one – the tool crate under the engine. But if you curl yourself into a ball you might fit in!' I agreed joyfully.

Now I had to go over to the boot-makers and ask them to fix new heels on my boots: how could I fly to Moscow with heels worn out to holes? As for my dark-blue breeches, I had been wearing them since my captivity, as well as the blouse once owned by Grigory Tretiak. During my time with the Partisans I had acquired a Polizei's jumper – snatched with some other stuff in one of our searches – plus Misha Chaikin's fur coat. Misha had given me the coat because I'd felt cold all the time.

Then I went to the Headquarters to report my departure. Korolenko and I parted warmly, and his kind words were the highest praise for me. It was difficult to deserve his commendation. Thus I saw Mitya for the last time. Six months later, in April 1944, he perished. On that day, the combat lasted twenty hours. Korolenko was on his horse the whole day, commanding the brigade's detachments, even engaging in combat himself. When the shooting stopped, a mine exploded nearby and Korolenko was hit in the stomach by a splinter. He died on the spot.

Kolya accompanied me to the airstrip. I was riding a bicycle and carried my little trunk in the makeshift luggage rack – a red record player case. All my possessions were inside. The flyer admired my bicycle: 'a wonder-machine!' The bike was new, Polish-made and very beautiful. I told him straightaway: 'Take it, it's yours now!' But how to take it on board? We decided Nikolai would keep it till the next flight. I presented my sub-machinegun to Kolya, taking it off my own neck and hanging it around his: Nikolai had no submachinegun, only a rifle. Klim Patseiko, the editor of our newspaper began scrutinizing the gift straightaway. The submachinegun was Czech-made and very reliable.

The aircraft was hidden in the bushes. The underbelly crate was cleared up, I crawled in, and rolled up, pressing my knees against my chin. They stuffed in my red record player case and shut the door. Oh God, how little space was needed to fit in a man with all he had done over 840 days of war! A man who had made so much effort, and who had risked so much! Films, glass negatives, and drawings – made in captivity and with the Partisans: the priceless memorabilia of a life I was leaving behind.

But the flight was ahead of me and I had to lie in my iron crypt for several hours. One enemy bullet would have been enough to pierce the duralumin, and in an emergency I wouldn't even be able to get out unaided. Under each wing the plane had a 'cradle', which could accommodate one lying man. The wounded – Nikolai from the cavalry squadron and another Partisan with a severe wound – were already waiting, warming themselves by a smouldering fire with the airstrip service crew. Two more Partisans were also to fly with us. There was not a single machinegun on the plane, and they would have to stand between the biplane's wings, secured by ropes, so as to shoot at the Germans.

Nikolai Goutiev and I began chatting. It seemed to us that we would meet again very soon, that tomorrow or the day after, a plane with ammo would arrive and Kolya would head off to Moscow and then to Rostov, to see his mum and wife. Who could know that it would turn out differently? Lobanok would return from Moscow to prepare our area for a big drop of paratroopers: the schedule of aircraft flights would change straightaway, and Nikolai would have to stay till winter.

It grew dark and the plane was moved to the runway. The woman with her six-year-old son was seated in the cockpit, in the second pilot's chair. When it was completely dark, bonfires were lit to mark out the runway. We were supposed to crawl over the combat zone in a low, grass-cutting flight, so as to stay out of the gun sights of flack artillery – it was the safest way. In the event, we would be shot at, but it worked out alright.

In two or three hours, and still in the dark, we landed on an airfield near the front line. It turned out that there'd been a snowfall during the night. Our P-5 stood on a white field lit by a searchlight as the passengers got off. First, the Partisans on the wings were untied and the woman and child were helped out. Then the cradles with the wounded were taken off. Only then did Kouznetsov jump off and release me. When I fell out of the crate, a colonel standing by the plane couldn't help observing: 'Wow, how many more do you have?!' Kouznetsov had exceeded all allowances for his two-seat 'liner'. On top of that, he had managed to take along my gift – the bicycle – attaching it, dismantled, to the undercarriage! I shook his hand and thanked him. The heavily wounded Partisan was dragged away on a sledge and Nikolai, Betta, and I were directed to Headquarters, accompanied by an armed soldier.

The day was breaking when our small group, having left the front line airfield, walked up a snowy road, following someone's footprints. On either side of the road were huge snowdrifts. It was becoming lighter and lighter, and suddenly I discerned a helmet, a hand, and iron-shod heels sticking out from the snow. There'd been fighting here recently, and many Fascists had been killed. They checked our papers at Headquarters and led us to a front-line village to rest. It was cold and damp in the shack, but we lay on the floor, huddling close for warmth. We had crossed the front line but we hadn't come to a peaceful land. Here it was smoking with fires and the snow was bumpy because of snowdrifts blown over corpses.

We were led to a station – or what remained of it – by night. There we boarded a train that was having its engine replaced. The train was heading to Moscow. We entered a cramped carriage, filled with soldiers and Partisans who'd distinguished themselves in combat and earned some leave. There were wounded men like our Nikolai, on their way to a Moscow hospital bed. A train loaded with tanks, about to head in the opposite direction, stood nearby. We looked at the tankers from our carriage, knowing that tomorrow, or the day after, they would go into combat: no one knew how many of them would remain buried under the snow. But they were laughing, slapping themselves on the sides, shoving each other, warming themselves up. At last an engine was brought and our train took off.

In the middle of the night the train stopped at a siding near Volokolamsk. Moments later, the darkness was lit by flares, an air raid siren screamed, and

'Junkerses' appeared overhead. People were jumping out of the cars and running down the embankment. I remembered that my red case with its precious load remained in the car and ran back. The planes swooped round for another pass. Again there were explosions and yelling. But the German fliers were driven away by our fighter planes. We returned to our car. The conductor was laughing: 'What warriors you are – you fell into the mud hiding from the bombs!' I told her: 'You know, I would have crawled to Moscow through that ditch just to see my wife. I haven't seen her for three years.' Soon, we discovered that the situation on the siding had been critical. Two open trucks containing shells had been attached to our train, while an oncoming troop train was next to us. No bomb was necessary to blow up both trains: a machinegun burst from a plane would have been enough. During the raid, our driver had detached the engine, and after a quick manoeuvre, got to the end of his train. Then he had attached the open trucks of ammo and driven them away from the siding, risking being shot or hit by a bomb at any moment and being blown up with his deadly load.

Meanwhile, everybody was excited after the bombing. Nobody was sleeping, and continued chatting. But I noticed that my neighbours were looking at me with animosity. The conversation was strained and I couldn't understand why they were being so cold. At last, one of them said: 'What's your problem? You told us you were eager to see your wife and yet you risked your life by running back for that red trunk. I reckon you've got gold in it!' And so I opened my case and showed them what it contained.

Later, photographs would be made from the negatives in this humble case – photographs that recorded the faces of Partisans and their way of life. But back then, sitting on that train, I couldn't imagine I'd left the Partisans forever: still less that I would live the rest of my life in my pictures and memories of that time . . .

Epilogue

By a strange chain of circumstances, almost all the comrades I'd found during the first squalls of war and captivity survived, and nearly all of them managed to escape to the Partisans or to the front.

As for my old friend Grisha Tretiak. I discovered his subsequent fate only after I found myself in Moscow, in October 1943, when I read his letter addressed to my wife. He'd written to Galochka that I was alive, in a POW camp, saying of himself that he'd escaped captivity and now was in the Red Army, working as a painter. He asked Galochka to send him paints and brushes. By the time this letter arrived, Galochka had already found out I was with the Partisans – I had managed to tell of my whereabouts and address. She wrote to Grisha about all that, but he obviously never received the letter. The second message we got from him was at the beginning of 1944: it was brought by his fellow-serviceman, Sergeant Soloviev, when my wife and I were not at home. It was signed 'Tretiakov G. F.'

Nikolai Orlov – the guy I had treated for typhus – also escaped POW camp at the end of 1942. He had got a German uniform, stood on the road like a traffic-controller, stopped a German vehicle, killed the driver, captured a colonel, and drove the vehicle to the Partisans. When I returned from the Partisan detachment I found out that Kolya Orlov had been called up to the Central Headquarters of the Partisan Movement in Moscow, where he reported on his detachment's conduct. That meant he was a good, prominent commander. I heard nothing more about him.

Tolya Vedeneev escaped and joined a Partisan brigade. The Partisans, having found out he was a good musician, got hold of a piano and he would give concerts in the detachments. After the war, Tolya returned to Moscow and worked in his institution.

Vanya Gousentsev – Vanya the Gypsy (he really was a Gypsy) – escaped with Dimka the violin player. They fought together in a Partisan detachment and formed a Partisan music band, which would travel to villages and other detachments giving concerts. The band enjoyed great success. It was led by Olya, the very same agent who had told me about Chistyakov. They fought in the brigade commanded by Alexei Donukalov, a legendary commander in the Vitebsk province.

Volodya Vekshin escaped twice. It was both a comic and dramatic story. He managed to escape the first time but lost his spectacles on the way, found himself in a hopeless situation, and returned to the camp asking to be taken back. Eventually he escaped again, but not alone, and he and his comrade reached the Partisans. They procured spectacles for him and he fought on.

Andreev the kitchen chef, and his deputy, Anatoly Kharlamov (Tolya Vedeneev's friend from polytechnic college), escaped as well. They poured poison in the food when cooking for the Germans and ran away.

Generally speaking nearly all of my mates who survived the horrors of dystrophy and typhus escaped.

Glossary

Ausweis	German identity card or travel pass
AWOL	Absent Without Leave
Babushka	Grandma or old woman
Banya	Wooden sauna shack
Bogatyr	Noble knight in a Russian epic
Chastushki	Simple, humorous folk songs, often sung in the form of a dialogue between two choruses
Dom Pionerov	'Pioneers' House' – i.e. youth clubs existing in the USSR till the late 1980s
Dracheniks	a type of thick potato pancake
Gefreiter	German Army rank, equivalent to a British lance corporal
Gymnasium	Secondary school
Hauptmann	German Army rank, equivalent to a British captain
Hero Star	Highest award in the USSR
Katyusha	Literally 'Little Kate' – Russian nickname for the BM-13 rocket launcher
Khokhol	Russian nickname for a Ukrainian
Kolkhoz	Collective farm
Kombat	Battalion commander
Kombrig	Brigade commander
Kommissar	Soviet Communist Party official, responsible for political education and organization
Komsomol	Young Communist League
Komsorg	Local organizer of Komsomol or 'Young Communist League'
Kubanka	Type of cylindrical Cossack hat
Kunstmaler	'Artist' or 'painter' in German
Lighters	Incendiary bombs

Limonka F-1 hand grenade nicknamed because of its characteristic 'lemon' shape
Makhorka Brand of cheap tobacco
Mauser a German-made pistol
Maxim Soviet machinegun, mounted on a wheeled carriage
Messers Russian nickname for the German Me-109 fighter plane
MTS Abbreviation of Machine Tractor Station, state-owned Soviet enterprise working for collective farms
Nagan Type of revolver, made in Belgium, but widely used in Russia
Nemka/Nemki Russian name for a German female/females
NZ (neprikosnovenny zapas) Reserve stock/rations
Obergefreite German Army rank, equivalent to a British corporal
Oberleutnant German Army rank, equivalent to a British first lieutenant
Oberst German Army rank, equivalent to a British colonel
Obkom Provincial committee of the Communist Party
Okruzhenets Russian nickname for a soldier from an encircled unit
Opolchenets Soldier of the Opolchenie
Opolchenie Territorial Army or Home Guard
Osoby otdel Security department of a Soviet military or Partisan unit
Pan/Panowie 'Gentleman/gentlemen' in Polish
Politruk Political kommissar
Polizei/Polizeitruppe German-organized police force of collaborationists
Polushubok Short sheepskin overcoat
PPD Soviet-made light machinegun
PPSh Soviet-made submachinegun
Pravda Main organ of the Central Communist Party Committee
Raikom District Communist Party committee
Rama literally 'frame' – Russian nickname for the twin-fuselage German FW-189 reconnaissance plane
Rasputitsa Season of thawing snows and slushy roads in autumn or spring
Samogon Illicitly distilled vodka or 'moonshine'
Schwester German term for sister
Soviet An elected local or national council in the former USSR
Sovinformbureau Soviet Information Bureau

Starosta	Village elder in German-occupied territory
Staroushka	Old woman
Starshina	Sergeant major
Stavka	Central Soviet Military Command
SVT rifle	Soviet semi-automatic weapon of the early war period
Tankette	'Light' tank used for reconnaissance
TNT	Trinitrotoluene, a type of high explosive
Trekhtonka	Soviet 3-ton lorry
Valenok (pl. valenki)	Soft felt boot(s)
Versta	Russian unit of measurement, equivalent to 0.66 miles or 1.07 km
Vlassovites	Followers of Andrei Vlassov, a former Red Army general who defected to the Germans. In 1943 Vlassov raised battalions of ex-POWs for service against Stalin, the so-called Russian Liberation Army (Russkaya Osvoboditel'naya Armija)
Voenkom	Military kommissar
Voenkomat	Commissariat office in charge of military affairs for a given district
Zootechnik	Skilled livestock attendant on a Soviet collective farm

Index